alcides lanza

Portrait of alcides lanza. Ink drawing by Otto Gal, 2001.
Reproduced by kind permission of the artist.

alcides lanza

Portrait of a Composer

PAMELA JONES

McGill-Queen's University Press

Montreal & Kingston • London • Ithaca

© McGill-Queen's University Press 2007
ISBN 0-7735-3264-9

Legal deposit fourth quarter 2007
Bibliothèque nationale du Québec

Printed in Canada on acid-free paper that is 100% ancient forest free
(100% post-consumer recycled), processed chlorine free.

This book has been published with the help of a grant from the
Canadian Federation for the Humanities and Social Sciences, through
the Aid to Scholarly Publications Programme, using funds provided by
the Social Sciences an Humanities Research Council of Canada.

McGill-Queen's University Press acknowledges the support of the
Canada Council for the Arts for our publishing program. We also
acknowledge the financial support of the Government of Canada
through the Book Publishing Industry Development Program (BPIDP)
for our publishing activities.

The poem "The Children Like Marbles Tumble into Life," by Norbert
Ruebsaat, pages 116–17, first published by Pulp Press, Vancouver,
British Columbia, is reprinted by permission of the author.

Library and Archives Canada Cataloguing in Publication

Jones, Pamela (Pamela Anne)
   Alcides Lanza: portrait of a composer / Pamela Jones.

Includes bibliographical references and index.
ISBN 978-0-7735-3264-9

1. Lanza, Alcides, 1929–. 2. Composers – Canada – Biography.
3. Composers – Argentina – Biography. I. Title.

ML410.L297J78 2007   780'.92   C2007-902948-5

This book was typeset by Interscript in 10.5/13 Sabon.

to Agnes and Alexander
in memoriam

Contents

Introduction

The life and career of alcides lanza are a gift to a biographer. Over the course of his fifty-year career as a composer he has produced a major body of work consisting of more than 120 compositions and has achieved international renown, particularly in the domains of experimental music theatre, electroacoustic music, and music for percussion.

lanza has lived and worked in four important world centres. He was born in 1929 in Argentina and raised during a time of political upheaval and artistic ferment. During the 1930s and 1940s South America was overflowing with first-rate European musicians who had fled fascist regimes in Spain, Germany, and Italy. Their presence and interaction with native-born South American composers produced a great flowering of the arts in Argentina. lanza received his musical training and began his career as a composer in this stimulating milieu. A Guggenheim grant in 1965 enabled him to travel to New York – at that time, a cauldron of wild experimentalism in the arts – to work at the Columbia-Princeton Electronic Music Center, and in 1972 he spent a year in Berlin, another hotbed of avant-garde artistic activity. He moved permanently to Montreal in 1973 during a period of nationalism and expansion in the arts. Thus lanza has had the good (or sometimes adverse) fortune to have truly lived in interesting places in interesting times.

This book will take readers step by step, in roughly chronological order, from Buenos Aires to New York to Berlin to Montreal. At each step of lanza's journey I will focus on three aspects of his career: the personal events of his life, the evolution of his musical style, and the influence of people, places, and events. The origin of this study can be traced back to a conversation I had with Mireille Gagné, director of the Montreal branch of the Canadian Music Centre, in which she expressed her concern about the serious shortage of books on Canadian composers. I proposed a biography of alcides lanza on condition that she would launch the book at the Montreal branch of the Canadian Music Centre. She agreed, but stressed that the book should be addressed to both scholars and ordinary concert goers. I have taken her advice to heart and have strived to make lanza's music understandable to a wide spectrum of readers.

I began my research by analysing many of lanza's compositions in order to distil the essence of his style at each point in his career. I have not attempted a comprehensive survey of his entire oeuvre but instead have chosen to zero in on representative works from each period. Indeed, this book is only an introduction: I discuss in detail only eighteen of the compositions listed in lanza's catalogue. For the most part I have chosen works that I consider among lanza's finest; although this book covers only about 15 per cent of his output, I have tried to present a colourful sampling from a variety of media that illustrate this composer's wide range of interests. There are also a considerable number of music examples. Since lanza's mature works employ a great deal of unconventional notation that involves graphic designs, I have also included a chapter explaining how to "read" lanza's idiosyncratic notation.

I felt it was vital to take advantage of the fact that both lanza and many of the performers associated with his career are still living. I had almost weekly discussions with lanza throughout my work on this book and recorded more than eighteen hours of interviews with him. In addition, I travelled to Argentina, New York, Houston, and several Canadian cities to record more than thirty hours of interviews with composers, performers, students, friends, and family members. Throughout these interviews I was concerned not only with gaining impressions of lanza but also with eliciting eyewitness accounts of events that help to bring to life the cultural and political background of the various centres in which lanza has lived and worked. These recorded interviews are now deposited in the alcides lanza fonds (ALF) in the Richard Johnston Canadian Music Archives Collection at the MacKimmie Library, University of Calgary. Some of the quotations from interviews with lanza are verbatim; others were revised or expanded by the composer while the book was a work in progress. Since 1960 alcides lanza has used lowercase letters for his name and for the titles of his compositions; I have respected his preference in this book. Titles of his earlier works have standard capitalization. All translations into English throughout the text and the notes, unless otherwise indicated, are my own. I have made every effort to identify, credit appropriately, and obtain publication rights from copyright holders of illustrations in this book. Notice of any errors or omissions in this regard will be gratefully received and correction made in any subsequent editions.

I have known alcides lanza for more than thirty years. Although I have made every effort to make my presentation as objective and factually correct as possible, conducting extensive research in three countries on two continents, this work is, at its core, rooted in my personal experience and understanding of the man and his works. This book is indeed a "portrait" of alcides lanza, and like all portraits, it is one person's interpretation of the essence of the subject.

Acknowledgments

I want to thank Mireille Gagné for suggesting that I write this book. Strongly worded letters of support from her and from Professor Bruce Minorgan of McGill University did much to persuade the Social Sciences and Humanities Research Council of Canada to award me a research grant that paid for my travel to Argentina, Texas, New York, Toronto, and Calgary. I am also grateful to the Canadian Federation for the Humanities and Social Sciences for awarding a grant from the Aid to Scholarly Publications Program to help with the production costs of the book.

lanza's archives are housed in the Richard Johnston Canadian Music Archives Collection in the MacKimmie Library at the University of Calgary. The extensive collection includes vinyl records, tapes, CDs, concert programs, reviews, videos, films, sketches, drawings, scores, letters, photographs, and much more. I am indebted to Apollonia Steele, the librarian in charge of the archives, for helping me to negotiate the abundance of this material.

I was deeply touched by the whole-hearted support I received from so many composers and performers in Argentina, the United States, and Canada (all are listed in Sources, pp. 253–4). They gave generously of their time for interviews and answered my questions fully, with honesty and, in some cases, with courage. They all gave permission for the recordings of these interviews to be deposited in the ALF, thus making it possible for future researchers to benefit from their first-hand knowledge of a variety of times and places.

lanza supplied me with scores and recordings of nearly all of his works, and he has read the book at each of its many stages. What I appreciated most of all, however, was his superlative memory. lanza is a font of information not only on South America and its institutions but also on New York in the 1960s and Montreal since 1970. I am grateful for the opportunity to present some of this precious information in book form.

There were a number of hurdles to jump between the first submission of my manuscript and the book now in your hands; I can truly say that the advice and support of the staff at McGill-Queens University Press was immensely helpful. I especially want to thank Jonathan Crago for his help in obtaining the ASPP grant, and my copy editor, Ruth Pincoe, for her encouragement and wisdom.

Lastly, I am deeply grateful to my husband, composer Robert F. Jones. I owe a great deal to his eagle vision, perfect ear, and remarkable sense of what works and what does not.

alcides lanza

preludio (preludio)

In 1938 Antonio Lanza, a barber in a small town in Argentina, won a modest sum of money by collecting the prize-winning coupons in a contest run by a cigarette company. He asked his two sons what they wanted with their share of the money: the elder boy, Edgardo, wanted a bicycle; the younger, the nine-year-old alcides, without a moment's hesitation, asked for a piano.[1]

alcides lanza was a child who loved music. When he was four years old, a cousin of the family who lived in a neighbouring town purchased a player piano and invited the Lanza family to see his new acquisition. Young alcides watched in fascination as his cousin put a piano roll in the instrument and pumped the pedals with his feet to produce, as if by magic, a flashy arrangement of a popular tune. The rest of the family soon tired of the novelty and returned to the dining room for supper and conversation, but alcides spent the entire evening not only pressing the keys to produce sounds but also trying to figure out the mechanics of the player piano. This telling incident in his early life sums up lanza's future career: he was to become an internationally respected composer of electronic music, interested as much in the technical aspects of sound production as in the sounds themselves.

lanza began to study piano at age seven during a period of convalescence from a serious illness. His parents, searching for ways to occupy the sick child, thought that music might be a good distraction, but since they could not afford a piano, the boy could only practice now and then at his teacher's house. So at first it seemed that his musical interests were unlikely to prosper. The prize money from the cigarette contest changed everything. lanza's parents could not have predicted how important music would become to him. When he first began piano lessons they were unaware that their son's convalescence would last until he was thirteen years old and that what might have been a dreary childhood would instead be a happy and productive one, mainly because of music.

I

no ouvido do tempo / in the ear of time

Timbúes

alcides lanza was born on 2 June 1929 in Rosario, the second largest city in Argentina. His mother moved to the city for the birth because there was a good maternity hospital there, but the family lived in Timbúes, a small town some sixty kilometres north of Rosario.[1] lanza's paternal ancestors came from Europe. His grandfather, Pablo Lanza, had emigrated from Italy to Argentina in the 1880s; his son Antonio, lanza's father, was a first-generation Argentinean. The Lanza family had musical talent: in his youth Antonio had supported himself by playing guitar and directing a tango band that played for local dances and tango evenings.[2] After he married, however, he decided that music was not a sensible career for a man with a family, so he dissolved the band, gave his guitar to a distant relative, and settled down as the town barber. lanza remembers his father as a gregarious man. His barbershop was always overflowing with men, only a few of whom had come for a haircut. Most of them were in the shop to argue about politics – always a favourite pastime in Argentina – and to bet on horses.

The maternal side of lanza's family had deep roots in Argentina. His mother's family may originally have come from Spain in the early eighteenth century, but at some point (the exact generation is hotly disputed in the family) there had been intermarriage with the Guaraní, an indigenous people who lived in northern Argentina. Several of lanza's uncles could read Guaraní, but this knowledge was lost in alcides's generation.[3] The only surviving photograph of lanza's maternal grandmother, Victorina Figueroa de Ayala Gauna,

Antonio Lanza, father of alcides lanza. Photograph
from the personal collection of alcides lanza.

shows a woman with unmistakably strong Guaraní features. It
seems likely that lanza's somewhat dark complexion, high cheek-
bones, and limited facial hair are part of a rich inheritance passed
down from his native ancestors.

Most of lanza's maternal relatives were teachers or writers. His
mother, Ernestina Ayala Gauna, was headmistress of one of the
two schools in Timbúes. She seems to have been a rather serious
woman, quite the opposite of her gregarious husband. Although
there are many photographs of her, she is not smiling in a single
one. Her mind and hands were constantly occupied, and it would
never have occurred to her to while away a day doing nothing.
She channelled her energy and focus into her job, running the
school by day, and at night teaching the local girls how to weave.
She even bred her own silkworms in the back garden. lanza, the

Ernestina Ayala Gauna, mother of
alcides lanza. Photograph from the
personal collection of alcides lanza.

indefatigable organizer of music festivals and founder of concert
groups, is a true son of his very active mother.

Nephritis – a Child in Distress

The seminal event of lanza's childhood, one which was to affect his
entire life, took place when he was four and a half years old. Within
hours of receiving a smallpox vaccination, he began to vomit and to
urinate blood. The local physician, Dr Simonetti, diagnosed nephritis, an inflammation of the kidneys. This disease can vary in severity
from a mild attack to a fatal illness: symptoms in severe cases include
fever, body swelling, blood in the urine, fluid retention, headache, infections, and visual disturbances. lanza's attack was acute. Today nephritis is treated with antibiotics, but in 1933 there was no easy cure.
The child was put to bed; ice packs were placed on his head and kidneys, and he was forced to drink enormous quantities of water. This
ritual cleansing of his kidneys continued for eight months.

lanza's cousin, Enriqueta Ayala Gauna, who was thirteen at the
time his illness began, told me that the boy adjusted well to this

grim routine and was the easiest of patients. Perhaps this is what she genuinely recalls, or perhaps her memories may have been coloured by the fact that I was writing a book about her cousin. (I failed to get any of lanza's relatives to say a single negative thing about him in any of my interviews.) lanza's version, however, is quite different. He vividly remembers dry lips, pain, and a feeling of miserable restlessness that sometimes erupted into tantrums. On one occasion – it was the middle of winter in Argentina where the houses are not well insulated – he threw the hated ice packs across the room in a rage. His mother calmly picked up the ice packs, gave him an Ayala Gauna stare, and placed them back on his kidneys.

During this period lanza was isolated from other children, and we can only guess at his frustration and fear. Children do not live for the future. In a somewhat spiritual sense, they live the moment. So it must have been little comfort to hear his relatives' constant assurances that someday he would get better and be able to play with other children again. Children are also observant, and the young lanza must have sensed his parents' deep-seated worry – there was no guarantee that he would ever get better.

Out of boredom he started looking through comic books and asking everyone to read to him. The house contained a large extended family, many of whom were teachers, so he was often lucky enough to get a reader; but during school hours and other times when everyone was busy, his attempts were frustrated. He kept pestering his relatives with questions – "What is this word? What is that one?" – until someone, in exasperation, would sit down to give him a brief lesson. Thus, out of a mixture of boredom and curiosity, the sick child learned to read and write before the age of five. Whiling away the long hours at home, the young boy also took up drawing with a passion; he eventually became so proficient in draughtsmanship that his family thought he might become an artist. Today, the legacy of those years of endless drawing can be seen in lanza's meticulous and refined graphic scores – works of visual art in their own right.

If the four-year-old lanza had known what his future held, he might well have been very depressed. At first, even his family did not understand the extent to which the illness would change his life. After eight months Dr Simonetti pronounced the child out of danger but insisted that because his kidneys were so weak he should still not be allowed to play with other children, for fear that he might be hurt or cause further damage to his kidneys; he was forbidden to run, bike, swim, climb, or play any games involving physical activity. For nine long years, young alcides was isolated from other children. He attended school, but the other children were warned never to be rough with him: he could not run home with them after school or join in their games; he was a child apart.

lanza was nine when his father won the cigarette contest.[4] When the piano entered the house his previous interests in reading and drawing became less important. Music was now his central focus. His cousin Enriqueta remembers that he never had to be forced to practice: quite the opposite, it was hard to get him away from the instrument! In a moment of insight she said, "I think the piano was the child's saviour. It helped alcides accept his illness and its restrictions." One cannot help but agree. The young lanza developed a positive and enthusiastic character that has served him well throughout his life. When one considers the difficulties of his childhood, it seems clear that this positive attitude can be attributed in large part to his love of music and his sense that he "belonged" at the keyboard.

lanza's childhood illness was pivotal to his artistic development. As a young child he had no choice but to pursue mental rather than physical activities, and all the boundless energies of childhood were pointedly directed toward art and music. A number of lanza's compositions revolve around children: the child-woman that no one listens to in *penetrations VII*, the children singing and at play in *ekphonesis VI*, and the mysterious disappearing child in *ekphonesis V* and *un mundo imaginario*. The composer's childhood illness, and the later traumatic experience of the illness and death of his first child, are deeply etched in his psyche. He knows what it is like to be a child in distress; he has known it since the age of four.

Rosario

When lanza reached school age he was exempted from the first two grades because he had learned to read and write during his eight-month convalescence from nephritis. This meant that throughout grade school and high school he was always younger than his classmates. Later in life lanza would be older than most of his fellow students – he did not begin the study of musical composition until his mid-twenties – but because he had been so much

younger than his classmates for so many years, he got into the
habit of seeing himself as young. I believe this has kept him youthful throughout his life.[5]

He began his formal education at his mother's school, Escuela Nacional no 12 in Timbúes, but, since it had only four grades, he completed the program in two years. At this point the family had to
consider where the eight-year-old boy should continue his education.
The other school in the village offered seven grades, but since it was
the rival establishment to his mother's school, this alternative was unthinkable. Instead, lanza was sent to Rosario, where he could live
with his uncle Velmiro Ayala Gauna. He stayed in Rosario during the
school week, returning home for some weekends and on holidays.

Rosario is a major metropolis on the Paraná River, about an hour
south of Timbúes.[6] In the late nineteenth and early twentieth centuries, it was one of Argentina's major ports and was sometimes referred to as "the Chicago of Argentina" or "la ciudad de los
millionarios." Evidence of the city's wealthy past can still be seen in
some streets where nineteenth-century mansions – long ago con-
verted to business premises – boast magnificent wrought-iron balco-
nies and massive bronze doors. In its heyday Rosario's active cultural
life included two symphony orchestras, a chamber orchestra, a resident string quartet, and two opera houses. By the 1930s, however,
the city had lost its international port status, and thereafter declined
in wealth, prestige, and culture. When lanza arrived in 1938, there
was only one orchestra and one opera house; the resident string quartet and chamber orchestra had disbanded, and the other opera theatre had been turned into a cinema. Nevertheless, after life in a small
village, Rosario presented a golden opportunity. The city was still on
the route of many international touring artists; lanza recalls hearing
piano recitals by Claudio Arrau, Wilhelm Backhaus, Aldo Ciccolini,
and an elderly Alfred Cortot. Today the city is still musically active,
with composers such as Dante Grela teaching and conducting there,
but it is known more for its popular culture: in the words of Enrique
Belloc: "Rosario is an odd place; it has produced all of Argentina's
leading rock stars – and alcides lanza."[7]

Tío Velmiro

The single most influential person on lanza during his childhood
was his uncle Velmiro Ayala Gauna (1905–67),[8] a man of such

extraordinary ability and character that one would be hard pressed to come up with anyone more suitable to guide and inspire an artistic child. Velmiro taught languages and literature at a private school and was a well-known author of novels, poetry, and plays. He is also fondly remembered in Argentina for his detective novels featuring the much-loved Don Frutos Gómez, a provincial sheriff who always defeated the wicked city slickers with his homegrown wisdom. One of these novels was even made into a popular movie.[9] Many of his novels and short stories are set in the Corrientes district in northeastern Argentina, a region rich in Guaraní history and culture. Velmiro credits his father, Ramón Ayala Gauna (lanza's maternal grandfather), as the mentor who inspired his love of native culture: his book *La selva y su hombre* [The Forest and Its Man] is dedicated, "To the memory of my father Ramón Ernesto Ayala Gauna, who perfumed the days of my childhood with the earthy scent of the legends of my Indian land."[10] Just as Ramón inspired his son Velmiro, so too Velmiro inspired his nephew alcides. It would be many years, however, before lanza would turn his attention to his native heritage: after nearly a lifetime of almost denying it, he composed several works, including *acúfenos III* (1979) and *vôo* (1990), that would embrace the "scent of his native land."

lanza's artistry owes much to his uncle's extraordinary mind. For example, Velmiro invented a type of theatre that he called "Teatro de lo Esencial."[11] These plays were designed for performance in a puppet theatre (minus the puppets) where only the actors' hands were seen. Everything was expressed through vocal intonation and dramatic hand gestures, with lights and music kept to a minimum so that the drama emerged in stark black and white. The scripts were based on serious subject matter; for example, one is titled *What Is the Colour of God's Skin?* The young lanza, new to the city and to artistic enterprises in general, was totally fascinated with his uncle and his writing. He absorbed the Teatro de lo Esencial scripts and was struck by the way their emotional directness was reinforced by the complete absence of sets, costumes, and colour. lanza later became a leading composer of music theatre and many features of these works – the importance assigned to the voice, the texts written mostly by the composer, the economy of musical means, the gut-wrenching emotional content, and the emphasis on black and white – clearly show the lasting impression that his uncle's Teatro de lo Esencial made on the young boy.

Velmiro Ayala Gauna, uncle and mentor of alcides lanza. Photograph from the personal collection of alcides lanza.

Velmiro was also a strong influence in the area of ethics. In character he might be compared to an eighteenth-century intellectual, an Enlightenment figure of sorts. An agnostic, an antifascist, and an anticleric, he possessed a deeply rooted personal sense of ethics and justice. One example is telling. One day lanza found the entrance to his school blocked by student protesters. Influenced by rumours flying outside the school, he went home and said to his uncle, "The kids are bad – they're a bunch of communists." Velmiro's reaction was immediate. He turned to the thirteen-year-old lanza and said, "True, it's not the best form of government – but, what are *you* doing when you say those students are bad because they're communists? You are denying them the right to their beliefs. What does that say about you?"[12]

While Velmiro might defend the right of everyone to their own beliefs, there was no question that he was staunchly opposed to both communism and fascism. His widow, Enriqueta Ayala Gauna, spoke about the difficulties they faced. At the time of the above incident fascism was on the rise in Argentina, and those who protested tended to be labelled as communists. It was prudent not to say too much in public. During the first dictatorship of Juan Perón (1946–55) there was considerable government interference in the classroom. As a history teacher, Enriqueta was in an even more difficult position than her husband because she was expected to "rewrite" history in order to glorify Perón and his regime, a policy so repugnant that both she and Velmiro chose to avoid the issue by teaching nothing at all about the dictator. To Enriqueta's horror, a school inspector appointed by the Perón government paid an unexpected visit to her classroom to assess how much the children had learned. Much to her surprise, the children gave all the correct responses to the questions the inspector posed. They knew about Perón's childhood, military career, government policies, and also a great deal about his wife, Evita. At the end of the session the inspector congratulated her on how well she had accomplished her task. Ianza, then about seventeen, remembers their discussion of this incident that evening over the dinner table. Enriqueta and Velmiro were disturbed by the evidence before them: clearly the children could parrot back information about Perón without hesitation. This was exactly the kind of brainwashing and government interference that they both detested.

Velmiro Ayala Gauna's influence on Ianza was immense. During the ten years that he lived with his uncle, Ianza absorbed Velmiro's sense of outrage at injustice and his scepticism about governments and organized religions. Ianza commented, "I don't need a religion or a government to tell me how to behave. For me it comes from the inside out ... I don't like governments and politics. It doesn't really matter if they're left or right, I just don't like them."[13] Velmiro, ever the man of reason, was intelligent, creative, rational, and prudent – much like Don Frutos Gómez, his fictional detective. Ianza was fortunate to have such a mentor, and a close rapport developed between uncle and nephew. Since Velmiro had no children of his own, perhaps Ianza was a substitute for the son he never had.

Velmiro firmly believed that one of the best ways to learn to write in one's native tongue was to study foreign languages, since it forces the student to think about how language works. With this in mind, he sent lanza to a language school to learn English. The boy quit after only three months but spent his evenings laboriously reading through an English version of Dumas's *The Man in the Iron Mask* with the help of a dictionary. Ever the pragmatist, Velmiro realized that this autodidactic approach would probably serve better than official lessons. Thus lanza taught himself to read basic English almost the same way that he had taught himself to read his native Spanish. With Spanish his interest had been comic books; with English, it was an exciting adventure novel. lanza was next sent to study German, which, much to his uncle's surprise, he seemed to relish. What Velmiro did not know was that his thirteen-year-old nephew had developed a schoolboy crush on the beautiful young teacher; lanza's love, needless to say, went unrequited but he did learn some German.

Age thirteen was special for another reason. After nine long years, lanza regained his physical freedom; Dr Simonetti finally gave him permission to engage in physical activities. lanza took up tennis and pursued it with such vigour that he began to win local competitions. To this day, lanza still plays tennis once or twice a week, and once jokingly remarked, "It is my only vice."[14]

The Ayala Gauna household was crammed with thousands of books, at least half of which were in English. lanza was a voracious reader, and Velmiro hoped that this love of literature might lead the boy to follow in his footsteps and become a professional writer. His uncle helped him develop his skills as a writer. There were no formal lessons; rather, it was more of an apprenticeship: lanza picked up the writer's trade from the work they did together. Velmiro was the producer and host of a weekly half-hour radio show in which he expounded on a theme. The program might include interviews, readings from great literature, original writing, music, or anything else that highlighted the theme of the week. lanza helped his uncle prepare the show. At first he merely typed the scripts but eventually he graduated to research assistant and co-writer; after several years Velmiro, who was often swamped with work, handed over the entire program to his nephew. Thus at seventeen lanza had his own radio show. During the first Perón dictatorship, complete scripts of all radio programs had to be submitted to the state censor at least a week before each broadcast. Such artistic censorship was repugnant to Velmiro – yet another trait he passed on to his nephew.

Early Musical Training

When lanza was thirteen years old his uncle invited a man named Nicolás Alfredo Alessio to his home to discuss music he wanted to play on his radio show. Alessio's family had emigrated from Italy about twenty years previously and ran a private conservatory of music in Rosario. During the course of the discussion between the two men, lanza was improvising on the piano in another room. Alessio suddenly stopped in mid-sentence and said, "Whoever's playing, he's really good."[15] After this conversation, Velmiro decided to send his nephew to the Alessio conservatory. The Alessios were what might be called "old world" teachers – strict, disciplined, dogmatic, and not prone to praise. lanza would not likely have tolerated their rigidity later in life, but at age thirteen it was exactly what he needed. The Alessios gave him a solid foundation in theory, counterpoint, ear training, and piano. After three productive years they informed the sixteen-year-old lanza with complete frankness that they had taught him everything they knew and that they felt he had the potential to become a professional musician. This was the first time in lanza's life that a musical career had been suggested and it set him thinking. Velmiro decided to find more advanced instruction and, after some inquiries, learned that Ruwin Erlich was considered the best piano teacher in the region. Erlich had no time available for a new student, however, and instead suggested that lanza study with his former student Arminda Canteros. At first lanza was disappointed, but in fact he had quite fortuitously ended up with a teacher who was perfectly suited to his needs and temperament.

At sixteen lanza had already developed a highly individual personality. In addition to his musical abilities, he had a frame of mind normally associated with scientists or engineers. Canteros had the insight to understand that there was no paradox in his multiple talents: she was open minded enough to appreciate his originality and sufficiently quick witted to argue her points in return. Canteros herself was quite a vivid character. As a young child she studied classical piano, specializing in the music of Mozart and Brahms, but when her father came home from work exhausted, he would say, "Arminda, please don't play that music; it makes me tired. Why don't you play some tangos?" – and she would oblige.[16] At age eighteen she was given a contract to perform weekly classical recitals on the radio, but when she was off air she played tangos for the production crew. One day the station manager overheard her playing tangos and immediately offered her a more lucrative contract for a weekly show of tango music; the producer, who had a flair for public relations, gave her the pseudonym "Juancho" (big John) because he wanted the radio audience to associate the performances with a macho personality. The broadcasts were a great success but listeners would have been quite surprised to discover that the pianist was a delicate young woman! Canteros went on to a long career as a chamber musician and a teacher in Rosario. She was in her late thirties at the time lanza studied with her.

Both lanza and Canteros have forceful wills, and lesson times were dynamic and lively. "alcides was stubborn," she remembered, "very stubborn. But I always put up with it because he had such well-thought-out reasons whenever he disagreed with me. He was so intelligent, so musical, that I was usually won over by his arguments. We read through enormous amounts of music together, but he was best at playing Bach."[17] Canteros and her family became lifelong friends with lanza. Canteros's daughter Arminda Farrugia remembers lanza at eighteen: "He was the only boy my mother would trust to escort me at night if I wanted to go out to something. I was only twelve years old but he was a twelve-year-old girl's best friend: tall, handsome, treated me like an adult, and always kept the secrets I told him strictly to himself."[18]

In her early fifties, many years after lanza studied with her, Canteros was involved in a serious accident. She was a passenger on a bus when the driver lost control and the vehicle plunged off a bridge into the Paraná River. When the authorities were recovering bodies, to their amazement, they found her still alive and took her to hospital. Tragically, she had broken her spine. The doctors said she would never walk or play the piano again, but Canteros began a monumental struggle to rebuild her life. With great determination and an indomitable will, she gradually learned to walk, and then taught herself to play the piano all over again. She later moved to New York where she became a respected teacher at the City University of New York. At age seventy-five, she surprised everyone by renting Alice Tully Hall and presenting a concert to celebrate her birthday. Her program included the twenty-four Chopin études. Suddenly, she was embraced by New York audiences and for a short while enjoyed the concert career she had been denied after her accident. By this time, lanza was teaching at

McGill University in Montreal, and he invited his former teacher to McGill to record a CD of the tangos she had played so well in her youth.[19] The recording was a best seller for McGill Records.

During the years that lanza was studying with Canteros, he was a student at the Escuela Industrial de la Nación in Rosario, where he majored in electrical engineering – a choice that later served him well when he became a composer of electronic music. After completing a diploma in electrical engineering he enrolled in the faculty of architecture at the Universidad Nacional del Litoral in Rosario. At the time it must have seemed a sensible choice, since he was artistic, drew well, and was good at math, but although he made tentative efforts for two semesters, the desire to study music soon overwhelmed him. At the beginning of his third semester, when his parents gave him money for his university fees, he banked the money, quit university, and took a number of odd jobs to pay for music lessons. Once he was sure that music was indeed his calling, he returned the university money to his parents, and then asked if the funds could be put toward music studies. They were astonished but, much to their credit, they agreed.

At this point, when he was looking forward to the joy and satisfaction of finally studying music full-time, he instead found himself frustrated and disappointed. He enrolled in the Profesorado Nacional de Música of Rosario, an institution that trained music teachers. It was a conservative, dogmatic, and uncreative place, and lanza had moved beyond the need for this type of instruction.[20] Even at age eighteen he was more in tune with experimental thought than with anything traditional. He was an exceptionally original thinker, and felt trapped in an archaic, narrow, and stifling environment. Several personal incidents added to his discomfort with the institution. The school's art history teacher was Angel Guido, a noted Argentinean architect who had designed the Monumento a la Bandera, a large square in front of the government houses in Rosario, built to commemorate the creation of the Argentinean flag. Guido's square, with its rows of white neoclassical columns and gigantic statues, closely resembles monuments built by Mussolini's fascist government in Italy. According to lanza, Guido was blatantly anti-Semitic and continually made disparaging remarks against two Jewish students in class. lanza, who had been raised to view racial prejudice as not only unethical but also irrational, made an official complaint, but was told by the administration to mind his own business. Thereafter, relations between lanza and the administration were strained.

His other troubles at the Profesorado were somewhat comical. At the end of the two-year program lanza was required to play a graduation recital. The printer who received the program information was confused by the uncommon name "alcides" and identified the pianist as "Señorita Alcides Lanza." When the school refused lanza's request to have the program reprinted, he in turn refused to play the recital. Today lanza would tolerate just about any absurdity in a printed program, but at the sensitive age of nineteen, with all his relatives and friends attending, he felt humiliated by the error. lanza never completed his diploma. He simply walked away from a school that did not fulfill his musical needs and where he was deeply unhappy.

Troubles with the Law

Trouble of a more serious nature was on the horizon. When lanza was eighteen he participated in a concert organized by some friends to raise money to send delegates to a peace conference in Moscow. lanza admits that these friends had leftist views, and considering the times, the enterprise was ill advised. Soon after the concert he was told to report to the police. During the Perón dictatorship a summons to the police station was indeed a serious matter. He and his uncle had a long discussion about how to proceed and decided that it would be even worse for lanza if he did not go; he would likely be arrested. So lanza reported to the police station as ordered, while his current girlfriend and his uncle anxiously waited outside. It turned out that the police had brought him in for questioning because they wanted to know who had organized the concert and what their political affiliations were. lanza, who was quick witted, decided on the spot to lie, so he told the interrogator that he was an artist and had no idea where the money was going or who had sponsored the concert; he simply wanted an opportunity to further his career by playing in public. He stuck to this story for more than two hours, after which the interrogator finally allowed him to leave. Much to the relief of his uncle and his girlfriend, lanza emerged from the station exhausted but unharmed.[21]

The incident, however, plagued lanza for several years. At that time many job and scholarship applications required a "certificate of good conduct" from the police. Since lanza's name was on file, the authorities refused to issue a certificate for him; Velmiro managed to "cleanse" lanza's record only after Perón lost power. It was several years before lanza learned how close a call he had had. After the fall of the Peronist regime in 1955, the man who had interrogated him was put on trial and found guilty of torturing and murdering prisoners.

It could be argued, however, that regardless of this brush with the law or the unpleasant personal incidents at the Profesorado Nacional, lanza's dissatisfaction with Rosario lay principally with the inadequacy of the teaching. He instinctively knew that he was not receiving the training he needed to prepare for an international career.

Any decisions about his future career, however, had to be postponed when he was called up for his compulsory military service. He served in the Argentinean army in Rosario for almost two years (1949–51). It was during this time that he ended up in jail.[22] Since lanza was tall and presentable he was often posted as part of the honour guard for VIPs. In 1950, during the visit of an apostolic nuncio (the pope's diplomatic representative) to Rosario, lanza was assigned guard duty in the cathedral, and was told that when the nuncio made the sign of the cross, he should also do so. lanza agreed to guard the priest but refused to make the sign of the cross on the grounds that he was an atheist. His commanding officer was unimpressed with this argument and sent him to the brig for two days for insubordination. lanza, however, felt that he won his point: "After I was released from the brig, they never assigned me duty in a church again."[23] There were no further incidents and lanza was decommissioned on schedule.

For the next two years he pursued a career as a solo pianist and accompanist in the Rosario area, but there was always something churning inside him. He started composing music in his early twenties. The moment he began to compose he felt the kind of excitement one experiences at moments of truth in one's life. He knew he wanted to become a composer, but that he had exhausted the resources Rosario had to offer. He realized he would have to move to Buenos Aires, the artistic centre of Argentina, one might even say of South America, to seek out the teachers he needed to pursue his dream.

Buenos Aires: The Disappearing Child

When lanza was twenty-four he was hired to accompany a choir for a concert in Rosario. One of the singers in the choir was an attractive, cultured young woman of twenty-two who loved music, dance, and art. Her name was Lydia Tomaíno. At the time she was studying to be a speech therapist for people with impaired hearing, a somewhat rare career in Argentina in 1953. lanza remembers that she was wearing a long yellow dress. Tomaíno remembers how well he played. After the concert, there was a dinner in honour of the choir and somehow, by accident or design, lanza and Tomaíno ended up side by side at the table. The attraction was instant and overwhelming, a veritable *coup de foudre*. Tomaíno and lanza were married less than a year later in a civil ceremony, and shortly afterwards moved to Buenos Aires.

Life was full of promise for the young couple. lanza was studying with teachers he respected, and after years of fruitless searching felt he was finally moving in the right direction. His new wife was equally content with her studies in speech therapy. At first, their financial position was precarious, but Tomaíno had a modest government grant, and they worked at a variety of jobs from dawn to 2:00 a.m., gradually upgrading their lifestyle. Both were hired as translators for an Argentinean publishing company that was anxious to sell American cookbooks and comic books in Argentina: Tomaíno translated cookbooks while lanza was given the comics – soon his English vocabulary was enriched by such colourful expressions as "Wham!" "Bang!" "Kaboing!" and "Kabooie!"

Their financial position improved dramatically when lanza was awarded a grant to study at the Di Tella Institute and was hired as a répétiteur at the Teatro Colón. The couple moved up step by step from a room in a pension to a rented apartment twenty-five kilometres outside Buenos Aires, to a rented apartment in town, to buying their own apartment. Tomaíno told me that at the time she and lanza were full of dreams of their future life together: "Among those dreams," she said wistfully, "were the babies to come." lanza composed a song for his young wife on Pablo Neruda's poem "Angela Adónica," and later a lullaby on a Portuguese text in honour of the baby they were planning. Part of this lullaby later surfaced in *penetrations VII* (1972) in a section where a child-woman, on the verge of a mental breakdown, sings a jazz improvisation on the melody.

Tomaíno became pregnant as planned and, after a normal and healthy pregnancy, gave birth to a severely handicapped baby boy.[24] It is not clear what went wrong during the birth, and even today neither Tomaíno nor lanza have an accurate understanding

Lydia Tomaíno and alcides lanza in Puerto Rico, 1967. Photograph from
the personal collection of alcides lanza

of exactly what happened. Tomaíno remembers that suddenly, toward the end of her labour, the doctor could no longer hear the
child's heartbeat; forceps were used to hasten the birth. The hospital claimed that the forceps had been applied with skill and that
the birth defects were the result of a lack of oxygen in the womb,
but it is unlikely that hospital staff would have readily admitted to
any error on their part. Whatever the cause, the baby was born a
quadriplegic with severe cerebral palsy.

Immediately following the birth the young couple were in too
much shock to ask probing questions, and they certainly didn't have
the resources to hire anyone to investigate the matter for them. In addition, they had no energy to spare on the past; the present was all
consuming. They had been presented with their severely ill child and
cursorily dismissed by the hospital with the words, "Look after
him." Their situation was desperate. There were almost no government or hospital support systems in Argentina at that time to assist
parents of severely handicapped children. lanza and Tomaíno were
completely on their own, with no experience, and in traumatic shock.

Pablo Alcides Lanza lived for six years (1958–64). His brain was
normal but he was unable to move a single muscle in his body by

his own volition. His parents desperately tried to keep him alive and well, but the task was impossible. In addition to a damaged central nervous system, Pablo also suffered from seizures and frequent infections. The couple worked out a system of care: Tomaíno looked after Pablo from about 8:00 a.m. to 2:00 p.m., lanza took over from 2:00 to 8:00 p.m., and they took turns through the night. For six years Pablo was almost constantly ill. He was never able to sleep through the night, and there was one medical crisis after another. His parents were wracked with fatigue, guilt, remorse, and despair; it was not long before their marriage began to fall apart.

Tomaíno believes that her husband blamed her for their son's illness. In a recent conversation lanza candidly admitted that perhaps she was right, but that he never did it consciously. Nevertheless, he began to distance himself emotionally from his wife. Tomaíno stresses, however, that lanza never rejected the child. She fondly remembers him playing the piano while holding Pablo under his arm, practicing the left hand while cradling the child with the right arm, and vice versa. Tomaíno and lanza never lost sight of the fact that Pablo's brain was normal. They made great efforts to stimulate his intelligence by reading to him and playing with him. They took him to parks, to see Christmas decorations, and to any interesting events in the city that might appeal to his young mind.

Tomaíno also felt it was important to have a second child. She said, "I knew we needed another child: for the child we had, for us, for everything." lanza was reluctant at first but eventually agreed. Their second child, a healthy baby boy named Guillermo, was born on 13 April 1960, about two and a half years after Pablo's birth. His arrival, however, did not mend the troubled marriage. It might be said that Pablo's poignant life had had a dual effect on the couple: the child's illness was both the catalyst that destroyed the marriage and the glue that kept it together. For six years Tomaíno and lanza directed all of their energies toward nurturing a child who was slowly dying. After Pablo's death, despite the presence of Guillermo, the marriage lost its raison d'être.

Shortly after Pablo's death, lanza was awarded a grant from the Guggenheim Foundation to study in New York. Tomaíno and Guillermo accompanied him to the United States but after two years returned to Buenos Aires. On the breakdown of the marriage Tomaíno commented, "Between us there wasn't anything left. He was living his life; I was living mine. My work was waiting for me [in Buenos Aires]. I returned home." The couple eventually divorced in 1972 and Tomaíno later married a successful Buenos Aires businessman.

lanza made efforts to keep contact with his remaining son. Every second year, from the age of nine to sixteen, Guillermo came to North America for January and February (the summer months in Argentina) to live with his father, and lanza also spent time with him during his annual concert tours of South America. It proved almost impossible, however, to maintain a healthy relationship at a distance of 11,000 kilometres. Guillermo Lanza has commented that for most of his youth he experienced a feeling of abandonment.

It is unfortunate that after Pablo's death it didn't seem to occur to anyone – parent, relative, or friend – that the four-year-old Guillermo needed counselling. With his brother's death he had lost his daily companion and friend, and he may well have been suffering from "survivor complex." The loss of Pablo, coupled with his parents' separation, was a staggering blow. Guillermo suggested that the reason he did not receive medical help at the time was perhaps because he was the type of child that tried to please and always appeared happy on the surface. Today Guillermo Lanza is an electrician with his own small company in Buenos Aires. The industrious way he drums up business is reminiscent of his father's similar skills in drumming up concert tours. There remains much love between father and son, but they are rarely comfortable together – their history is too painful.

Pablo's brief life had a strong influence on lanza as an artist. It is interesting to note that during the period of Pablo's desperate struggles, lanza made enormous strides as a composer. Despite the almost constant fatigue and crises, or perhaps even partly because of them, his music developed a distinctly personal flavour. He moved from works in which the influences of other composers are patently obvious to strikingly original compositions such as *plectros I* (1962) and *cuarteto IV* (1964). After Pablo's death lanza wanted, but was unable, to express his feelings about his son in a composition. He was too frozen with grief, too close to the memories. Decades later, he was finally able to put his son and his interior world into two compositions. Pablo appears in *ekphonesis V* (1979), an autobiographical work with a cast of characters from lanza's early life including his grandmother, grandfather, uncle, and "un niño ilusorio." This "illusory child" reappears in 1989 as the focus of the

choral work *un mundo imaginario* (1989); lanza's text evokes subtle images of his lost son, "un imaginario mundo interior ... un
niño ilusorio que se aleja en la niebla ... and vanishes" [an imaginary interior world ... an illusory child who drifts into the mist ...
and vanishes]. After twenty-five years of being unable to voice his
grief, lanza was finally able to express in music the poignant life
and world of his lost son.

2

Buenos Aires: The Music

When lanza moved to Buenos Aires in 1953, he found himself in one of the most important cultural centres of the Western Hemisphere.[1] Up to this point he had heard practically no contemporary music. In Rosario there was no interest in recent music in the symphony orchestra, the chamber music groups, or any of the schools he attended, and although he had explored a large repertoire of piano music with Arminda Canteros, practically none of it was contemporary.

In Buenos Aires, however, lanza was surrounded by opportunities to hear the most recent music. The city boasted five symphony orchestras, all of which had a serious commitment to performing contemporary music. Two of the orchestras – the Orquesta Estable and the Filarmónica Municipal – were associated with the Teatro Colón where, every Sunday morning, the multitalented Juan José Castro (1895–1968) conducted the Estable in a free concert with at least two modern pieces on the program. Castro, a noted composer who came from a family of musicians (his two brothers were also conductors and composers), had established free contemporary music concerts fifteen years previously with a private orchestra and had gradually worked his way up to the Orquesta Estable. On Sunday mornings lanza and his young wife would eat breakfast and head off to Castro's concert. Here for the first time lanza heard live performances of orchestral works by Honegger, Hindemith, Ravel, and Stravinsky.

The Orquesta Filarmónica Municipal played mainly nineteenth- and early twentieth-century repertoire, but each year devoted the entire month of April to new music. lanza particularly remembers the noted Italian avant-garde composer Bruno Maderna, who was invited to conduct the new music month in 1964. Maderna chose, among other repertoire, works by Stockhausen and Xenakis. Since lanza had been hired to translate at rehearsals, he attended all the rehearsals and absorbed the orchestral sounds of his European contemporaries.

The Orquesta Sinfónica de Radio Nacional also offered a concert season at the Amphitheatre of the Law Faculty of the University of Buenos Aires and nearly always included recent works. Other performing organizations included the Orquesta de la Asociación Wagneriana and the Orquesta de la Asociación Amigos de la Música, the latter of which had a strong commitment to commissioning works from contemporary composers.

lanza revelled in the opportunity to hear so much contemporary music and he attended an enormous number of concerts, some free, others with cheap student seats. Even today lanza insists that he acquired his vast knowledge of twentieth-century repertoire not by listening to recordings and radio broadcasts but by attending two or three concerts each week. He still believes this is the best way to learn and urges his students to hear as much live music as possible.

The quality of his teachers in Buenos Aires also expanded lanza's musical horizons. At this time Argentina was overflowing with first-rate musicians who had fled fascism in Europe during the 1930s and 1940s. lanza was studying piano with Ruwin Erlich, a well-known émigré who had studied in Warsaw and Odessa with Josef Silwinsky (a former student of Leschetitzky) and Leo Sirota (a former student of Busoni).[2] Erlich had taught at the Meisterschule of Vienna between 1926 and 1938. During that time he had come in contact with Schoenberg, Webern, and Berg and had performed some of their works. As a Jew, Erlich automatically lost his job in 1938 after the Anschluss, and most certainly would also have lost his life had he not immigrated to Argentina that year. Once in Buenos Aires Erlich allied himself with the Grupo Renovación, a contemporary music ensemble prominent in the 1930s and 1940s whose members included the composers Juan José Castro, José Maria Castro, Gilardo Gilardi, and Juan Carlos Paz.[3] lanza studied advanced piano technique with Erlich, whose bravura piano tradition could be traced back through Silwinsky and Sirota to Czerny and Liszt. He learned the challenging classical and romantic repertoire but also inherited, as did so many piano lines that trace back to Liszt, a great respect for living composers and a strong belief that one should perform their music. This belief is the bedrock on which lanza built much of his performing career.

By the time he arrived in Buenos Aires lanza had been composing for several years. Much of this music is now lost, but the few surviving works include settings of two poems by Pablo Neruda: "Angela Adónica" (1953) for voice and piano, and "La ahogada del cielo" (1957) for mixed chorus.[4] These early compositions show skill and imagination in writing idiomatically for voice and for piano but, despite occasional striking melodic and harmonic details, fail to fulfil the potential implied in their best passages because of awkwardness in the harmonic progressions and in the harmonic rhythm. lanza knew he needed a good solid professional teacher of composition. Erlich suggested Jacobo Ficher but after only one lesson lanza knew that this composer of neoclassical and neoromantic works was not the instructor he was seeking. Then a friend suggested he try Julián Bautista.[5]

Bautista, yet another European refugee, had left Spain to escape Franco's fascist regime. Ironically, on the day of lanza's first lesson, 16 June 1955, there was a major uprising against Perón. lanza remembers an unearthly silence in the streets, with military planes flying overhead and a radio blackout. He was hesitant to risk travelling downtown from the suburbs but decided to attempt it. Getting into town was easy but the usually bustling streets of central Buenos Aires were deserted. After the lesson, however, the streets had began to fill up and the Peronist government had commandeered all the municipal buses to transport workers from across the city to the Plaza de Mayo (the square in front of the presidential mansion) to mount a demonstration in favour of Perón. lanza had to walk miles to get home, but he felt little annoyance because he was buoyed up by the pleasure at having found a good teacher: "Bautista was delightful, very intelligent, and very cultured. One could have a conversation about anything with him."[6]

Bautista, who had inherited his method of teaching from his own teacher in Spain, Conrado del Campo, taught a three-year program of advanced harmony, counterpoint, fugue, analysis, and composition. His theoretical teaching was closely allied to music history in that chromatic harmony and atonality were viewed as natural and inevitable extensions of traditional harmony. This philosophy appealed to the young lanza, as did Bautista's vast knowledge of both music and the visual arts. lanza studied with Bautista between late

Julián Bautista and Alberto Ginastera, ca. 1950. Photograph published in Pola Suárez Urtubey, *Alberto Ginastera* (Buenos Aires: Ediciones Culturales Argentinas, 1967), 8 pp. after p. 76. Reproduced by kind permission of Georgina Ginastera.

1955 and early 1959, when Bautista moved to Puerto Rico.[7] It is worth noting that lanza was studying privately with Bautista. In North America and Europe most music students are trained at large-scale institutions such as universities or conservatories. While such institutions did exist in Argentina, it was common, indeed almost standard, for well-known musicians to offer three- or four-year programs of study in a number of subjects in their own studios, and today, although advanced musical training is taught in universities, the system of a master teaching in a private studio is still quite prevalent.

First Mature Works:
A Period of Exploration.

During this period lanza composed what he considers his first mature work: a toccata for piano (1957). He believes that at the time he was working on this piece he had been analysing works by Bartók with Bautista,[8] and indeed lanza's toccata displays the

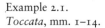

Example 2.1.
Toccata, mm. 1–14.

additive rhythms, polyrhythms, ostinatos, and chromatically in-flected modality typical of Bartók's music (see example 2.1). The work has the drive and energy associated with toccatas (at least since Schumann). The form is rondo-like, with several sections that return more than once, either verbatim or slightly varied. Anyone familiar with lanza's later style would be hard-pressed to identify the toccata as his work – clearly the young composer was still searching for a personal style – but the piece has the sense of drama, urgency, and exaggeration often heard in lanza's later works. It won first prize in the Iriberri Composition Competition, a national award that included publication of the winning work by Ricordi in Buenos Aires. Ricordi thus became lanza's first publisher.

lanza was also writing a series of six preludes and fugues and no-ticed that the material in one of the preludes was strongly related to his toccata. With some small motivic adjustments he linked the two works cyclically and began to perform them together in concert as *Prelude and Toccata*. The prelude, however, was never published, and over the years lanza lost the score. In 1988, when his former teacher Arminda Canteros visited him in Montreal, she asked for copies of his early piano music. He produced the toccata but told her that the prelude was lost. "But," he suggested, "I can still re-member quite a bit ... I can improvise it for you." "No, alcides," she replied, "if you can remember it that well, I want you to write it down again for me."[9] lanza complied; today the composition bears the curious title *preludio (preludio)* because, in a sense, it was composed twice. Canteros premiered the re-composed prelude in New York City at Alice Tully Hall on 18 March 1990 and performed it with the toccata for several years on her concert tours.

Toward the end of their work together, lanza and Bautista explored the techniques of twelve-tone writing. In 1959 lanza wrote a sonata for violin and piano that included a strict twelve-tone movement. *Transformaciones*, a work for chamber orchestra also written that year, explores various twelve-tone idioms but is particularly influenced by a Stravinsky-like brand of neoclassical dodecaphony. lanza remembers that works such as Stravinsky's *Agon* were influential in South America at that time. But lanza was still searching for a musical language that would suit him. Of this period of exploration, he commented, "I was after something. Using the twelve-tone technique, though in a free manner, was one way to get the dissonances I wanted – to get away from diatonic things ... All through those early years I was looking for some sort of language to express myself, a language with which I would feel comfortable stylistically."[10]

In the late 1950s lanza became friends with a group of young musicians working in Buenos Aires that included composer-pianists Gerardo Gandini and Armando Krieger, conductor Antonio Tauriello, and the teenaged composer Mariano Etkin. In 1959, with lanza, they founded the Agrupación Música Viva, a contemporary music ensemble that performed concerts throughout Latin America.[11] The principal raison d'être of this group was to perform their own compositions but they also programmed works by Bartók (*Sonata for Two Pianos and Percussion*), Varèse (*Ionisation*), Messiaen (*Harawi* and *Cantéyodjayâ*), and Riccardo Malipiero (*Preludio, adagio e finale*). The work by Malipiero was written for the group, who were proud to have commissioned a work from such a distinguished European composer. This was the first time lanza was involved in the commissioning of a new work.

plectros I (1962)

While preparing the Música Viva concerts lanza went through a crisis in his stylistic development: "I started feeling the pressure of what was contemporary and what was not ... I think I was too concerned about what my colleagues would say about my music. I was the newcomer. I came from a town where there was not much instruction. I felt I had to prove myself."[12] He had just completed *Concierto de cámara* (1960) an angular, dissonant work for chamber ensemble, and felt the writing was awkward and forced, but was in a dilemma as to how to move forward. One afternoon Gerardo Gandini, who was to become a life-long friend and performer of lanza's music, offered this advice: "Your writing is too difficult. You are forcing it. There must be easier ways to get the sounds you want – and you have to be more yourself."[13]

Whether lanza was already poised for the artistic leap he was about to make, or whether Gandini had prompted him to reassess his style, the advice certainly fell on fertile ground. lanza proceeded to compose *plectros I*, his first original work in his own style. lanza recalls that the piece was written as a birthday present: "I don't remember whether it was Krieger or Gandini's birthday, but this piece was my gift ... I began to explore the inside of the piano – sound as sound, not as notes. The work was more graphic, more theatrical ... Slowly, I was becoming aware that I was thinking in terms of musical colours – timbral situations – and not in terms of notes or intervals."[14] *plectros I*, scored for two pianists, is a highly interactive piece: player 1 plays on the inside of the piano, exploiting the percussive qualities of the instrument, while player 2 controls the keyboard and pedals. The preface to the score includes a list of twenty-four symbols, each representing a way to produce a specific timbral effect. There is a wide range of effects: the strings inside the piano, for example, are plucked, struck or strummed with timpani and side drum sticks, with the palm of the hand, with the fist, or with fingers wearing metal thimbles. There are also effects using harmonics, sliding wood against steel, using a plectrum to pluck the strings, and a host of other devices. Example 2.2 shows seven of these symbols and what they represent.

plectros I consists of five miniature pieces played in approximately four and a half minutes. lanza is interested not in producing random effects but rather in creating different soundscapes or atmospheres for each movement. He chose his sounds carefully: each movement has an individual character that contrasts strongly with the others. Example 2.3 shows the complete third and fourth movements. (I have added letters in square brackets so that the reader

Example 2.2.
plectros I, excerpt from prefatory instructions.

 Striking [the strings] with the palm of the hand.

 Playing [single notes] with thimbles.

 Striking with the four thimbled fingers at a time.

 With "legno" (side-drum stick).

 With "legno," but striking with the side of the stick horizontally on the strings.

 [Drop] the side-drum stick on the strings from a height of about four inches.

 Glissando "col legno," sliding the stick on the strings [in] a waving motion.

can identify which part of the example is under discussion.) In the third movement, marked *quasi ad libitum*, player 2 (the pianist who plays on the keys of the piano) has only a few notes to play; the movement is dominated instead by the sound effects produced by player 1 (the pianist who plays on the inside of the instrument). The part for player 1 consists almost completely of sounds produced by wooden sticks striking strings. At the opening, player 1 strikes the side of a stick against the strings [a]; then drops a stick from about 4 inches above the strings allowing it to bounce about on the strings [b]; later he slides the stick over the strings from low to high [c]. In the closing gestures he again drops the stick two times in a row [d] followed by a sliding motion from low to high to low [e]. While each of these gestures produces a distinct effect, the movement consists almost entirely of sounds produced by wood on steel strings. Most of these gestures are harsh and loud and, with little else happening, each effect has time to resonate before the next one begins, creating a harsh yet sparse soundscape.

The fourth movement, marked *presto ed accelerando al fine*, has an entirely different atmosphere. Here player 2 is extremely active, playing rapid, free-flowing, quiet (*pp* or *ppp*) notes on the keyboard.

Example 2.3.
plectros I, third and fourth movements.

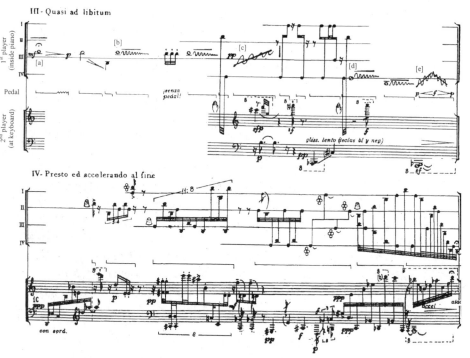

Inside the piano player 1 is equally active, playing a rapid series of notes by striking the strings with thimbles on the fingers, producing, for want of a better comparison, a sound somewhat reminiscent of a zither. These two movements create their own contrasting islands of sound: sparse, long resonating, thick, percussive sounds (wood against strings) followed by rapid, zither-like, quiet tinkling (metal against strings).

lanza obscures the metre throughout *plectros I*. Although most of the work is notated fairly exactly, lanza's use of complex irregular groupings (for example, ten notes in the time of eight, of which we hear only the fifth and sixth notes) combined with frequently changing tempi eliminates any perception of regular pulse.

plectros I is the first work in which lanza focuses more on purely sonic qualities than on pitch organization. The work exhibits two features that were to become signposts of his first mature style: the creation of unconventional sounds using traditional instruments, and a rhythmic language that avoids any sense of metre. The score also includes a hint of the graphic notational style that he was soon to embrace so fervently. Alberto Ginastera, the foremost composer in Argentina at the time, loved *plectros I*, arranged for its immediate publication by his Argentinean publisher, Editorial Barry, and used the work as a symbol of the Argentinean avant-garde during his lecture tours in South America and Europe.

lanza completed his studies with Bautista in 1959, and over the next few years pursued an active career as a pianist, conductor, and composer. In 1959 he formed a piano duo with the composer and virtuoso pianist Armando Krieger.[15] They performed frequently in Argentina and made several concert tours travelling to Washington, D.C., Quito (Ecuador), Lima (Peru), Montevideo (Uruguay), Mexico City, and Santiago de Chile. In addition to their own works, they performed music by Bartók, Boulez, Cage, Pousseur, and a host of Latin American composers. This intrepid duo once played Boulez's *Structures II* in Quito, Ecuador – probably the highest elevation at which the work has ever been heard. Their duo piano recitals and the concerts he gave with the Agrupación Música Viva did much to establish lanza's career as a performer of new music.

In 1959 lanza accepted a position as répétiteur at the Teatro Colón, one of the world's most magnificent opera houses. He was hired to accompany opera and ballet rehearsals, and over the next six years he observed the theatrical techniques of leading directors and choreographers while developing an instinctive feeling for how great dramatic composers of the past used music to enhance drama.

Ginastera and the Centro Latinoamericano de Altos Estudios Musicales

It is possible that with such a full agenda of concertizing and accompanying, lanza might never have pursued further studies, had it not been for the vision of Alberto Ginastera. The late 1950s and early 1960s were exciting times for contemporary music in Buenos Aires. During this time the Argentinean new music scene was divided into two opposing musical camps: one containing the disciples of Juan Carlos Paz, and the other, those of Ginastera. The roots of this hostility date back to the 1940s. Although the conflict between Paz and Ginastera is usually understood as the result of differences in musical style and aesthetic – Paz's music was atonal, whereas Ginastera's, at that time, was tonal and folkloric – at a deeper level their antagonism stemmed from a profound difference in artistic temperament: Paz was a sober intellectual, and Ginastera, a man of the theatre. Because of this fundamental difference, their mutual antipathy continued even after Ginastera himself embraced atonality. In the 1960s Ginastera's theatrical temperament enabled him to support his students in quite radical experimentalism (including indeterminacy and theatrics), while Paz's disciples continued to explore complex extensions of Schoenberg's twelve-tone method. This split between serialists and experimentalists was prevalent in many music centres around the world at this time.[16] Francisco Kröpfl, who founded the first electronic music studio in Argentina in 1958, commented that the two schools were sometimes referred to as "the Montagues and the Capulets."[17] The rift between the two schools was based not only on aesthetic differences but also on personal hostility between Paz and Ginastera. In his *Introducción a la música de nuestro tiempo*, Paz refers to Ginastera as an opportunist who writes domestic music fit only for Argentinean audiences and not for consumption abroad.[18] This sort of rhetoric fanned the flames of intolerance between the two camps. But as early as 1958 Kröpfl and Antonio Tauriello organized a concert series including works representing all the latest musical styles in Argentina. Kröpfl commented that following these concerts there was a gradual acceptance of each other's styles, and that the hostility between the two schools ended more quickly in Argentina than it did, for example, in New York.[19] lanza agrees with Kröpfl: "We, the younger composers, did not want the Montague-Capulet quarrel. We had inherited it from a previous generation and were not anxious to continue it."[20]

For some time Ginastera had felt that Latin America needed a school for advanced musical studies that would teach the most up-to-date styles of Europe and North America. With this in mind he approached the Di Tella Foundation, a philanthropic organization founded by Don Torcuato Di Tella, an Italian immigrant who had become wealthy in his adopted country and expressed his gratitude by endowing educational projects. The Foundation had created the Di Tella Institute of Buenos Aires. At the time that Ginastera approached the foundation they were already supporting research in economics,

Meeting at the Centro Latinoamericano de Altos Estudios Musicales of the Di Tella
Institute, 1963. *Left to right*: Enrique Oteira (director of the Di Tella Institute Foun-
dation), Olivier Messiaen, Maria Robiola de Di Tella, Riccardo Malipiero, Alberto
Ginastera. Photograph published in Pola Suárez Urtubey, *Alberto Ginastera* (Buenos
Aires: Ediciones Culturales Argentinas, 1967), 20 pp. after p. 76. Reproduced by kind
permission of Georgina Ginastera.

biology, and mathematics. In 1962 Ginastera persuaded them to support the training of composers by creating a music branch at the Institute. The Rockefeller Foundation of New York also contributed
a substantial grant. The Centro Latinoamericano de Altos Estudios
Musicales, which offered a two-year diploma in advanced musical
studies, opened in March 1963.

Competition to get into the program was fierce. Only applicants
who were already professional composers were considered. The sti-
pends offered to students were exceptionally generous (us$200 per
month) and funding was ample enough to invite a host of first-rate
visiting professors, including Olivier Messiaen, Luigi Dallapiccola,
Aaron Copland, Riccardo Malipiero, and Bruno Maderna. lanza felt
this could be the opportunity of a lifetime and applied. The twelve
composers accepted as the first composition class were Marlos Nobre
(from Brazil), Edgar Valcárcel and César Bolaños (from Peru), Mesías
Maiguashca (from Ecuador), Alberto Villalpando (from Bolivia), Blas
Emilio Atehortúa and Marco Aurelio Vanegas (from Colombia),

Mario Kuri Aldana (from Mexico), and Armando Krieger, Miguel Rondano, Oscar Bazán, and alcides lanza (from Argentina). A number of these composers – most notably Nobre, Valcárcel, Maiguashca, and lanza – were later considered to be among the leading contemporary composers of their generation in Latin America. In addition to accepting the student composers, the Di Tella Institute also hired Gerardo Gandini as pianist and assistant to Ginastera and Antonio Tauriello as conductor.

Ginastera was the right man in the right place at the right time. Only someone with his rare combination of vision, drive, organizational skills, and social connections could have managed to drum up the support needed for the new school. But it was his pedagogical approach – a philosophy that appreciated so many different views of contemporary music – that made the school so enlightened. Within reason, students were free to choose whatever type of composition they were inspired to work on. Ginastera's composition students met for a group lesson once a week during which they presented their "compositions in progress." Gandini would sight-read them at the piano, and the group would make comments. This extraordinarily talented group, the best that South America had to offer, was free to bounce ideas off one another and to prod and influence one other with little interference from Ginastera. Ginastera's contribution lay in the insights he had drawn from decades of hearing his music rehearsed and performed. His comments about notation and orchestration often helped students express their musical visions more efficiently and practically. Ginastera insisted that his students compose music that was well organized, professional, and creative, but the style was basically left up to them. One need only listen to the music of lanza, Gandini, and Etkin to know that Ginastera's students do not sound alike. Perhaps this is the best recommendation for any teacher.[21]

lanza vividly remembers the richness of the education he received from visiting professors at the Di Tella:

Aaron Copland gave lectures in which he played tapes of computer music (which was virtually unknown in South America at the time). Yvonne Loriod taught a fabulous course on contemporary piano techniques and repertoire. Olivier Messiaen guided us through a gruelling three-month investigation of his techniques, including analysis of Indian rhythms and ragas, Greek prosody,

Luigi Dallapiccola, with some of the Di Tella Institute students and their friends, 1964;
left to right, standing: Oscar Bazán, Mrs Bazán, Gerardo Gandini, Juan Carlos Zorzi,
Antonio Tauriello, Mrs Nobre, Marlos Nobre, Mesías Maiguashca, Jorge Arandia
Navarro; *seated*: alcides lanza, Mario Kuri Aldana, Esther Pires, Luigi Dallapiccola,
Alberto Villalpando, Mrs Villalpando, unidentified friend of Mrs Villalpando. Photo-
graph from the personal collection of alcides lanza.

and birdsong – all of this at a ghastly early hour of the morning
(at least for South Americans)! Malipiero was interested in music
and mathematics concentrating on works employing the golden
mean and the Fibonacci series. Dallapiccola, I remember, was a
man in constant motion, writing on the board, playing the piano,
chanting from *Ulisse*, with his tongue sticking in and out like a
snake. He stressed over and over again that we were not using
our memories to their full potential. I especially remember that he
taught us to love languages and would keep us on our linguistic
toes by switching back and forth in class between Spanish, Italian, German, and French with little or no translation.[22]

It was Bruno Maderna, however, who seems to have made the
strongest impression on lanza, perhaps because they shared so
many interests and beliefs. Maderna played a great deal of electronic music in class, mainly from Europe, and stressed that, like
any good composition, electronic works should have convincing

musical phrases and a sense of structure. It was an ideal lanza took to heart. In addition, Maderna was interested in the spatial distribution of sound and in mixed media. When we consider lanza's love of theatre and his training in electrical engineering it is not surprising that he found special stimulation in Maderna's classes. lanza's comments on Maderna's personality are touching: "I remember him as a most humane, tender human being, the nicest person. All soft edges, gentleness personified, a great conductor and tremendous musician."[23]

The music branch of the Di Tella was run along admirable lines. It seems that great efforts were made to keep the institution free of social, political, and in some ways even cultural (although this is hardly possible) prejudices. Fernando von Reichenbach, who was hired in the mid-1960s to design and build electroacoustic instruments, vividly remembers his interview for the job. "I was asked, 'Do you hate Jews? Negroes? Homosexuals?' I answered, 'I don't hate anybody.'"[24] The interviewers, somewhat naively, were attempting to avoid hiring anyone with overt prejudices or extreme political views. The Di Tella Institute was also determined to hire the type of people that could work together to produce the highest musical standards. It was a somewhat idealistic community that succeeded, at least for a short while. Reichenbach commented: "The Di Tella Institute was not polarized in any way. And that was fine … We were very, very happy. We were free to invent anything we wanted … And we could go to the [café] and eat and not worry about money. That's very important. [Money] works in other countries. In this country, never. There was only that one time: at the Di Tella. We could all work in one place for one purpose … Only the best was brought to the Di Tella."[25]

There are times in history when certain cities dominate the cultural direction of a country or even a continent: Paris in the 1830s, Vienna at the turn of the twentieth century, Berlin in the 1920s. In the 1960s, for a brief shining time, Buenos Aires was a leading light for contemporary culture in the Americas. I am referring here not to artistry, for South America has always had plenty of that, but rather to the confluence of money, opportunity, and talent. lanza has the highest praise for the man who founded and directed the music department of the Di Tella: "Ginastera had vision, he was a builder, he was positive."[26]

One example of the open-mindedness of the staff and students at the Di Tella is telling. In 1959, as mentioned above, lanza and several other Argentinean musicians had founded the Agrupación Música Viva. Although lanza had performed several pieces of contemporary Brazilian music, the group had a strong bias toward Argentinean works. Late in 1963, the eight student composers at the Di Tella who were not Argentinean requested a meeting with the Música Viva directors, namely lanza, Gandini, and Krieger. The students complained about the bias of the group and asked that their music be included in future concerts. Maiguashca, an Ecuadorian who was the ringleader of the protesters, angrily said, "We are guests in your country. You invite us here and then ignore us!"[27] lanza and Gandini listened carefully to their objections and concluded that the students had a legitimate grievance. Thereafter the agenda of Música Viva was consciously expanded to include contemporary music from all of Latin America. This crucial meeting marked the beginning of lanza's lifelong efforts to promote music of the Americas.[28]

three songs for soprano and chamber ensemble (1963)

The first composition lanza wrote at the Di Tella was the *three songs for soprano and chamber ensemble* (1963), scored for voice, flute, clarinet, bass clarinet, trombone, and percussion. Ginastera had suggested he choose a Latin American poet, and lanza spent several weeks perusing various books of poetry but, in the end, decided to write his own texts. Thus he set a precedent he was to follow for decades. His uncle Velmiro Ayala Gauna, who had hoped that lanza would become a writer, would not have been disappointed. With the courage of youth, lanza decided to write his text in English. Since Ginastera spoke little English, he had to trust that his student knew what he was doing. lanza's verse is simple, but displays accurate grammar, imaginative imagery, and a colouristic sense of the sound of individual words. The musical setting, however, reveals that he had not yet fully mastered the natural inflections of the language.

At this point lanza was continuing his exploration of irregular and nonperiodic rhythms, but was still notating rhythm with great precision. He seemingly wanted to create a quality of freedom and unpredictability but was still tied to traditional notation. Perhaps he had not yet fully understood the breakthrough he had made the previous year with *plectros I*; or, in another sense, he may not yet have been willing to trust performers with more freedom.

let's stop the chorus (1963)

Given his background, it is not surprising that lanza's music has always been inherently dramatic. His uncle Velmiro had written and produced avant-garde theatre, and for many years lanza had been an accompanist for opera and ballet at the Teatro Colón. It was probably only a matter of time and opportunity before he combined his interests in music and theatre. *let's stop the chorus*, composed in 1963, is his first piece of music theatre.

All the students at the Di Tella were required to sing in the choir, but since lanza's singing voice was considered unpleasant, he was exempted from this requirement on condition that he write a work for the choir to perform. lanza decided to write a theatre piece with a text consisting of a series of tongue twisters in various languages. The conductor speaks each phrase, and, after he has mastered it, signals for the chorus to attempt it. When the conductor judges that the chorus has spoken the line properly, he begins the next twister. The "catch" lay in the fact that Antonio Tauriello was to conduct the piece. Tauriello had a broken tooth, a large moustache that covered his mouth, and a tendancy to mumble when he spoke. lanza was counting on Tauriello's inability to master the twisters to produce the drama: the different speeds he would try, his various accentuations, the humourous effect of his failures. Tauriello, who was a good sport, was delighted with the idea.

The work was already scheduled for rehearsal when Ginastera heard about it. He was so horrified that he cancelled it. In his defence it must be said that he was walking a thin line. The Centro had just opened and had yet to prove itself, and Ginastera, like many other department heads, had to contend with difficult and inconsistent governments that often interfered with the arts. Put simply, lanza's piece smacked of frivolity and anarchy, and this was the last message Ginastera wanted his department to send.

Ginastera was not overreacting. Only a few years later the artistic branches of the Di Tella Institute were shut down. In 1970, during the dictatorship of General Juan Carlos Onganía, the art department of the Di Tella presented an exhibition in which they displayed a *pissoir*: the public was invited to go into the toilet, shut the door, and write graffiti on the walls. People being people – especially Argentinean people – they could not resist such a splendid opportunity to write antigovernment slogans![29] Onganía's reaction was swift. His government closed down both artistic branches – visual arts and music – of the Di Tella Institute.

I interviewed two members of the Di Tella about those traumatic days. Fernando von Reichenbach, the technical designer in charge of the electronic music studio, remembered the beginning of the trouble: "At first they just harassed us … They broke windows … There were attacks with [tear] gas … Then they tried a different tactic: they accused us of having drugs on the premises." Francisco Kröpfl, the director of the electronic music studio of the Di Tella, admitted, with some resignation, that the music department might have had to close within a few years in any case because of financial difficulties. Whether or not the school could have raised the necessary funding, we will never know. Kröpfl had a premonition that a shutdown was imminent and hurriedly assembled teachers, students, and staff who worked all night to move as much of the equipment and music as possible to the home of a wealthy woman. The following morning the music department of the Di Tella Institute was forcibly closed. The doors have never reopened, and today alcides lanza's alma mater is the home of an upscale shoe store.

This account of the closing of the music department differs strikingly from the version given by both Kröpfl and Gandini to John King for his book on the Di Tella Institute,[30] in which financial problems are cited as the sole reason for the school's closure. No one spoke about a government shutdown of the music department. Only Kröpfl, in the midst of a long discussion on finances, adds, almost after the fact, that there were also "problematic relations with the type of government that existed at that moment."[31] One possible reason for the discrepancy between the version published by King and the one I describe above is that the two sets of interviews occurred under very different political conditions. King interviewed Kröpfl and Gandini in 1978, at the height of Jorge Rafael Videla's dictatorship, probably the most dangerous time to speak out in the entire history of Argentina. Between 1976 and 1981 some 30,000 persons "disappeared." No sane person living in the country was giving interviews criticizing a government action or admitting to leftist views.[32] I interviewed Kröpfl, von Reichenbach, and Gandini in 1996, when there was no longer fear of losing one's job or one's life. Although all three mentioned the financial problems of the music department, they also courageously spoke about what had happened to them and why. Von Reichenbach told me that the music department had leftist views, but Kröpfl vigorously denied it. The extent of leftist leanings in the music department, however, is somewhat irrelevant, since even a suspicion of antigovernment views would have been enough to produce a strong reaction from Onganía.[33]

lanza, who was living in New York at the time of the shutdown, was saddened and appalled by the event. This incident, more than anything else, convinced him that he had made the right decision in leaving Argentina: "I have nostalgia for Argentina, but no regrets at leaving."[34]

cuarteto IV (1964)

lanza's next work, *cuarteto IV* for four French horns, makes a momentous leap forward in confidence and originality, and is indeed one of lanza's finest compositions. lanza had been working as a répétiteur at the Teatro Colón and had impressed several members of the orchestra with his musicianship. Guelfo Nalli, the principal horn in the Orquesta Estable, commissioned him to write a work for his newly-formed horn quartet, the Cuarteto de Trompas Wagner.

cuarteto IV is a three-movement work of extreme difficulty: the piece exploits a range of more than four octaves (from A^1 to B-flat[5]), and all four players are required to jump rapidly from one register to another, with great agility, in dynamics ranging from *pppp* to *ffff*. The work is somewhat reminiscent of Varèse in its wild exuberance. lanza requires the players to make many interesting modifications of the "normal" horn sound, calling for mutes, cuivré playing, flutter tonguing, glissandi, exaggerated vibrato, and quarter tones, as well as a variety of techniques to create "acoustic interferences" between the players. The work has a quasi-electronic character, as if lanza is pushing traditional instruments into another dimension. However, it is the complexity of the rhythmic component, rather than the extreme technical difficulty of the individual parts, that causes the greatest problems for players. lanza continues, even more forcefully in this piece than in previous works, his attempt to eliminate any sense of metric regularity. The rhythms – written in precise notation – are carefully crafted to sound random and unpredictable, and it is an enormous challenge to coordinate the parts. In his preface to the score, lanza states that he is "very interested in the 'atomization' of time values and rhythm, trying to practically eliminate the feeling of metric accentuation."

Example 2.4.
cuarteto IV, opening of third movement.

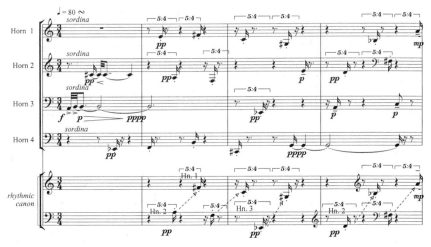

The opening of the third movement serves as a typical example
(see example 2.4). Here lanza uses five sixteenths in the time of four
(5:4), but because of the unpredictable placement of rests, it is impossible to sense where you are in the beat or the bar. In the 5:4
groups in mm. 2–3, horn 1 plays only the third sixteenth of the first
beat and the fifth sixteenth of the second beat; beat 3 is silent. In the
following bar, horn 1 plays the second sixteenth of the first beat and
the fourth sixteenth of the second beat. The other three parts are
just as unpredictable. Heard together the listener is awash in a sea
of seemingly random blips, with no discernable sense of downbeat,
upbeat, or syncopation.

But while the listener hears the rhythmic patterns as random, the
players must play these rhythms exactly as written, because in some
places there is an intricate rhythmic interplay between the parts. For
example, in mm. 2–4 there is a rhythmic canon between the
pp notes in horns 2 and 3 and those in horn 1. On the first beat of
m. 2, horn 2 plays on the fifth sixteenth of the 5:4 group; horn 1 repeats this rhythm one beat later. On the third beat, horn 2 plays on
the second sixteenth of the 5:4 group; horn 1 again repeats the pat-
tern. On the first beat of m. 3, horn 3 plays on the fourth sixteenth
and horn 1 echoes a beat later. In other words, horn 1 always echoes the rhythm played by one of the other parts a beat earlier. This

rhythmic canon is extracted from the score on the two lower staves of example 2.4. Although *cuarteto IV* contains quite a few of these miniature rhythmic patterns, they are too brief, change too often, and pass too quickly for our ear to catch them. Instead, we hear constant change and, with all the special effects, fantastic variety. My impression is that lanza used traditional notation principally as a means to keep the players together; in later works, when he was no longer interested in strict synchronization, he dispenses with standard rhythmic notation and substitutes forms of spatial notation that make it easier for players to achieve a sense of unpredictability without the enormous struggle of counting complicated ever-changing subdivisions of beats.

lanza uses graphic notation in two climactic moments of *cuarteto IV*: in the second movement, mm. 46–51, and in the third movement, mm. 34–41. Let us examine the first of these passages. The second movement, according to lanza, is based on "slowly evolving clusters." Example 2.5 shows much of the movement: the whole tone cluster C–D–E–F-sharp (mm. 23–7) contracts into a chromatic cluster, C-sharp–D–E-flat–E (mm. 28–34), which further contracts into a group of microtonal clusters (mm. 36–42, the arrows indicate quarter tone inflections), followed by an explosion of glissandi indicated with graphic notation. In other words, lanza narrows the cluster sense from whole tone, to semitone, to quarter tone, and finally, just as we expect a further contraction, the players erupt into faster and faster free improvisation. There is a sense of ever-increasing tension, and of something mysterious (the microtonal section has a Ligeti-like otherworldly feel), that builds until it is released in the improvisational passage. Here lanza wants ferocious energy, and uses graphics as a means to free the players from exact pitch, rhythm, and coordination in order to obtain the no-holds-barred effect he wants. It is interesting to note that the two timbral soundscapes mentioned above – microtonal otherworldliness and ferocious wild improvisation – are effects that lanza will favour all his life.

cuarteto IV is a grand summing up of lanza's stylistic interests of this period. As in *plectros I* sonic exploration becomes the primary focus. More specifically, while *cuarteto IV* has no electronic component, the waves of ever-changing sonic textures, including sections with pitches outside the tempered system tend to sound almost electronic. Colour and timbre now direct lanza's musical

Example 2.5.
cuarteto IV, end of second movement.

Example 2.5.
(cont.)

choices. Pitch is secondary, almost incidental. What makes this work stand out in lanza's development is the sense of fully-assured mastery that it projects. In most of his previous compositions, passages of striking audacity and inventiveness are found side by side with passages that mark the music as the work of a student composer. *cuarteto IV* triumphantly overcomes this problem. The premiere in December 1964 made a lasting impression on lanza's teachers and fellow students at the Di Tella. Mariano Etkin commented that, "it is one of the landmarks of Argentinean music of that time." Gerardo Gandini states even more boldly: "It is one of the best pieces ever written in Argentina."[35]

New Interests

Part of the impetus for lanza's creative breakthrough in Buenos Aires
came from listening to experimental music. As early as 1960 lanza
and his duo-pianist partner Armando Krieger had a weekly radio
show in Buenos Aires specializing in contemporary music. In the
course of his search for interesting works to discuss and play on the
show, lanza visited the American and French embassies, both of which
supplied him with books, scores, and recordings of avant-garde music
from their countries. The French contribution included a recording of
Messiaen's *Turangalîla Symphony*, while the American embassy lent
recordings of works by Ives, Cowell, Partch, Cage, Feldman, and
Brown. lanza played these works for his fellow composers in the
Agrupación Música Viva. As they pored over the scores, a number of
them became attracted more to developments in the United States
than those in Europe. lanza recalls that this switch in focus evolved
gradually, almost without them realizing it:

> I don't know if it was truly clear in our minds; but we had be-
> come aware that we were more interested in the New York school
> and California ... in Ives, Cage, Cowell, and Partch, rather than
> what our teachers were offering us from Europe ... The consulate
> of the U.S. and the Lincoln Library would lend us recordings of
> American composers and scores and books. So this [became] part
> of our training. I speak in plural because I think that Tauriello
> and Gandini had a more or less similar reaction ... But we didn't
> get together in coffee shops discussing "Shall we reject Europe?"
> No, it just happened. It was natural.[36]

When we consider the musical path lanza travelled in Buenos Aires, it
is not surprising that he was fascinated by the American experimental
tradition. As a student he had experimented with several musical languages, including various dialects of serialism, but he soon came to realize that a pitch-centred language would not answer his artistic needs.
He was becoming more interested in sonic qualities (texture and colour)
than in pitch organization. In *plectros I* (1962), his breakthrough piece,
two pianists explore a range of timbral effects created by touching the
strings of a piano with fingers and a variety of objects. Similarly, *cuarteto IV* (1964) is in many respects a sonics-first/pitch-secondary piece.

When lanza discovered the experimental American tradition ex-
emplified by composers such as Ives, Cowell, Partch, and Cage, he

recognized a band of kindred spirits. These composers were strongly focused on sonic qualities and, consequently, on stretching traditional instruments to their limits or inventing new instruments. They were also interested in sounds outside the tempered system. lanza was delighted to discover a group who believed that any possible sound was worthy of being used in a musical composition. It is lanza's interest in sonic effects that led him to investigate electroacoustic music.

Electroacoustic Music

lanza became attracted to electroacoustic music through his exposure to the most advanced music coming out of the United States and Europe. The first electroacoustic music studio in Argentina was established by Francisco Kröpfl in 1958 at the University of Buenos Aires. Pierre Boulez had visited Buenos Aires in 1954 as music director of the Jean-Louis Barrault theatre company. During that visit he met Kröpfl and gave him a recent publication from the Südwestdeutschesrundfunk (Cologne) containing technical information by Stockhausen, Meyer-Eppler, and others. Kröpfl had absolutely no funding, but was so enthusiastic that he began to look for a place to set up an electronic music studio.

I was lucky because I became acquainted with people at the Architecture School of the University ... I was teaching acoustics at the university and I found out that the architecture studio had an acoustic laboratory which was almost unused. But it had incredible equipment: oscillators, filters, analysers, mixers. They used it for measurements. So I proposed to the faculty that I could offer services in measuring material in exchange for the use of the laboratory. I called the laboratory the Studio of Musical Phonology.[37]

lanza's visit to Kröpfl's studio in the early 1960s reawakened his interest in combining music and electronics. "In a way," he said, this interest "stems naturally from my character. I remember at eight years of age I asked my piano teacher, what are the sounds between C and C-sharp?"[38] Even before he chose electrical engineering as his major in polytechnical school, he was combining his interests in electronics and in music. At thirteen his brother Edgardo showed him that if you reversed the polarity of the motor on a record player, the records would play backwards. Edgardo quickly tired of this trick but lanza would experiment for hours with all manner of music.[39] In 1955 he first saw a sine wave generator. His first wife, Lydia

Tomaíno, a speech therapist for the hearing impaired, used a number of electronic devices for audiometric tests. When lanza visited her laboratory, he realized the musical potential of this equipment. lanza began to compose electronic music in 1964:

> I had managed to buy a Grundig monophonic half-track tape recorder. One could play things backwards; speed variation was also possible. I also had a good microphone and it was with my equipment that the first Di Tella concerts were recorded. My first 'electronic' music was composed in 1964 when the composer Armando Krieger hired me to realize a tape to accompany his two-piano piece, *Contrastes*.[40]

In the same year as lanza's first private efforts to create electronic music, the music branch of the Di Tella Institute opened a rudimentary electronic music studio under the direction of the Chilean composer José Vicente Asuar.

lanza was determined to move to the United States because he felt philosophically attracted to developments in experimental music there. Using his knowledge and interest in electronic music as a lever to achieve his goal, in 1963 he applied for a Guggenheim grant to study at the Columbia-Princeton Electronic Music Center. His application was rejected. Later that year Aaron Copland came to the Di Tella Institute as a visiting professor. Copland was a good friend of Ginastera, had promoted his music in the United States, and felt that it was important for Latin American composers to visit their colleagues in North America. Copland liked lanza and his music, and suggested that he reapply for the grant and offered to supply a personal recommendation. Copland's support carried sufficient weight for the committee to award a grant to lanza early in 1965, and soon he was on his way to New York.[41] At that time, he did not realize that he would never again live permanently in Argentina.

Retrospect

In Argentina, as in other countries during the postwar years, many composers rejected the folkloric, populist, and nationalistic elements of previous generations, and some even rejected their own earlier styles. The pendulum had swung from proudly wearing one's ethnicity on one's sleeve to a distaste for sounding local and a fear of being seen as provincial. By the time lanza's generation reached adulthood this rejection of nationalism was well established in the Argentinean cultural climate. His generation wanted to sound "international." But what exactly did that mean? For the followers of Paz, it meant some form of serialism, but lanza and a number of his fellow students at the Di Tella were not interested in serial techniques. lanza's statement that he and his companions "rejected Europe" was in fact a rejection of serialism. They wanted instead to emulate the experimental composers of the United States.

What sort of musical style did lanza take with him to New York? Like many other advanced composers of the time – extreme serialists and aleatorists alike – lanza favoured a style characterized by constant surface unpredictability: no dominant patterns of pitches, no sense of metre, no sense of musical recall, a dissonance that is constant yet unpredictable, with extreme dynamics and range. But unlike the works of many of his contemporaries, each of lanza's works has a clear sonic plan – a succession of carefully chosen timbres – that defines the form and gives the work a sense of narrative. Underlying much of lanza's music from this period is a desire to saturate the acoustic space with contrasting sound experiences. To achieve this saturation he uses instruments unconventionally, tunes them in untraditional ways, explores sounds outside the tempered system, and introduces multitudes of microtones, glissandi, and "special effects," either one after the other in breathless succession or in complex layered textures. None of these diverse elements seem random: lanza's powerful dramatic flair directs his choices and gives a musical logic to the overall design. Even in his most abstract works the listener has the sense that a latent drama is unfolding.

New York offered opportunities that were unavailable in Argentina. lanza had already developed an avid interest in the theatre through his uncle's plays and radio shows, and through his years as a répétiteur at the Teatro Colón, but his only theatrical piece, *let's stop the chorus*, had been suppressed before its premiere. New York was to provide him with ample opportunities to compose music theatre and have works in this genre performed frequently. His travels abroad would also deepen his knowledge of languages and give him the confidence to mix, match, and splice words and syllables in his compositions. His studies at Columbia would open up a new world of sonic possibilities through electronics – a "new" bag of tricks soon modified to fit into his already highly developed musical style. And finally, in New York he developed better ways of writing down his musical intentions. His particular brand of graphic notation and his courage to use it even under great criticism represent the next step in his career.

3

New York

When lanza came to New York in 1965 to study electronic music composition at the Columbia-Princeton Electronic Music Center, he found a rich and lively but highly fractured artistic scene. Just about any musical style could be found there, practiced at the highest level. There were establishment musical institutions, such as the New York Philharmonic and the Metropolitan Opera, and jazz legends such as Thelonious Monk and Charles Mingus. *Hello Dolly*, *Funny Girl*, and *Fiddler on the Roof* had opened on Broadway the previous year and were still going strong. In addition there were a phenomenal variety of "new music" events – electroacoustic music, happenings, music theatre, avant-garde dance – featuring many of the most influential figures from the United States and abroad. There was also, as lanza was soon to experience, a bitter stylistic and aesthetic gulf between the "uptown" and the "downtown" composers. These labels, assigned much later, reflect the areas of the city where each group was active: loosely speaking, the "uptown" composers were active north of midtown, while the "downtown" composers were more likely to be found in the southern parts of Manhattan. The uptown group was largely associated with the Columbia-Princeton Electronic Music Center, which at that time was dominated by composers firmly committed to the use of serial principles to organize nearly all aspects of their compositions, not only pitch but also rhythm, dynamics, texture, and timbre. The downtown composers were major players in New York's experimental music scene. Because this group was so avant-garde, so unstructured, and so unacademic, no single set of characteristics can be used to define them as a whole, but the following list sets out some of their typical beliefs:[1] any sound is acceptable in a composition; anything can be used as an instrument; traditional instruments should be used untraditionally; the untrained amateur may be as inspired as the trained musician; the audience need not be physically separate from the players and might participate in the piece; it is no longer desirable for a composer to control all aspects of a composition; and, consequently, the end result of a work should in some way be unpredictable. In a loose sense, it could be said that the uptown composers favoured highly complex atonal music in which a central importance was given to pitch relations, while the downtown composers preferred music with some form of unpredictability and were often more interested in noise than in exact, clearly heard pitches. It is a major irony that both groups were equally alien to the mainstream musical community, which was largely hostile to both on the rare occasions they came into contact. When Leonard Bernstein programmed Stefan Wolpe's *Symphony* and John Cage's *Atlas Eclipticalis* in an avant-garde series with the New York Philharmonic in 1964, both Wolpe's highly organized atonality and Cage's random sounds were loudly and equally booed.

lanza as Outsider

When one considers lanza's work and interests in the early 1960s, his association with the avant-garde experimentalists in Argentina, and his rather expressionist free-flowing noise-like music, it seems odd that he chose to study electronic music composition at the Columbia-Princeton Electronic Music Center, the hotbed of "uptown" musical academia. It appears to have been an unwise choice that destined him to be an outsider in his own place of study.

So why did he make this decision? lanza has admitted that when he applied to the Center he was completely ignorant of the uptown-downtown rift in the city's new music scene. There had been similar divisions in Buenos Aires but nothing near the animosity that he found in New York. The other factor is that in 1963, when lanza first applied for a grant to study in New York, there were only a few institutions in North America (he never considered Europe) that had facilities for teaching electronic music: of those few, the Columbia-Princeton Electronic Music Center was considered the most important. Had he chosen the Studio for Experimental Music at the University of Illinois (founded in 1958 by Lejaren Hiller) or the San

Francisco Tape Music Center (founded in 1959 by Morton Subotnik and Ramón Sender), his musical style would not have been so jarringly opposed to the prevailing ideals of the institution. But in 1963 lanza, a young man thousands of kilometres away in Argentina, had never heard of these studios. He had gained much of his knowledge of the music scene in the United States from the recordings of contemporary experimental music provided for him by the American embassy and had noted that much of the music he admired had come out of New York. Since lanza wanted to find a way to study in New York, he approached Mario Davidovsky for advice. Davidovsky was an Argentinean composer who had studied at the Columbia-Princeton Electronic Music Center in the early 1960s with the aid of a Guggenheim Fellowship. He met with lanza during a visit home to Argentina in 1962, and suggested that lanza should apply for the same grant and study at the same institution.

lanza had listened to recordings of music by Otto Luening and Vladimir Ussachevsky, the co-founders of the Columbia-Princeton Electronic Music Center. Both composers had recorded traditional instruments and experimented with altering the natural sounds through electronic manipulation; they did not appear hostile to the type of experimentation that interested lanza. What lanza did not realize, however, was that his perspective was several years behind the times. The Center was now dominated by a new generation of composers totally committed to serialism. lanza also failed to take into consideration the fact that he and Davidovsky had quite different approaches to composition. Davidovsky had been allied with the twelve-tone milieu in Argentina whereas lanza was more interested in experimentalism. This crucial difference lay at the root of the opposite experiences of the two Argentinean composers at the Columbia-Princeton Center: Davidovsky's music was accepted, but lanza's was not. The Columbia-Princeton Electronic Music Center was in many ways dominated by the ideals of Milton Babbitt, Charles Wuorinen, and Harvey Sollberger. While all three are composers of merit, there is no doubt that their primary interests were fundamentally opposed to those of lanza.

The hyper-serialist composers' interest in electronics was rooted mainly in their desire to have complete control over all aspects of a composition. Much of the music being written at this time was ferociously difficult to play because the total serialization used by many established composers resulted in compositions of terrifying rhythmic and dynamic complexity, far beyond the skill of ordinary musicians. These works became the property of performers who specialized in contemporary music, and even these highly skilled specialists had difficulty giving musically convincing performances while maintaining anything close to technical accuracy. One reason that these composers embraced electronics was that they knew the machines could give them the kind of accuracy that human performers were unable to provide.

In many ways lanza was the diametric opposite of composers such as Babbitt, Wuorinen, and Sollberger. Their primary concern was the serial organization of the equal-tempered pitch system; lanza was completely uninterested in using serial techniques, was opposed to total control (he had introduced graphic notation, with its inherent freedom for the performer, as early as 1962), and favoured breaking free of the equal tempered system. Because of the serialists' concern with exact pitch, in their electronic music they tended to favour noticeably clear and clean distilled sounds; lanza, on the other hand, preferred murky and often noise-like timbres. All of these contrasts stem from a fundamental difference of aesthetic: the Columbia-Princeton serialists desired total control of a large but limited repertoire of sounds, lanza preferred an intuitive and expressionistic exploration of an infinite universe of sound.

In view of these fundamental differences it is not surprising that lanza felt alienated from the composers in power at Columbia-Princeton, and that these men in turn probably considered his music lacking in intellectual rigour. lanza's alienation from the Columbia establishment, however, was part of a more wide-spread problem. lanza's fellow students Jon Appleton and Charles Dodge have also stated that they felt ignored and oppressed by the institution.[2] Many younger composers wanted to use electronics to create special effects, to enhance mood and character, and, in some cases, to break free of equal temperament. These composers had little interest in serialization even of pitch, let alone of other musical parameters. The composer George Flynn, who also studied at Columbia around that time, expressed it succinctly: "Concerning twelve-tone, every time the note was supposed to go one way, my ear would invariably want to go the other; I ended up following my ear."[3]

In the mid 1960s the opposing groups could see no common ground. At Columbia this resulted in a significant generation gap between the older and younger composers. Jon Appleton remembers that in classes at Columbia the students "were never played a piece of French electroacoustic *musique concrète*, never played any electroacoustics except those done by Davidovsky, Ussachevsky, Bülent-Arel, and Milton Babbitt ... and we were told to emulate that style ... I felt very uncomfortable around those people. Everybody did."[4]

Joseph P. Straus questions the widespread assumption that the serialists dominated the new music scene by controlling academic advancement and the purse strings of awards, grants, and commissions.[5] Straus's statistics, which show that the serialists had about 15 per cent of the academic appointments in composition and received a similar (or slightly lower) percentage of awards, publications, recordings, and press coverage, has caused many to re-examine the ways in which the serialists made the "others" (tonal composers and experimentalists alike) feel bullied. However, Straus admits that his statistics do not measure "prestige."

> Certainly serialism in this period commanded an intellectual interest out of proportion to its actual measurable presence on the musical scene. Its outsized prestige derived from a number of factors, including its scientific aura, its association with the most recent European developments, and its simple novelty. It came to seem intellectually chic, in certain circles, and composers active at the time may have felt some internal pressure to stay abreast of the latest fashions.[6]

Testimony from "survivors" of the serialism wars confirms the observations in Anthony Tommasini's response to Straus's article.

> [T]he history of the world, from the Roman Empire to modern South Africa, is filled with examples of minorities controlling majorities ... You had to be caught in the battle to understand the tyranny ... The trenches were the classrooms, recital halls and lunch hangouts of every American university with an important music department. On these campuses, the most formidably complex serialist and 12-tone composers were intimidating figures. And vulnerable composition students were easily intimidated.[7]

The Columbia-Princeton Electronic Music Studio was on the front lines of this war. Babbitt's now infamous article "Who Cares If

You Listen?" sums up the intellectual position of the serialists with particular clarity. Babbitt argues that the progression of musical style from tonality to atonality to twelve-tone serialism to hyper-serialism was a historically inevitable development and that composers of "advanced" music contribute to the advancement of the frontiers of knowledge in some "scientific" way. His argument leads to a controversial corollary:

> The time has passed when the normally well-educated man without special preparation could understand the most advanced work in, for example, mathematics, philosophy, and physics. Advanced music ... scarcely can be expected to appear more intelligible than these arts and sciences to the person whose musical education usually has been even less extensive than his background in other fields.
>
> I dare suggest that the composer would do himself and his music an immediate and eventual service by total, resolute, and voluntary withdrawal from this public world to one of private performance and electronic media, with its very real possibility of complete elimination of the public.[8]

There is no question that if lanza had known that the dominant composer at the Columbia-Princeton Center believed this, he might have thought twice about studying there. lanza was certainly capable of writing a "difficult" piece, but he had long ago begun to look for ways to make music easier to perform and had always believed that contemporary music could be enjoyed by a wide audience. He had toured all over South America playing contemporary music to a wide variety of audiences because he believed the music could reach them. lanza is first and foremost a composer-performer determined to reach as many people as possible. Babbitt's elitist views would have struck him as alien.

In fairness, there was also much that was positive at Columbia. Vladimir Ussachevsky, who was in charge of the Electronic Music Center, was a gentle, cultured man who was encouraging and welcoming to foreign students. Composer Pril Smiley, Ussachevsky's colleague in the Center for many years, suggests a reason for this attitude: "Ussachevsky was a Russian emigrant. He knew what it was like to be a foreigner. He also had had to build a new life. lanza, and indeed many of the other students, had a positive experience with him."[9]

alcides lanza at the Columbia-Princeton Electronic
Music Center, 1967. Photograph from the personal
collection of alcides lanza.

The Columbia-Princeton Electronic Music Center had grown
out of a private electronic music studio established in 1951 by
Ussachevsky and his former teacher, Otto Luening. Luening was
very eclectic in his musical tastes, and Ussachevsky was to some degree influenced by this. Ussachevsky had a dual role at Columbia.
As a teacher of electroacoustic music he had a somewhat narrow
approach; in his classes, where composer-students learned to use
the machinery, he tended to toe the stylistic "party line." As director of the Electronic Music Center, however, he was much more
open, and was determined to make the Center an important international studio. The Center was founded in 1959 with the aid of a
$175,000 grant from the Guggenheim Foundation. The foundation
stipulated that the studio should have an international open-door

policy. With this in mind, Ussachevsky collected recordings of many different styles of electronic music from all over the world, so that the Center became a library as well as a working studio. Since these recordings were available to anyone, students who were not exposed to other styles of electroacoustic music in class could listen to these tapes on their own time. In addition, Ussachevsky opened the doors of the studio to composers of many different styles and backgrounds, including Varèse, Babbitt, Berio, Druckman, Dodge, Mimaroglu, and lanza, to name only a few. As lanza was later to discover, this "open-door" policy was not the case in European studios.

lanza had a good rapport with Ussachevsky. In the summer of 1966, when lanza had been at the Center for only a year, Ussachevsky recommended that he be hired as a technician and part-time teacher. For the next six years lanza had a regular salary. More importantly, at a time when there were only about a dozen top-notch electronic music studios worldwide, he had access to one of the very best.

lanza as Insider

Although lanza was creatively ill at ease with the Columbia-Princeton milieu, he was not unhappy in New York. Quite the opposite. This was due principally to the fact that he found a group of musicians who embraced him wholeheartedly – the so-called "downtown" experimentalist composers.[10] They seemed to know each other well, support each others' projects, and inspire each other. And it was an easy group to join: it didn't require a degree, a particular nationality or language, a university position, or even a specific style. The only requirement was a frame of mind open to experimentation. lanza drew enormous inspiration from the experimental movement in New York. There is no doubt he had been heading in this direction before his arrival in New York, but the explosion of experimentalism he found there and the considerable encouragement he received from other composers in the scene inspired him to follow his ideas with courage.

Who were the composers attached (however loosely) to this milieu, and how did lanza meet them? lanza had met John Cage at a party in Buenos Aires in the mid-1960s and the two composers developed a genuine rapport. Their friendship is documented in a wonderful interview done in 1970–71. lanza and American art historian Barbara Rose dedicated an issue of *Revista de Letras*[11] to the

John Cage in lanza's apartment in Berlin, 1972. Photograph by alcides lanza, reproduced by kind permission.

work of John Cage. lanza contributed a transcript of a recorded interview he did with Cage in New York.[12] The interview took place in Cage's apartment and it is obvious from the recording that both men were very much at ease with each other; their conversation has a gentle easy flow, and with the accompaniment of Cage's birds twittering in the background, it sounds like a Cage composition.

The musical styles of lanza and Cage, however, are quite dissimilar. lanza's music has an overall sense of development leading to climax, as if a drama is unfolding, and it exhibits a passionate in-your-face emotional intensity. Cage's music, on the other hand, is more likely to unfold in discrete events with no sense of narrative or purpose; it exhibits a Buddhist-like restraint and emotional distancing. Where the two composers are alike is in their love of using instruments in strikingly unconventional ways, in their use of graphic notational elements, in their collage-like approach to the tape medium, and, most importantly, in the way they explore, break up, and reassemble spoken languages, and create new languages in their compositions. All of these elements can be seen in lanza's works from the late 1960s onward. lanza and Cage had enough in common – and enough respect for what they did not have in common – to be happy in each other's company.

Another New York composer to befriend lanza was Earle Brown. lanza had experimented with graphic notation in a few brief passages of *plectros I* (1962) and *cuarteto IV* (1964), and was now itching to explore the use of graphics on a larger scale. In the early 1960s he studied the graphic notation of a number of composers, including Berio, Brown, Cage, Ligeti, and Stockhausen, but it was Brown's work that interested him most. A comparison, for example, of Brown's instrumental notation in *Available Forms II* (1965) with any of lanza's early graphic pieces reveals a similarity of design and thought. The two composers also shared a similarity of purpose: both wanted to free musicians from the constraints of complex written rhythms and pitches in order to achieve greater spontaneity and drama in performance. There is, however, a distinctive difference in their approach: Brown was interested in "open form" – in allowing performers to choose the order of events in a piece. lanza, on the other hand, does not usually allow musicians to re-order major sections of a work, because in each of his pieces there is a sense that a specific drama is unfolding. lanza was determined to meet the composer with whom he shared so many interests, and in 1966 attended a lecture given by Brown. After the lecture he introduced himself and was invited to visit Brown at his apartment the next day. This visit marked the beginning of a long and fruitful friendship and artistic collaboration.

lanza began to program Brown's works in his concerts – he conducted *Event: Synergy II* in Washington, D.C. (1967), in Malmö, Sweden (1972), and in Montreal, Canada (1974) – and was also responsible for inviting Brown to be composer-in-residence at McGill University in 1974. Brown was the director of the Contemporary Sound Series of Time Records (later Mainstream Records) at the time he met lanza, and in 1969 he invited lanza to make a recording of new music from South America for the series.[13] Thus *penetrations II* was lanza's first work to be recorded in North America. It was also through Brown that lanza met Lukas Foss, and through Foss that he met Morton Feldman.

lanza feels that he owes a great deal to this experimental group. "These were the people who gave me positive feedback. They played my works and gave me many opportunities to perform in their concerts. As a composer and performer I was accepted without discussion. This acceptance gave me a new confidence in myself, and a determination to write the way I wanted. Once I had tasted my freedom, I didn't want to get back into the box."[14]

New York Performance Groups

One of the main problems faced by student composers at Columbia was getting performances of their music. While there was a forum for performance of purely electronic music, it was extremely difficult to arrange concerts requiring live musicians. This problem is common in smaller faculties that specialize in the "academic" side of music (theory, composition, musicology) but have few, if any, performance majors. In larger faculties that offer programs in education and performance, there are always a few performance students who want to specialize in contemporary music, and others who can be enticed or pressed into performing student compositions. At Columbia, Wuorinen and Sollberger, both excellent performing musicians, had formed the Group for Contemporary Music. lanza's *interferences I*, scored for two groups of wind instruments and tape, was actually composed with the resources and technical abilities of this group in mind, but since his aesthetic was so different from theirs, they never performed the work. lanza was one of many in this situation, but the sharp stylistic divide at Columbia may have been more of a shock to him because of his recent experience at the Di Tella Institute where there was an emphasis on toleration and a family-like commitment to mutual support.

Eventually the Columbia Composers Group was formed; they performed at least two of lanza's compositions – *exercise I* and *trio concertante* – but their funding and their technical level were limited. In 1966 lanza solved the problem of getting performances by forming his own group outside the official Columbia-Princeton sphere, a typical strategy that lanza was to repeat at various points in his career: when a door is closed to him, he simply constructs a new door elsewhere. One should also note that many of the "downtown" composers had formed their own performance groups or were loosely connected members of one another's groups.

lanza's ensemble – the Composers Group for International Performance (after 1969, the Composers/Performers Group) – focused on music of the Americas, bringing Latin American music to the United States and North American music to Latin America. He shared the directorship with composers Edgar Valcárcel (Peru), Gitta Steiner (U.S.), and William Hellermann (U.S.). The musicians included David Gilbert (flute), Efrain Guigui (clarinet), Per

Brevig (trombone), Rogelio Terán (percussion), Carla Huebner and lanza (pianos), and later Meg Sheppard (voice). The following program, presented in both Puerto Rico and New York, is an telling example of the healthy and vibrant "no borders" approach of this group:

Eduardo Mazzadi (Argentina): *3 preludios sobre una serie de Dallapiccola* (1965)
Fernando García (Chile): *Estática* (1961)
Jacob Druckman (U.S.): *Animus I*, for trombone and electronic sounds (1966)
Gerardo Gandini (Argentina): ... *l'adieu*, for piano, 4 percussionists, and conductor (1967)
Alberto Villalpando (Bolivia): *Evoluciones*, for piano (1965)
Gitta Steiner (U.S.): *Five Pieces*, for trombone and piano (1965)
Rafael Aponte-Ledée (Puerto Rico): *Presagio de pájaros muertos*, for narrator and electronic sounds (1966)
William Hellermann (U.S.): *Formata*, for trombone and 4 instruments (1967)

During the six years that the group was active (1966–72), they gave more than fifty concerts in the United States, Puerto Rico, Mexico, Argentina, Peru, Canada, and Europe. Their two commercial recordings attest to the high calibre of the musicians. *Música contemporánea de América* (1969) was produced in Argentina and contains music by Mesias Maiguashca (Ecuador), Edgar Valcárcel (Peru), Gitta Steiner (U.S.), David Gilbert (U.S.), Marlos Nobre (Brazil), and lanza (Argentina).[15] *New Music from South America* (1970), recorded in New York for Time/Mainstream Records under the sponsorship of Earle Brown, includes works by Marlos Nobre (Brazil), Manuel Enriquez (Mexico), César Bolaños (Peru), and Gerardo Gandini, Oscar Bazán, and lanza (Argentina).[16] The Composers/Performers Group was an extraordinary ensemble. In the late 1960s and early 1970s hardly anyone had heard the recent music of Latin America's young composers. This lacuna was a two-fold gift: it gave the group its entrée into many festivals and series and, in turn, the group gave its audience a breath of something they had never heard before. Unfortunately, in the early 1970s, members of the group moved far away from one another and it proved too difficult to continue performing together.

exercise I (1965)

exercise I (1965) was lanza's first composition created at the Columbia-Princeton studio.[17] In it he explores through electronic means many of the features of his recent instrumental music: clusters evolve through slow glissandi; irregular bursts of staccato sounds are contrasted with slowly evolving sustained sounds; extremes of range, from low rumbling to high shrieking, are exploited; equal temperament is abandoned, and timbres are often noisy and distorted. The sound sources are completely electronic in origin, but the work has so many "realistic" noises that it could easily be mistaken for a piece of musique concrète (electroacoustic music based on the manipulation of pre-recorded real sounds). lanza stated that he deliberately intended it to sound that way: since Columbia-Princeton did not approve of musique concrète, he wrote a completely electronic piece disguised as musique concrète.[18]

exercise I was composed in two stages. The original four-and-a-half-minute piece was completed in 1965. In the fall of 1969 WKCR, the Columbia University radio station, invited lanza to appear on a program in which a famous composer interviews an aspiring composer (a switch from the usual situation where a notable figure is interviewed by someone who is less well known). WKCR had invited Luciano Berio to interview lanza[19] and in this case it gave both composers a chance to speak about their music. Berio listened to exercise I, which he had been told was lanza's first electronic piece. While he found the work "very interesting and very skilful," he claimed he could hear which section had been created first and which had been completed after the composer had acquired more experience. Berio urged lanza to rework the piece and make it longer. lanza took Berio's comments to heart and returned to the studio to rework and extend the composition; the revised version is about eight minutes long.

Although exercise I was originally conceived as a tape piece, lanza later added optional parts for dancers performing what he terms a "self-developing" choreography. After the interview with Berio, lanza attended a performance of Berio's Visage, an electroacoustic composition based almost entirely on the voice of the American singer Cathy Berberian.[20] On that evening the performance included a male dancer. The choreography consisted of only three gestures: the dancer walked across the stage, took off his jacket, and placed his jacket over his shoulder. The remarkable thing was that these three simple gestures took up the entire twenty-two minutes of the music. The dancer had tremendous control and an uncanny sense of timing. Each movement was performed so slowly and the changes were so subtle that it took some time for the audience to understand what was happening. "It made a big impression on me," lanza said. "I left the concert mesmerized. It was magical."[21] Inspired by this example, lanza decided that it might be interesting to add a dance element to *exercise I*. Soon afterward he met Mary Fulkerson, a modern dancer who expressed an interest in working with him.

The choreography for *exercise I* involves a minimum of four dancers. Each dancer chooses a particular path across the stage and repeats this path as many times as needed throughout the performance. The dancers choose their own steps and gestures, but the speed at which they move is fixed: dancer 1, who is the first to enter and the last to leave, moves in slow motion; dancer 2 uses rapid arm gestures but takes only one step every two seconds; dancer 3 uses slow arm gestures but slightly faster steps than dancer 2; dancer 4 uses extremely slow arm gestures with rapid footwork. In other words, the slower the arm movements, the faster the footwork. The choreography is concerned primarily with contrasts of rhythm and tempo; the dancers differ from one other because they move at different speeds and, in addition, the upper and lower body of each dancer also contrast in rhythm and tempo. Although the choreographic gestures are random, lanza is not averse to a more fixed choreography evolving during rehearsals, provided it is not preplanned but develops naturally out of the directional paths and separate rhythms of the dancers. lanza also specifies an effective lighting plan, consisting of soft backlighting and a number of spotlights focused so as to cast moving shadows on a back screen as the dancers enter and leave these islands of light.

lanza admits that he was also influenced by the artistic collaboration between Cage and the American dancer and choreographer Merce Cunningham. lanza had seen a Cunningham/Cage collaboration when the Cunningham Company came to Buenos Aires, and had continued to follow their work after he moved to New York. In the Cunningham/Cage choreographies the music is not intended to accompany specific dance gestures, and conversely, the choreography does not "represent" the music. Both are independent entities

with their own pulse, form, and character. In one sense this inde-
pendence of dance and music appealed to lanza, whose musical
scores of the period show a strong preference for loosely synchronized instrumental and vocal parts. In another sense, however, lanza
is too much the expressionist dramatist, too much the artist want-
ing to explore deep-seated emotions, to enjoy working with anything so completely abstract for long. lanza does not have Cage's
Buddhist attitudes: it is not in his character to step back and allow
the visual component of his work to develop independently with no
reference to the emotional content of his music. It is not surprising,
therefore, that he did not continue in this abstract vein.

The longer, choreographed version of *exercise I* was premiered by
the Mary Fulkerson Dance Company at the University of Rochester
in 1970. *exercise I* was to be lanza's sole foray into the field of
avant-garde dance. In the late 1960s he began to compose highly
personal works of music theatre, a genre he chose to develop over
the following decades.

plectros II (1966)
and interferences I (1966)

During his first year at Columbia-Princeton lanza composed two
pieces: *plectros II*, for piano and electronic sounds, and *interferences I*, for two groups of wind instruments and tape. The instrumental parts for both works are written almost entirely in
traditional notation and exhibit a great concern for pitch organization. Both pieces show an influence of the Columbia-Princeton establishment composers, with their concern for control of pitches
and complicated rhythms – although lanza in no way takes their
techniques to their extremes. The two pieces are more like impressionistic portraits of "totally organized" works: they could not be
mistaken for the genuine article.

At this point lanza was trying to fit in with the ideals of his faculty without sacrificing his personal vision. It was a dangerous
tightrope to walk and he only attempted it for one year. *interferences I* was composed with the forces and skills of the pro-serialist
Group for Contemporary Music in mind, but while his "conces-
sions" to their stylistic preferences were certainly enough to make
him uncomfortable, they were not enough to impress the group. In
a sense, he had got himself into the same hole he had climbed out of

back in Argentina; there he had been writing works of such extreme difficulty that his friend Gerardo Gandini suggested that there must be another way to achieve the sounds he wanted. "Be more yourself," Gandini told him. This conversation had been the springboard for *plectros I*, lanza's first work in which the primary focus was on timbral effects rather than pitch and rhythm.

In New York he had no need for a friend to point out his predicament; he came to the same conclusion on his own, and in response, immersed himself in the musical styles, notations, and ideals of his new friends in the "downtown" experimental scene. Although he was teaching at Columbia, there is no question that in less than a year he had shifted allegiance to another milieu where he felt much more at home. lanza soon realized that rhythmically complicated, pitch-centred works were not what he wanted to compose. During the following year he abandoned control over pitch and rhythm. In his more extreme works of the late 1960s there are often no precise pitches, and musical notation is replaced by graphic designs. Tone colour, texture, and dramatic shape – all highly significant factors in lanza's earlier work – come to replace pitch and rhythm as the primary means of musical organization.

I do not mean to suggest that *plectros II* and *interferences I* are not pieces of merit. In fact, *plectros II* was quite successful and has a long history of performances by pianists who want to dip into avant-garde techniques (plucking strings, use of harmonics, playing with a tape) without having to learn an unfamiliar graphic notation system. In this book, however, I am tracing lanza's evolution as a composer and prefer to concentrate on works that propelled that evolution. As such, these two pieces can be seen as intermezzi to the overall picture.

lanza was dissatisfied with traditional notation but up to this point had been unwilling to make a clean break with it. He had begun to give serious consideration to the limits of traditional notation in 1963 when he attended the rehearsals and performance of Stockhausen's *Gruppen* – a work scored for three orchestras and requiring three conductors – at the Teatro Colón. The problems he witnessed during the lengthy rehearsals made him rethink the question of notation, and he came to the following conclusion:

I decided that's not the way to do it. Stockhausen is writing complex music but it has to be played by human beings, and human

beings cannot be that precise. Because no matter how many rehearsals, people cannot play with that degree of accuracy … so it
becomes random … I made the decision that the more complex-
sounding music I had in my imagination, the easier I had to make
it for performers via graphic notation and randomness. Because
the result, in the end, is the same: they are all approximations.[22]

lanza did not immediately put this philosophy into practice, but
he let it germinate in his mind, and in the meantime he wrote *interferences I*, a work containing some of the same concepts he later
used in *eidesis II*, but written almost entirely in traditional notation.
interferences I, lanza says, "is very tough; it is so difficult to play. I
had not yet solved how to obtain the sounds I wanted without asking for the moon in terms of technical demands and number of rehearsals." Perhaps this, his most difficult work, finally made him
realize that if he continued to write music of such complexity, few
musicians would play his works. He became increasingly convinced
that graphic notation and specific improvisatory freedoms would
produce the type of high drama, complexity, and dense textures he
was hearing in his head.

eidesis II (1967)

In his next major composition lanza found the courage to notate the
sounds he wanted in the way he wanted, with no self-consciousness
or apology. It took only the catalyst of a commission from the right
kind of person, for the right kind of circumstance, to propel him in
the direction he had wanted to move for some time.

   In the summer of 1966 lanza and the Peruvian composer Edgar
Valcárcel went to Tanglewood to visit Gunther Schuller. lanza
played him a recording of *cuarteto IV*. Schuller had been a professional horn player for many years and had also composed a horn
quintet. He loved lanza's work, and said, "alcides, if you write a
piece for large ensemble, I'll play it next year at Tanglewood."[23]
With a certain courage, lanza began work on the commission using
mostly graphic notation. For most of his career, he has continued to
use the notational system he developed at this time. (A brief outline
of the basic elements of his system is given in chapter 4.) He visited
Schuller several times to warn him about his decisions regarding notation. Schuller was encouraging, and essentially gave lanza carte

blanche. Because of scheduling difficulties, however, the work was premiered at Tanglewood with Paul Zukovsky conducting.

eidesis II is a masterly summation of many of lanza's interests at the time. It is scored for thirteen instruments: two horns, three trombones, tuba, three percussionists (playing xylophone, vibraphone, timpani, finger cymbals, temple blocks, and woodblocks), three cellos, and two double basses. Most of these instruments are drawn from the low end of the orchestral spectrum, reflecting lanza's love for low-pitched sounds. In its exploitation of microtones, *eidesis II* is lanza's most extreme work to that date. Several instruments are deliberately tuned a quarter tone higher or lower than normal. Moreover, the parts for instruments that easily play microtones – trombone, timpani, cello, and double bass – are written entirely in graphic notation: not a single exact pitch is notated for them. Microtones are rarely exploited systematically but instead are used to create an ambience in which the concept of "out-of-tuneness" does not exist.

In lanza's first electronic pieces he adapted compositional techniques of his instrumental music of the time, but in *eidesis II* the influence is in the opposite direction. Specific details suggest electroacoustic techniques. In several places (pages 7, 10, and 15 of the score) short sequences of notes are to be repeated over and over, suggesting the use of tape loops. The musical continuity features both sudden changes of texture, as in a tape splice, and more gradual transitions, as if one type of material is faded out while another fades in. The exploitation of extreme timbral effects suggests the timbre-modifying effects of ring and frequency modulation, and frequent glissandi in the strings suggest the use of variable-speed tape recorders. Filtering effects are also found; for example, on page 8 of the score, the only musical event for a full minute (or more) is a double stop played by the first cello with the bow pressed heavily into the string and drawn slowly to create a scratching sound, making a gradual crescendo from near silence to extreme loudness and then fading down. As the volume changes, so does the timbral quality: the treble component of the sound increases as the crescendo progresses, as if one were gradually filtering out the low frequencies. The many other shifting timbral palettes that occur from moment to moment throughout the work are not "special effects" heard only at isolated moments, but rather are the essence of the piece. Most are achieved by exploiting unconventional ways of playing traditional instruments. This timbral manipulation, together with the microtonal harmony, creates the illusion of electronic music. In fact, a good performance of *eidesis II* in a good hall sounds as if it has an electroacoustic component.

  eidesis II contains a superabundance of energy, passion, and drama. The question of sexual energy was on lanza's mind. The controversial *Human Sexual Response* by sex therapists William Masters and Virginia Johnson, which had been published in 1966, includes along with much else, graphs recording the ebb and flow of energy during sexual activity. lanza admits that he never read the book, but that he found the undulating flow of energy in these graphs inspiring, and decided to "translate" the energy patterns into sounds. The overall effect – the outstanding characteristic of *eidesis II* – is that the audience experiences a force of energy. This force is directly linked to the graphic notation. lanza expects the musicians to use the freedom allowed by graphic notation to produce this energy. In his instructions to the performers, he says: "You don't have to count, you don't have to follow a conductor. [The music] is like waves, and the conductor is just cueing you; but it's not strict counting ... I am removing that restriction because I want you to use the energy you would ordinarily have put into counting or getting a precise interval ... Instead, play any high pitch or any low pitch, but give me more energy. Always more energy!"

  Example 3.1 shows the last minute of the buildup to the interior climax of *eidesis II*. We see that the players are given a range of notations with varying degrees of specificity. Sometimes they are given exact pitches (for example, the horns), sometimes relative pitches (indicated by notes that have the spacing and contour of notes on a staff but not actually written on a music staff – for example, trombone 1, opening), and sometimes wavy lines, indicating the contours of glissandi. There are no precise rhythms but the texture is controlled: the players build a crescendo from *p* to *ffff* over more than a minute, with each instrumental group added gradually to the texture to support and augment the increase in sound: the vibraphone, xylophone, and timpani begin at *p* and gradually increase the dynamic; in the middle of their buildup the double basses and brass enter in quick succession with much louder dynamics; with the final increase from *ff* to *fff*, the cellos are added. Then, at a cue from the conductor, all the players simultaneously reach or jump to the final box playing *ffff*.

Example 3.1.
eidesis II, p. 11.

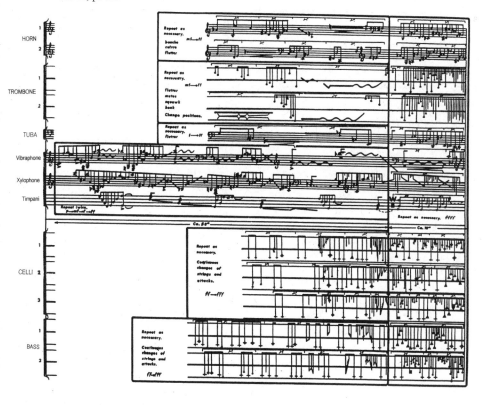

There is also a continuous increase of activity: some of the players are given a series of small fragments with a repeat sign above each fragment (see example 3.2). The players jump back and forth among the fragments, repeating them over and over again, becoming louder, quicker, freer, more intense, and finally frenzied. Once the musicians become accustomed to lanza's notation (which happens quite quickly in rehearsal) they can easily produce the frenzied buildup of energy that he wants.

This climax is followed by a momentary lull, after which lanza adds the sounds of human voices: for four seconds the musicians speak, sing, and shout a series of words, letters, or syllables. Again there is an expectant pause, broken by the voices for three seconds; another pause, then the voices for two seconds. The introduction of voices three quarters of the way through a work that has been entirely instrumental thus far is unexpected and startling. lanza says

Example 3.2.
eidesis II, horn parts from p. 11.

he wanted to add the colour of the human voice – in a piece that is all about colours – and the element of language after the interior climax not only to contrast with what was heard before, but also to react to it. The voices cry out, in cryptic fashion, the names of people or things lanza either loves or detests. Hidden among them is Wuorinen's name. Concerning this bit of mischievousness lanza says, "The whole idea comes from [my old teacher] Bautista who believed that critics of all sorts should be responded to. I was in the middle of that hornet's nest, Columbia-Princeton … [I felt] like I was a leper or something … so this was a kind of little revenge."

After the successful premiere of *eidesis II* at Tanglewood, lanza met Mario Davidovsky, a fellow Argentinean composer, in Manhattan. Davidovsky had attended the performance and praised the work, but suggested that lanza could have achieved the same effect by writing everything in traditional notation. Here, in a nutshell, was the gulf between the establishment and the experimental composers at Columbia. Davidovsky could not see the point of graphic notation, whereas lanza felt it was liberating.

lanza has described *eidesis II* as a series of waves. It is a good analogy, but I would like to propose another highly personal metaphor. The work has always struck me as a musical depiction of the ebbs and flows of an active volcano: at first the force of nature is quiet, with far-off rumblings. Then jets of activity pour out at intervals, only to quiet down once again. This is followed by a long sustained buildup to an eruption, after which human voices, shouting hysterically, lead to a final cataclysmic explosion.

eidesis II was published by Boosey and Hawkes shortly after the premiere. It has been very successful and has been performed numerous times in Canada, the United States, and Europe. According to Nicolas Slonimsky's exuberant description, "the title [is] derived from the Greek word 'eidos' (idea) and from the oneireic phenomenon known in medicine as 'eidetic dreams,' wherein the kinetic energy of enormous charges of sensuality leads to a series of sonic orgasms, with some instruments tuned in quarter tones resulting in orgiastic icosite-traphonic implosions."[24]

It is significant that *eidesis II* gave lanza another kind of break-through when he later moved to Montreal. When lanza first began giving concerts of his music and the experimental music of other composers in Montreal, he received more than a fair share of nega-tive reviews, but a performance of *eidesis II* changed at least one critic's mind. On 18 March 1972 Jacques Thériault commented on the work in *Le Devoir*:

It is not every day that one has the occasion to revise one's opin-ion of a composer. After a concert of the Performers [sic] Group of New York last January, I wrote that Alcides Lanza was strug-gling in the wilderness ... But now a single concert of the SMCQ has totally eliminated my initial reticence with regard to Lanza ... The work which has reconciled me to this young Argentinean composer is called "Eidesis II." Scored for thirteen instruments, the music explores and probes "the spectral analysis of sound" with a great deal of acuity. But, what struck me the most was the electroacoustic character of the work, the manner in which Lanza brings out new properties of the instruments, and the way in which he balances all the masses of sounds.[25]

Music Theatre

When lanza first arrived in New York in 1965, the city was a verita-ble cauldron of experimental dance, visual arts, music, and film. These different experimental disciplines often came together in vari-ous permutations to present inter-art collaborations involving some form of theatre. Some "events" were basically vehicles for experi-mental visual arts, with music relegated to a minor role; others were dominated by music. lanza first attended inter-art performance in New York with two Argentinean friends – the poet Eduardo Costa and the painter Juan Carlos Aznar – both of whom were interested in the lively New York "happenings" scene, which at the time was largely driven by visual artists. lanza also began to attend perfor-mances of what has come to be known as music theatre.

This term "music theatre" has a number of meanings but, in rela-tion to lanza and his interests, it can be defined as a musical work for a soloist or a small ensemble that has an important theatrical component. During the 1960s composers in a number of different countries were trying their hand at writing music theatre. The theatrical content might range from the peripheral – for example, players wearing masks and speaking – to the overwhelming – a dramatic extravaganza involving musicians, dancers, visual arts, complex lighting effects, slides, and so on. It is important to note that most composers tended to follow their own style of composition in their music-theatre works, but a few, including Peter Maxwell Davies, made significant changes in style when they began writing theatrical works. Some composers delved into the music-theatre genre only once or twice, while others, such as Mauricio Kagel and John Cage, made the genre a major component of their compositional output. lanza was to join the ranks of Kagel and Cage, producing music theatre works throughout his career.

It is tempting to draw connections between Kagel and lanza: both are of the same Argentinean generation, both worked at the Teatro Colón, and both are noted for their music-theatre compositions. However, they were not at the Colón at the same time. By the time lanza was hired at the famous theatre, Kagel had already moved to Germany. The two met only briefly in Buenos Aires. Their sole contact in Argentina was in 1957, when Kagel hired lanza to play Roger Sessions's Second Piano Sonata in a concert. It is important to remember that lanza came to composition somewhat late in life. In the mid-1950s he was only known as a pianist, and his first major composition, the *Toccata* for piano, dates from 1957, the year Kagel settled in Cologne. Thus these two composers – so similar in their interests in music theatre, in the sound rather than the meaning of words, and in their noise-like approach to electroacoustic composition – barely knew each another. Moreover, while the two Argentinean composers share a similar background and interests, their music theatre is fundamentally different. Kagel's work is somewhat Dadaesque in style, and often involves a series of irrational, seemingly random, and unconnected events. He wants to provoke the audience, but not necessarily to get them emotionally involved. lanza's theatre works, on the other hand (with the exception of a now-lost student work) always include some sense of narrative, of a story being told; he wants his listeners to become deeply involved with his dramatis personae.

When lanza was still living in Buenos Aires, he had read about experimental music-theatre works in the United States – particularly those of Pauline Oliveros, John Cage, and the ONCE group. Reading about these productions had inspired him to write his first piece of music theatre, *let's stop the chorus* (1963), while he studying at the Di Tella Institute. This piece is a farcical and an irreverent turning of the tables on authority figures: the conductor is made to look foolish while the chorus patiently waits for him to give them a chance to get the music right. Ginastera cancelled the premiere of the work because he rightly feared that government officials might think his music department was producing radicals.

Whether or not we consider a piece of theatre as radical often depends on what we are used to seeing and hearing, and on the current social norms of the time and place. lanza's music theatre could hardly be considered radical in New York. When he first considered writing a music-theatre piece in 1967, an "anything goes" climate had been in the air for some time, resulting in a wide variety of music-theatre works ranging from light-hearted thumbing of the nose at tradition to violent, angry, anti-establishment protests. Some music theatre was abstract and totally indeterminate: chance operations were used and no specific outcome was desired; John Cage's *Musicircus* (1967), a work he "produced" at the University of Illinois, is a good example. This piece involved simultaneous performances of rock, jazz, piano, vocal, and electronic music as well as pantomime, dance, film, and slides in the same space. The performers were free to do or play whatever they wished, and the audience was free to move about among the performers. The event was well attended; the multisensory experience struck some as anarchic, while others found it liberating.

Many music-theatre pieces, however, did not employ chance elements in a predominant way and were based on some sort of plot or episodes of a story. Peter Maxwell Davies's *Eight Songs for a Mad King* – a theatre piece that revolves around the life of England's King George III during his incarceration as a lunatic – which lanza first heard in New York in 1967, is a good example. lanza's theatre works are more like the Davies piece. They are not abstract or predominantly indeterminate but instead follow an implied narrative; we may not be fully aware of the details but we understand there is a drama taking place. lanza controls the overall form and content of his theatrical works in several ways. All of lanza's theatre works have a tape part that guides the action. The electronic component sets the initial mood and changes it at key points throughout the drama. The performer either enters into the mood or character of the tape music or occasionally struggles against it. In a sense lanza uses the electronic component to direct the drama. Performers are often cued by an electronic motive or sound, and loosely synchronize their parts, often in graphic notation, with the tape. lanza is unwilling to relinquish control over the overall form. He does not allow the musicians to change the order of the major sections of the work because there is a specific dramatic content that must unfold. While he leaves many local choices to the discretion of the performer (who might be directed, for example, to sing any high note, to mumble, or to elicit a few low sounds from the instrument), what happens in the dramatic continuity is carefully planned.

lanza was living in the United States during the height of protests against the war in Viet Nam, and these protests often spilled over into a general tendency to question any authority or tradition. lanza absorbed some of the defiance that was in the air, with the result that today his New York theatre pieces seem dated, very much products of the rebellious late 1960s. However, these pieces work well as theatre. lanza learned his theatrical craft in Argentina. As a child he had been fascinated by his uncle Velmira Ayala Gauna's Teatro de lo Esencial plays that were performed in a marionette theatre using only hands, voices, and lighting effects. lanza admired the fact that strong emotions and deep thoughts could be expressed powerfully with such economy of means. Later on, as a répétiteur for ballet and opera at the Teatro Colón, he was involved in theatrical productions on a daily basis. Although he knew that he did not want to compose traditional opera, he nevertheless absorbed the tricks of the trade. He had seen, heard, and absorbed a lot of theatre and theatrical craft before he arrived in North America, but it was in New York that he found his own theatrical "voice."

strobo I (1967)

strobo I, commissioned by noted bassist Bertram Turetzky, is scored "for double bass, miscellaneous percussion instruments, lights, audience, and electronic sounds." Turetzky, who had a strong interest in contemporary music, had heard lanza's eidesis II and was sufficiently impressed to ask him to compose a piece for the double bass. In 1967 lanza was young and somewhat defiant, and was totally enamoured of new electronic instruments. He told Turetzky that he no longer believed in writing for the double bass or any acoustic instrument. He said, "I will probably write against the instrument and will end up asking you to destroy it." Much to lanza's surprise, Turetzky replied, "Go ahead, just do it, no limits."[26]

lanza rethought the matter. He couldn't bring himself to ask for an instrument to be destroyed. Instead he wrote *strobo I*, a piece of music theatre in which he presents a traditional instrument as something constricting, exhausting, and on the brink of extinction. He uses several visual aids to get this message across. The player spends most of his time in a wire cage, like a prisoner or caged animal. Masking tape with fluorescent paint is applied to the body of the double bass to make it look like a skeleton, an image only seen near the end of the work when the stage is lit with black light.

lanza had been struck by the number of police sirens and strobe lights in New York City at night. He also had visited the Electric Circus and was intrigued by the psychedelic effects created by lighting at that fashionable discotheque. Inspired by these sounds and sights, he decided to incorporate sirens, strobe lights, and coloured lights into his new work. Lighting changes throughout *strobo I* enhance the various shifts of mood. In fact, the lighting is notated as if it was another instrument. lanza indicates specific lighting cues – blue and red spotlights, flashing green, yellow, and orange lights, black light, and strobe light – by means of continuous coloured drawings that appear on two lines at the top of each system in the score.

The score is remarkable in that while stage directions, lighting effects, and indications of how the instruments should be played are specified with a great deal of precision, lanza never asks the performer to produce a single exact pitch. Even the tuning of the double bass is indeterminate: the upper two strings are tuned "as high as possible (very tense)," and the two lowest strings "as low as possible." To a large extent, the sounds produced by the performer are improvised according to specific guidelines given by the composer. The soloist is as much an actor as a musician. In his introductory note to the score lanza writes, "the performer must change his mood several times, and this must be done very distinctly – even 'over-acting.' these changes are very important, and should correspond to different actions, environments, or atmospheres created during the piece."

At the opening of the piece the performer comes on stage, bows to the audience, and makes exaggerated gestures to cue the entries of the

electronic sounds (on tape) and the blue and red spotlights. This is
followed by a solo accompanied by the electronic music on the tape.
After about thirty seconds the electronic music subsides and the lighting becomes more hallucinatory, as rapid flashes of colours kaleido-
scopically flood the stage. The change of lighting triggers a change in
the performer, who no longer seems able to produce sound on his instrument. He makes slow, exaggerated gestures with his arms and the
bow to no avail. He increases the speed of his gestures and eventually
produces an occasional sound on the double bass and on the percussion instruments suspended from the bars of the cage. As he increases
his activity he adds sighs, whispers, interjections, and clicks. When he
cannot get what he wants from the instrument, his anger and frustration increase. lanza instructs the performer to "get hectic, frantic.
play viciously until reaching the maximum amount of sound." At
this point, contact mikes on the double bass are activated so that the
performer's mad improvisation is amplified and projected throughout the hall. Eventually the tape part enters, again in competition
with the performer, who shouts, "I don't want to play this." As the
tape takes over, completely masking the sound of the bass, the frustrated performer lays the instrument on the floor. All stage lighting is
extinguished and the player, in total darkness, begins to bang on the
percussion instruments and on the body of the bass. The tape fades
out again and the darkness is pierced by flashing strobe lights. The
player stops playing the percussion instruments and takes up the bass
once again, screaming and shouting while playing at a wild and frantic pace. The tape part parallels the player's frenetic activity with an
equal violence and works up to what lanza describes in the score as
an "orgasm of sound."

      At this point there is a complete blackout, except for the black
light, so that we see the double bass is a skeleton. The message is
clear: the instrument is dead. The performer opens his mouth but is
no longer able to speak. His long struggle with the instrument has
left him exhausted. He leaves the corpse of his instrument on the
floor and bows to the audience as if the piece has finished. When
they begin to applaud, their applause is then taken up on the tape
and distorted. The audience usually stops applauding in confusion,
at which time the performer begins to walk slowly offstage shaking
his head in bewilderment. The final gesture of *strobo I* is worthy of
the Marx brothers. Throughout the work, the player has tried repeatedly to strike a tamtam at one side of the stage without success,

Gerardo Gandini performing *strobo I* at the Di Tella Institute Contemporary Music Festival, 1967. Photograph from the personal collection of alcides lanza.

but as he slowly leaves the stage, the tamtam is struck by means of an invisible remote control mechanism.

Turetzky was genuinely delighted with the opportunities that *strobo I* afforded him. The premiere at the Festival of Contemporary Art in Cleveland in 1968 had a great reception from the audience, and Turetzky telephoned lanza to say that the piece stole the show. Even the newspaper critics enjoyed it: "The tour de force of the evening was Alcides Lanza's 'Strobo I (1967-V)' which had flashing and coloured lights and taped sounds all demanding of the performer a certain histrionic ability far above the requirements of the musicians' union."[27] "The Argentine composer stole the show with a theatre piece for bass, tape, strobe-lights and percussion. Despite the psychedelic gimcracks, the music was arresting, and it made one want to hear more from this composer."[28]

A year after the Cleveland premiere lanza's long-time friend Gerardo Gandini decided to perform the work in Buenos Aires.

Gandini is a pianist; he had never played a string instrument, let alone double bass, in his life, but lanza liked the idea of a non-bass-player performing the work. Gandini rented a double bass, took a few basic lessons, and learned how to elicit some good sounds, harmonics, and special effects. His rawness and awkwardness with the instrument became part of the overall effect. Gandini is a magnificent performer who puts his heart and soul into any project. He has a very physical approach to performance, and moves his entire body with the moods, rhythms, and nuances of any work he plays. All this made him a perfect performer for a work that requires the projection of violent mood swings. Gandini's performance was also enhanced by the special efforts made to follow lanza's lighting instructions accurately. Fernando von Reichenbach transcribed lanza's lighting score onto a celluloid film that was used to control two sets of coloured lights, so that the lighting was perfectly synchronized with the music. The effect was striking.[29]

ekphonesis II (1968)

ekphonesis II, lanza's second music-theatre piece composed in the United States, is scored for voice, piano, and electronics.[30] The setting is the studio of an opera coach. The coach, waiting for a soprano who is late, begins to practice. She finally appears – the epitome of an aspiring diva: beautiful, shallow, totally self-absorbed, and living in her own fantasy world. She sings or hums bits and pieces of operatic arias but ignores the suggestions of the coach. Eventually she breaks into a series of grunts, coos, cries, whispers, and screams. She is modern woman and modern music. When the pianist tries repeatedly to force her to return to her operatic repertoire, she takes out a revolver and shoots him, commenting, "Poor man."

In *ekphonesis II* the audience is inundated with sensory overload. In addition to the "modern" vocalises, the singer must improvise or quote traditional opera, pop tunes, tango, and jazz, while the pianist plays quotes from *Tristan und Isolde*, *Aida*, and *Rigoletto*, as well as a minuet, a waltz, and a samba. There are slides projecting images of stars, animals, Richard Wagner, and shortly afterward, a skeleton, along with coloured lights, blinking lights, dimmers, and strobe lights, all accompanied by highly amplified electronic sounds and city noises. The work is definitely influenced by the psychedelic events produced by Morton Subotnik, Donald Buchla, and Anthony Martin at the Electric Circus discotheque in Greenwich Village. Although lanza will allow the work to be performed without the slides and lighting effects, it is my opinion that if the piece is performed without them it loses much of its punch.

ekphonesis II was commissioned by Mexican soprano Margarita González, but she felt uncomfortable with both the ideas expressed in the work and the demands it made on her voice, and decided not to perform it. It was eventually premiered by soprano Judith Toensing, and although lanza enjoyed her performance, he felt that *ekphonesis II* had not yet found its ideal performer.

strobo I and *ekphonesis II* are connected in spirit. lanza – in his somewhat defiant *enfant-terrible* period – announces the death of acoustic instruments (represented by the double bass) in one, and of traditional forms (represented by opera) in the other. This attitude was part and parcel of the late 1960s experimental scene, but lanza did not take it too seriously. He has never stopped composing for acoustic instruments, although he uses them unconventionally, and his theatre works owe much to his six-year exposure to opera and ballet at the Teatro Colón. In this brief period he dabbled rather innocently in some of the more extreme views about music, but at heart he is both a man of the theatre and a pianist who loves to play an acoustic instrument.

Expanding Horizons

During the late 1960s there was a marked increase in performances of lanza's works. It is ironic that his music began to be played often and internationally just at the time when his own university chose to ignore him. At this time, hardly a month went by without lanza's music performed somewhere in the world. The following is only a brief overview of a few of these concerts. In 1967, for example, the Orquesta Filarmónica of the Teatro Colón (Buenos Aires), conducted by Pedro Calderón, played *eidesis sinfónica* (1960), and that same year the program for the Festival Internacional de Música Contemporánea in Mexico City included his *cuarteto V* (1967) for string quartet. In 1968 his first piano concerto, written in 1964 while he was studying with Ginastera at the Di Tella Institute, was premiered at the cultural celebrations during the Olympic Games in Mexico City. In the United States, Gunther Schuller commissioned *eidesis II* for the Tanglewood

Festival of Contemporary American Music, and *interferences I*, a work for wind ensemble, was taken up by the Hartt College Symphonic Wind Ensemble (conducted by Donald Mattram). In Buffalo the Group for Contemporary Music, conducted by Lukas Foss, programmed *acúfenos I* (for trombone and four instruments). Meanwhile two piano works, *plectros I* and *plectros II*, were performed in Montevideo, Buenos Aires, Lima, and at a number of North American universities. But perhaps the most significant event for lanza was the concert and lecture series devoted entirely to his music at his alma mater, the Di Tella Institute of Buenos Aires. Unfortunately this homecoming was marred by hostile comments from the Italian composer Luigi Nono who was a guest composer at the school. Nono, a rabid anti-American communist, could not forgive lanza for moving to New York, and condemned lanza's music as the product of American imperialism; somewhat illogically, Nono included works that lanza wrote in South America in this sweeping statement. Regardless of Nono's objection, however, it was clear to lanza that his move to the United States had catapulted his status from that of a composer of local stature to one of international renown.

In 1967 the Di Tella Institute offered lanza the directorship of its burgeoning electronic music studio. lanza hesitated, but after some soul searching, refused the position, mainly because of the small salary and the political instability in Argentina. This decision took some courage, as he did not yet have a permanent full-time position in North America, although he was optimistic that he would ultimately get one. Given the political repressions that were to convulse Argentina in the late 1960s and 1970s, lanza deserves some credit for presence of mind. Francisco Kröpfl, lanza's fellow composer and friend, was not so fortunate.[31] Kröpfl, the director of the electronic music studio at the Di Tella Institute, found himself without a job when the Institute was closed in 1970 by the government of military dictator Juan Carlos Onganía. lanza realized that had he accepted the position at the Di Tella, he would have shared a similar fate. Kröpfl went on to teach at the University of Buenos Aires, but when Perón returned to power in 1973, he was fired because the Peronist government considered him an "elitist." Whenever lanza returned to Argentina to play concerts, he visited his fellow composers; as he considered their troubles, he felt more and more grateful to be living in North America.

lanza had other reasons for not regretting his move to New York – reasons less dramatic, perhaps, but nevertheless important to him. In

Buenos Aires, he had been frustrated by the behaviour of local musicians. While they were excellent performers, he found them unreliable at rehearsals;[32] they would arrive late, or not at all, or sometimes sent substitute players who came halfway through. lanza found this frustrating and, in view of the difficulty in understanding his notation, it was also time consuming, since many details had to be explained two or three times. In New York musicians arrived on time, were present for rehearsals, and could be counted on to show up for the performance. It was just so much easier. While he missed the camaraderie of the Di Tella, the Latin temperament of Argentina, and the nurturing acceptance that a native-born composer often receives from his country and peers, he did not miss the struggles at rehearsals, the economic uncertainty, and the political oppression.

lanza's residence in New York came to an abrupt and unexpected end late in 1970 when the immigration authorities discovered that he did not possess an up-to-date visa. He was interned overnight at an immigration centre in New York. He called the Argentinean consul, who promised to obtain his release, but warned him that it would probably take about twenty-four hours. In a room with rows of beds he was reasonably comfortable, except for the fact that he got no sleep. The immigration authorities had arrested a gang of Colombian drug dealers who spoke a colourful dialect of Spanish incomprehensible to the authorities, so they woke lanza up, and he spent half the night translating back and forth between the Colombians and the authorities. The next day the Argentinean consulate informed him that his bail had been set at $1,000, an amount that his publisher, Boosey and Hawkes, much to their credit, agreed to pay. lanza left the detention centre accompanied by an Argentinean official, and was told that he would have to leave the United States and reapply for a visa from outside the country. lanza had been scheduled to fly to Madrid to conduct two concerts in October of 1970 at the third Festival Internacional de Música de las Américas, so he reapplied for entry to the United States from Spain, and once again received an American visa.

lanza, however, was destined to move to yet another country. Canada's representative at the Festival was the noted Canadian composer Bruce Mather, then a professor of composition in the faculty of music of McGill University in Montreal.[33] Mather attended lanza's concerts at the festival and was impressed with lanza's compositions and his abilities as a performer.[34] He invited lanza to lunch, and during the course of conversation, the composers discovered they had much in common: both were linguists, both were pianists who often performed new music, and most importantly, both had an international outlook on music. Mather was as curious about new Latin American music as lanza was about Canadian works. The two composers exchanged scores. At that time McGill University was searching for a teacher of composition and electroacoustic music, and Mather urged lanza to apply for the position. lanza asked his publisher to send a number of scores to the search committee, but for some reason the scores never arrived. On the day of the committee meeting to choose a candidate, Mather discovered that none of lanza's scores were on hand. He put the committee on hold for an hour, took a taxi home, picked up the scores lanza had given him, and hastened back to the meeting. Without Mather's generous act, it is unlikely that lanza would have been considered.

Mather, the prime instigator in getting lanza to Montreal, had a strong desire to give McGill's music faculty an international flavour. The year after lanza was hired, Mather was also instrumental in the appointment of Swedish composer Bengt Hambraeus as a professor of composition. Because of Mather's international outlook and contacts, for the next twenty-five years the music faculty at McGill boasted distinguished composers from three continents, an international "stew" that was to enrich the students beyond measure. In hiring lanza, McGill received a double gift. lanza was well able to teach composition and electroacoustics, but he was also a performer who had spent the last fifteen years of his life playing and conducting the works of living composers. He was to continue performing throughout his time at McGill, and many Canadian composers would reap the benefits. In the course of his thirty-year career in Montreal he has programmed more than two hundred compositions by Canadian composers. He has also brought Canadian music to South America and Europe, recorded it, written about it, and taught it. Columbia's loss was indeed McGill's gain.

4

lanza's Notation

In the late 1960s lanza began to use graphic notation regularly in his compositions, so at this point, I will interrupt the chronological narrative of his life and works to present a brief introduction to the type of graphic notation that lanza uses in his mature works. This will give readers a better understanding of the music examples that appear in the remaining chapters.

For much of the history of western music, beginning in the Middle Ages, innovations in musical notation have been prompted by the desire of composers to express their intentions with greater and greater precision. During the 1950s and 1960s, as a number of avant-garde composers began to relinquish control over various aspects of musical performance, they needed to find new ways of indicating these freedoms to performers. The use of graphic notation was fairly common in the late 1960s, and composers from quite different backgrounds (including Luciano Berio, John Cage, Karlheinz Stockhausen, Earle Brown, R. Murray Schafer, and Gilles Tremblay) experimented with it, working for the most part independently. As composers introduced a spate of new notations, their scores began to look less and less like traditional music, and more and more like works of graphic art. Performers were faced with a situation in which a new and unique notation might have to be learned for each new piece; often similar symbols were used in contradictory ways by different composers. Although a few highly committed performers rose to the occasion with dedication and skill – the extraordinary pianist David Tudor comes to mind – most musicians, already out of tune with the unconventional sound of new music, saw these new notation systems as yet another reason to avoid learning contemporary works. Therefore, lanza's difficulties with performers and his quest for a notation to express his ideas were not unique.

Trigram

lanza had been exploring new ways to notate his ideas throughout the 1960s. The method he developed toward the end of the decade is, in spite of its unconventional appearance, eminently suited for conveying his intentions to performers. Much of his notation is placed in a three-line staff that he calls a "trigram" (see example 4.1). The bottom and top lines of the trigram represent the extreme low and extreme high notes of the performer's range; the middle line represents an approximate midrange. Within the trigram lanza uses a variety of notational practices. Specific pitches are either written as notes on a conventional five-line staff or indicated as note names in parentheses added to a graphic notation. The excerpt from *eidesis III* (for two orchestras and tape, 1973) in example 4.2 is a good illustration of this procedure.

In the first bar the clarinet 1 plays a low D (placed near the bottom line of the trigram) which is sustained for two bars; in the second bar clarinet 2 plays a C-sharp sustained throughout the bar. The wavy line for the English horn and contrabassoon indicates a tremolo for those instruments beginning near the end of the first bar; since the notation appears near the top of the trigram, the notes are relatively high, but the exact pitches are left to the performers' discretion. The numerical indicators 1'45" and 2' (1 minute 45 seconds and 2 minutes) are "mileage markers" that indicate approximately how far into the tape part this passage occurs. Conductors and players use stopwatches during the early stages of rehearsal, but it does not take long for the musicians to become familiar with the sounds on the tape and the musical cues from other players. At this point, the stopwatch is often no longer needed and is used only in specific critical passages.

In the excerpt shown in example 4.2, lanza indicates two specific pitches and leaves a third to the choice of the performers. However, a number of his works contain few if any exact pitches; they are written almost entirely in graphic notation, with trigrams used to control range. lanza has also developed specific notational devices to indicate repetitions, dynamics, and performance directions. These

Example 4.1.
Blank trigram.

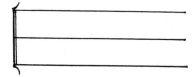

Example 4.2.
eidesis III, excerpt from p. 10.

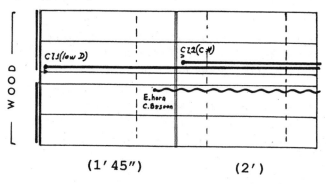

Example 4.3.
vôo, excerpt from p. 4.

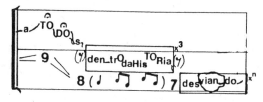

can be seen in example 4.3, a passage from *vôo* (1992, for singer, tape, and electronic extensions). The text consists of three fragments: "a todos," "dentro da historia," and "desviando."

The singer begins the "bar" singing "a todos" in her highest range (near the top line of the trigram), continues with "dentro da historia" hovering around the mid-range, and finishes with "desviando" in the lowest part of her range. lanza's notation indicates that the line moves from very high to very low, but allows the singer to choose the precise pitches. In most of his works lanza indicates dynamics with boldface numbers ranging from 1 (*pppp*) to 10

Example 4.4.
Possible realization of example 4.3.

(ffff). In this passage, the dynamic numbers 9, 8, and 7 indicate a diminuendo from *fff* to *ff* to *f*. The phrase is part of the climax of *vôo* and lanza wants a great display of emotional intensity from the singer. Her highest notes ("todos") are also her loudest and each syllable is marked with a fermata to prolong the tension. lanza also indicates repetitions of particular phrases of the text. The second segment, "dentro da historia," is enclosed in a rectangle with the rubric "x^3" (times 3) just outside the box. lanza uses this device to indicate that the material inside the box is to be performed three times. He also provides a rhythm in traditional notation under the text with a hint of a melodic line (the syllables "-tro" and "-to-" are higher pitches than "da his-" and "-ria"). The third segment of text, "desviando," is enclosed in a rectangle that is marked "x^n." This indicates that the singer must repeat the enclosed material but that the number of repetitions is left to the discretion of the performer (so long as the repetitions fit generally within the given time segment). Note also that the syllable "-vian" (from the word "desviando") is enclosed in an irregular curve; this indicates that the singer may repeat the enclosed material at will. In other words, rectangles indicate a required repetition whereas irregular curves indicate optional repetition. Example 4.4 shows one possible performance of the passage.

To those who take the trouble to understand its mechanisms, lanza's notation is remarkably clear. He wants to give the performers certain liberties but at the same time, to retain important creative decisions. He controls the overall scenario – the general sequence of music and text – and specifies when and for how long each event occurs within the drama, but leaves many of the moment-to-moment details up to the performer.

lanza could have notated the measure above using exact rhythms and pitches; after all, he used traditional notation almost exclusively for the first twelve years of his career as a composer. His early compositions, however, tend to be very difficult to perform because of the complexity of the rhythms, the wide ranges, and the extremes of dynamics. Using trigram graphic notation he can achieve much the same effect with a score that is much easier for musicians to learn and perform. lanza says that while he relinquishes certain controls, he expects something in return, a quid pro quo: musicians must direct all the energy that might have been spent counting beats and finding exact pitches to create a totally committed and passionate performance. This is the price of the freedom he offers.

Pure Graphic Notation

Although lanza uses trigram notation in the majority of his works, he does not use it exclusively. A few of his pieces composed between 1967 and 1971 are in what I call "pure graphic" notation; the scores are drawn completely in abstract graphic designs, with no notes, bar lines, or trigrams. In these works the tape part is preeminent, and the performer is given a set of instructions specifying what to do and when to do it. The performer's role is to react to the tape: to imitate the sounds on it, to "interfere" with it, or to create other sounds in counterpoint to it. Although lanza's pure graphic period was brief, a few pure graphic passages appear in later works.

In lanza's first compositions of this type, the "scores" did not contain graphic designs; they consisted only of the verbal instructions. When his publisher Boosey and Hawkes submitted these works to the Library of Congress for U.S. copyright registration, they were told that a set of verbal instructions could not be copyrighted as a musical composition. lanza added a graphic component that was essentially a pictorial representation of the music on the tape and the music to be created by the performers. The resulting score – drawings and instructions – was accepted.

penetrations II (1969), scored "for wind(s), string(s), percussion, and keyboard instrument(s), with voices, lights, electronic sounds, and electronic extensions," is a good example of lanza's pure graphic notation. The players sit in the dark and react to sounds on the tape in an improvisatory way. The "score" consists of three

Example 4.5.
penetrations II, p. 2.

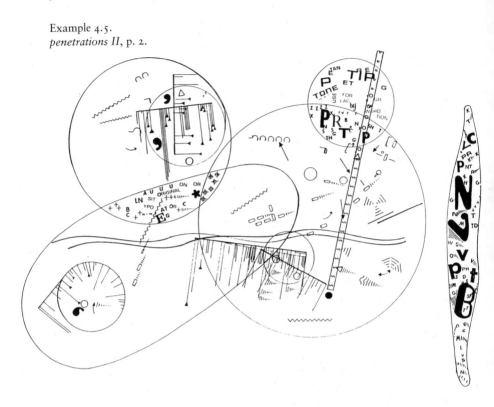

pages of drawings accompanied by a page of instructions. Page 2 of
the "score" is shown in example 4.5; the following paragraph is an
excerpt from the instructions.

listen to the taped electronic sounds, one sequence at a time. react
accordingly. this can be accomplished by exact or partial imitation,
or by playing materials completely opposed to the taped ones. listen
to the other players in the group and react accordingly. be imaginative and avoid the use of consonant chords or sequences related to
tonality. in this context special tuning for the instruments, microtonal intervals and multiphonics are also possible.

take advantage of the electronic amplification and modification
possibilities for your instrument or voice.

on page 2 isolated vocal sounds can be used ... fast sequences of
short vocal sounds, consonants, vowels, syllables, "choral
sounds" and speaking "as a mute trying to speak."

Hybrid Notation

Later in his life lanza again became concerned with exact pitches and harmonies. These later works employ a hybrid notation that combines conventional notation to indicate exact pitches or rhythms, trigram notation for approximate pitches, and pure graphics for improvisatory sections. This mixture of notations came to be the norm for lanza's later works.

The excerpt from *un mundo imginario* (for mixed choir, 1989) in example 4.6 is typical. Here the tenors and basses sing pitches and rhythms written in traditional notation. Their phrases are enclosed in rectangles with "x^n" in the upper right corner, indicating that the singers repeat the material enclosed in the boxes as many times as needed to fill the required time. The two soprano parts are notated in pure graphics: they sing fragments of the word "interior" beginning in unison and sliding up or down in pitch according to the shape of the curved lines. The alto part is more complex: they begin in unison, singing three exact pitches notated on a traditional five-line staff, then separate to form a microtonal cluster that expands and contracts [a]; after a six-second pause they sing three unspecified low pitches notated in a trigram [b]; they then separate once again to form a second microtonal cluster that expands and contracts to a single note which drifts upward into nothingness [c]. By the end of the passage the altos are divided into two groups, each singing a series of microtonal clusters. In this section lanza achieves a tightly controlled soundscape. The male singers repeat chromatic phrases obsessively, like a moto perpetuo; the altos are trapped in microtonal clusters that expand and contract in close formations; the sopranos slide up and down in improvisatory gestures. This layering of different sonorities comes out of the tradition of Ives and early Stravinsky, but here lanza takes it to another dimension by writing each layer in a different notation. More importantly, the various notations are not simply a means of indicating the sound; they also help the performers to create the sound itself. As such, lanza's notation is interactive performance art.

The above paragraphs present the briefest of introductions to lanza's notation. It is important for performers and those who study lanza's music to read the prefaces to his scores carefully for two reasons. First, these prefaces typically include a multitude of instructions about the tuning of the instruments and the electronic setup; most of lanza's works require amplification for both

Example 4.6.
un mundo imaginario, p. 3, second system.

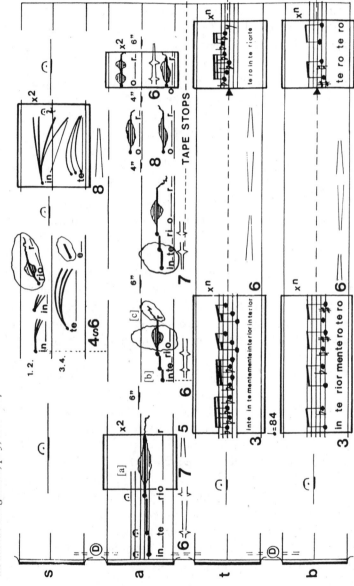

instruments and voices, and many works call for additional electronic effects, such as ring modulation, tape delays, and digital signal processing. Second, these prefaces explain the various symbols that lanza has devised to indicate unconventional uses of instruments and voices. Since many of these signs appear in a number of lanza's works, performers who have mastered one of his pieces will have a much easier time learning a second or third work. Indeed, lanza's notational signs signify recurrent components of his compositional language. The idiosyncrasies of his notation closely parallel the idiosyncrasies of his musical style.

5

Meg Sheppard and *trilogy*

By the summer of 1967 it was clear to both lanza and his wife Lydia Tomaíno that, after fifteen years, their marriage was at an end. Tomaíno left New York to return to her job and her life in Buenos Aires, taking their seven-year-old son, Guillermo, with her. lanza remained in New York to continue his work at the Columbia-Princeton Electronic Music Center.

Two years later, on a bright September morning in 1969, lanza met the young woman who was to change his life. Meg Sheppard, then eighteen years old, had just come to New York from the small mid-western city of Ashtabula, Ohio, to study acting at the American Academy of Dramatic Arts. She recalls their first meeting:

> One of my favourite things to do in New York was to take very long walks. On this particular day I walked from the midtown area, where I was staying, down into the Village. And as I was walking I was saying hello to people, and smiling, and doing my bit to make New York a friendlier place. And one of the people I smiled at was alcides. He was walking on the opposite side of the street, going in the other direction. So he crossed over and used the oldest line in the book: "Don't I know you from somewhere?"[1]

lanza and Sheppard found themselves walking for miles that day. During the course of their long conversation they both spoke of how much they enjoyed living in New York. lanza was glad to have escaped the formal strictures of Argentina with its political and economic problems and its Old World conventions of dress and etiquette, and he revelled in the casual dress and quasi-anarchistic society of the

Meg Sheppard in 1992. Photograph by André Leduc,
reproduced by kind permission.

New York arts scene. But most importantly, he felt liberated by the
breakthroughs he was making in his music. Sheppard had felt culturally suffocated by the small-town atmosphere of Ashtabula. She recalls, "There were certainly a lot of smart people there (as anywhere
else) but it was a culture where, if you fell outside the narrow boundaries, you were pretty much on your own. So when I arrived in New
York and found all those other people 'like me,' it was a tremendous
relief." Sheppard was a singer who was working towards a career in
musical theatre. On the day they met she somehow got the idea that
lanza was a struggling rock musician. lanza thought Sheppard was
simply an aspiring actress; he had no idea that he had met a woman
with an extraordinary singing voice.

A few days later there was a performance of lanza's *acúfenos I*
(for trombone and four instruments) at Carnegie Recital Hall, so
lanza invited Sheppard to the concert. She had had no previous experience of avant-garde music, but although some of it baffled her,

she also found it vitally interesting: "A lot of people hear new music and say, 'What is this? This isn't music!' … [But] luckily I wasn't closed off."

Neither Sheppard nor lanza can remember the first time he heard her sing, but soon after their first meeting, she asked him to help her make a demo recording. lanza was struck by the remarkable qualities of her voice – large, dark, velvety, dramatic, capable of astonishing emotional depth.

In April 1971 Sheppard attended a performance of *ekphonesis II*, lanza's music-theatre piece about a mad opera singer. He had had some difficulty finding a singer to perform this work. The soprano for whom it had originally been composed refused to perform it because she felt uncomfortable with the whole premise of the piece; a second singer agreed to do it, but her performance had been disappointing. lanza felt that the piece had not yet found its ideal interpreter: a performer, both actress and singer, who could project its strong message with humour and panache. Sheppard enjoyed the work immensely, and after the performance, leaned over to lanza and whispered, "alcides, I think I could do that." It was one of the most significant moments of his career. lanza took her up on her offer and she gave her first performance of *ekphonesis II* less than a month later, on 16 May 1971 at a concert in New York. Her interpretation was so stunning that lanza congratulated himself on having fallen in love with a woman who could perform his music so well. This concert was the beginning of a life-long musical partnership between composer and singer.

lanza had found it difficult to persuade conventionally trained singers to produce the wide variety of vocal sounds that he wanted. Some had been afraid to damage their voices, and most felt alienated from new music. In addition, many musicians were hostile – they still are even today – to unconventional notation. The requirements and sounds of new music were simply outside the realm of their experience, and many were unwilling to embark on something so different from what they were used to.

Sheppard's approach to learning a new work is basically theatrical: "I think every actor starts out by asking, 'What is happening to me during this period of time?' And I begin to form ideas about what I want to communicate with people … I create scenarios and then I live them." Her respect for her audience and her genuine desire to give her best at every performance is the hallmark of her style. She is committed to engaging her listeners at deep levels of experience; "I ask myself, 'Why did [the audience] come out tonight in minus-twenty-degree weather, or plus-thirty, or the monsoons? Why do people bother to go to a concert?' After all, CD technology is much cleaner, and it's easier to listen at home. No, they come for the experience. They come to connect – not only with the performer but also with the other people listening to the same piece in the same space." Sheppard has the ability, shared by all great performing artists, to take audience members out of their mindsets; they arrive at a concert with their worries, preconceptions, and fatigue, but the intensity, conviction, and drama of her performance draws them out of themselves and into the music and the story as she reels them into the unfolding drama.

penetrations VI and VII (1972)

In September 1971 lanza and Sheppard moved to Montreal, where lanza began teaching at McGill University. On 25 May 1972 they were married in her hometown of Ashtabula, and the following month they left for Germany. lanza had been awarded a Berliner Künstlerprogramm fellowship from the Deutscher Akademischer Austauschdienst (DAAD) that was to support him for a year's residence in Berlin.

The DAAD Berlin residency awards were extremely prestigious. In the 1920s and early 1930s Berlin had been one of the most important cultural centres of Europe, but with the rise of Nazism, and the accompanying hostility to avant-garde arts, the city lost its cultural status. The purpose of the Berliner Künstlerprogramm, administered jointly by the Ford Foundation and the DAAD, was to support leading artists (including painters, composers, filmmakers, etc.) for a year's residence in Berlin, with the idea that their presence would contribute to the city's cultural revival. lanza had twice applied for the grant while he was living in New York and was twice rejected. In 1970, while he was in Germany to make a recording, he visited Ecuadorian composer Mesías Maiguashca, an old friend who had been a fellow student at the Di Tella Institute. Maiguashca was working in Cologne as one of Stockhausen's assistants. When lanza told him about his failure to obtain a Berliner Künstlerprogramm award, Maiguashca arranged for him to meet Dr Otto Tomek (the director of the Donaueschingen festival)

and cellist Siegfried Palm, both of whom had considerable influence on West German music awards.[2]

These meetings had two positive results: lanza was awarded the
DAAD fellowship, and when he arrived in Berlin, Tomek commissioned him to compose a work for the next Donaueschingen Festival. Moreover, the work was to be premiered in an evening devoted
entirely to lanza's music. Both lanza and Sheppard vividly remember Tomek's dazzling visit to their apartment in Berlin. Tomek had
flown to Berlin from Baden-Baden in a private airplane, bringing
with him his assistant, the assistant to his assistant, and three secre-
taries. lanza recalls, "I couldn't believe it, everyone seemed to be
taking notes of every word I said." Tomek was also taken by Sheppard's abilities as a performer, and said, "Herr lanza, we would like
to commission a new work. Of course, you may do whatever you
please, but we hoped for a few instruments with electronic music
and theatre. And, you have to use Meg's voice, and include some
jazz for her to sing."

lanza agreed to this request. The new work, entitled *penetrations VI*,
is scored for voice, tape, and chamber ensemble. At the time he began
the Donaueschingen commission lanza already had a much larger
work in mind, centred on Sheppard's voice and acting skills. Since he
did not intend to use instruments in the other movements of the larger
work, he structured *penetrations VI* in such a way that it would be
complete with the instrumental parts omitted. The new version, *penetrations VII*, for voice, tape, and electronic extensions of the voice, was
to become the centrepiece of lanza's *trilogy*. The outer two movements
are *ekphonesis V* and *ekphonesis VI*.

Soon after accepting the commission, lanza ran into problems producing the tape part. He had planned to work at the electronic music
studio of the Technisches Universität, the only place in Berlin with the
technical resources he required. He had assumed that he would have
no trouble obtaining permission to work there; after all, he had seven
years experience at the Columbia-Princeton Electronic Music Center
and a growing international reputation as a composer of electroacoustic music, recognized both by the award of the prestigious Berliner
Künstlerprogramm residency and a commission from the Donaueschingen festival. He was shocked to be refused, and complained to Peter
Nestler, the director of the Berlin bureau of the DAAD. Nestler was
sympathetic but informed lanza that Fritz Winckel, the director of the
studio, was fanatically opposed to allowing outsiders to work there,

and had refused permission for everyone except for a few monumentally famous composers whose presence he tolerated only grudgingly. In Berlin later that month lanza met the composers Mario Bertoncini (of Italy) and Makoto Shinohara (of Japan), both of whom had also been denied use of the studio. "Don't feel too bad," Bertoncini said reassuringly, "It's the same with nearly everyone; Winckel is very possessive about the studio. He believes his job is to protect it." lanza, however, was unable to accept the refusal with such nonchalance, and somewhat belatedly began to appreciate the hospitality of the Columbia-Princeton studio, where Ussachevsky had welcomed all professionals regardless of nationality or musical philosophy. For lanza, the studios in Berlin and New York became metaphors for the Old and New Worlds: the New York studio was open and free, the Berlin studio was closed, hierarchical, and rigid.[3]

Faced with the dilemma of how to compose the electronic component of the Donaueschingen commission without access to an electronic music studio, lanza made one of the most important decisions of his life. He used the $6,000 he would be paid for the commission – a considerable sum in 1971 – to equip a studio in his own home. It proved a magnificent investment. Over the following decades lanza composed a number of works on the equipment he acquired that year, and in the long run, the machines paid for themselves ten times over. Later, when he was in charge of building up the studio at McGill University, he was careful to make the university studio compatible with his own equipment.

The tape part for *penetrations VI/VII* was composed in large part on lanza's new instruments, but there are a few sections that quote *penetrations I*, a tape piece composed in New York in 1968, for which he had recorded urban sounds (such as subway rumbling, sirens, and traffic) for an outdoor "happening" that fell through.[4] He has since used fragments of this urban soundscape for each work entitled *penetrations*.

penetrations VI/VII opens in darkness. We first hear distant low sustained rumblings that gradually grow louder. To this, lanza adds a four-note electronic motive that sounds vaguely like a woodwind instrument asking a musical question. Over the next minute he builds up layers of sound spanning a wide range and culminating in thick tone clusters. During this buildup a spotlight darts back and forth searching for the soloist. It finds her at the back of the hall and lights up her face. With all eyes now focused on her, she calmly weaves her way through the audience humming a few isolated notes that eventually coalesce into a melody as the tape part fades out. When she reaches the stage she begins a blues improvisation based on motives of the melody. lanza has said that these motives come from a "lullaby" he wrote in 1955 (now lost) when he and Lydia Tomaíno were planning to have a child; it is "the key to understanding [*penetrations VI/VII*], which is about a woman who reverts to childhood when she is crushed by memories."[5] At the opening of the improvisation lanza manipulates the singer's voice so that it sounds as if she is standing in a room with reverberant acoustics, but over the next two minutes, this maximum echo diminishes until we hear her voice in its natural state. At the end of the improvisation the singer speaks, beginning with the word "eidetic," which she defines as "pertaining to or constituting visual imagery retained in the memories," thus announcing the subject of *penetrations VI/VII*: memories and how they affect us.

When the tape re-enters we again hear the musical question first asked near the opening of the work. The mood changes. So far, the singer has been relaxed, but now, in brief half-sung, half-spoken phrases, she begins to remember the experiences of humanity and our inability to learn from them. As these memories penetrate her mind she becomes increasingly distraught. Her agitation is reinforced by the introduction of voices on the tape that speak simultaneously of "desperation," "communication," "memories," and "child." The voices – overlapping layers of Sheppard's and lanza's voices – are interested only in their own monologues, and blithely ignore the desperate woman. At the height of her anxiety, lanza directs the singer to "go berserk." "Nobody listens ...," she screams repeatedly, "no, no, no ..." As the "no"s reach maximum volume (10 on lanza's dynamic scale of 1 to 10) they are grotesquely distorted by ring modulation, and the singer collapses on the floor in spasms. The voices on the tape disappear and lanza highlights the woman's mental and physical collapse by accompanying her spasms with a wonderfully apt fragment of *musique concrète* that sounds somewhat like an old door squeaking on rusty hinges in the wind.

The woman lies still for a few moments. Then, as she drags herself onto her knees, we hear the four-note questioning motive for the third time. The woman is so traumatized she can no longer sing

Example 5.1.
penetrations VII, excerpt from p. 2.

or speak; she can only emit inarticulate, guttural noises. lanza has said "she must sound like a mute trying to speak."[6] She can no longer endure the present, and reverts to her childhood, returning to the pitches she sang during her entrance. In a lilting childlike voice she sings of dreams, memories, and time, ending with the word "listen." Slowly and rhythmically she breathes into the microphone. As the tape fades away, we are left with the sound of her breathing in, out, in, out, in, out. I believe this could be interpreted as the breath of a person who has retreated so far into the past that her consciousness disappears and she falls into a deep primordial sleep, the breath of life continuing in spite of all. When I spoke with lanza about this interpretation, however, he replied, "That's a very beautiful idea, Pamela, and perhaps it is true. But it could also just be sound for the sake of sound."[7]

To summarize, the work begins in near silence, builds to an intense climax, and then gradually subsides to near silence – a structure that Berlioz (reviewing Wagner) called "crescendo-diminuendo form," and that lanza has used in a number of works since the late 1960s.

Let us consider the work in greater detail. After the "instrumental" tape introduction, the woman sings a few isolated pitches that gradually coalesce to form hints of motives (see example 5.1). Although this passage, notated in traditional staff notation, is not composed in a strictly systematic manner, each new fragment evolves from the previous one. lanza is creating an evocative image. Above the passage he writes, "Free and hesitantly, as a child trying to remember." The

Example 5.2.
penetrations VII, excerpt from p. 3.

Table 5.1

Performance Directions	Dynamics	Text
Getting nervous	7 (*f*)	"a human-uman experience, being a child dreaming"
Exasperated	8 (*ff*)	"but I was a child with all the memories"
Trembling	9 (*fff*)	"from the beginning of time and"
Go berserk	*crescendo*	"nobody listens" [at least 6 times]
Screaming	10 (*ffff*)	"no" [at least 11 times]

minimal repetitions and hesitations are all part of the story, almost as if the singer is trying to remember a long-forgotten melody.

The intense climactic section that follows is strikingly different. It consists entirely of a series of words drawn in graphic fashion on trigram notation with only designs to outline the approximate contour of the phrases. The maximal feel of this section contrasts with the minimalist introduction. Here, we are bombarded with one new idea after another in quick succession, in a constant gradual buildup of dynamics and intensity (see example 5.2). The summary of this passage in table 5.1 includes lanza's directions to the singer, the dynamics, and the text. Note the increase of dynamics from 7 to 10 (*f* to *ffff*), the rapid changes of text, the density of ideas, and the multiple hysterical repetition of the words "nobody listens" and "no" at the climax.

At the end of the work the singer returns to quiet humming, eventually singing a musical line that is notated in exact pitches (see example 5.3). Here again, lanza uses traditional staff notation because he wants the singer to hover around the same pitches she sang during her entrance. At her entrance the woman was hesitant but she was able to elicit a full melodic motive that eventually even gained a rhythmic identity, and she confidently sang a jazzy improvisation that grew out of the motive. In these final moments, however, she never quite elicits a real motive, only isolated notes with uneasy pauses, a sad skeletal recollection of the lullaby motive heard in the opening.

Sheppard did not enjoy the premiere of *penetrations VI* at the Donaueschingen Festival. "I felt that I was performing to an audience

Example 5.3:
penetrations VII, p. 4 (conclusion).

of 600 critics," she said. She was anxious to take the piece "on the road" to listeners for whom music was a less esoteric experience. Sheppard's performances of *penetrations VII* in Europe and North and South America were resoundingly successful, leaving her listeners stunned and breathless at each stop. It was a tour de force, and even critics who had reservations about lanza's music were unanimous in their praise of Sheppard's performance.[8] It could be said that this piece put Sheppard on the map as a music-theatre specialist.

ekphonesis V (1979)

In May 1973 lanza and Sheppard returned to Montreal and settled into domestic life. Their first child, Adriana Sheppard-Lanza, was born in Montreal on 4 April 1974; their son – named Antonio Edward Sheppard-Lanza in honour of lanza's late father (Antonio) and Sheppard's uncle (Edward) – was born four years later, on 24 September 1978.

By 1979 Sheppard had performed *penetrations VII* more than a hundred times and wanted another piece to add to her repertoire: "I nagged alcides repeatedly about the new work, but he was too busy with his official commissions."[9] Finally Sheppard decided to apply to the Canada Council for a grant to commission her own husband, and, to their credit, the Council agreed. After the gut-wrenching, harrowing shock value of *penetrations VII*, Sheppard wanted a gentler, more introspective work. Her feelings coincided with lanza's: he had always planned to make *penetrations VII* part of a larger work and he too felt that a gentler piece was needed for contrast.

Whereas *penetrations VII* focused on the memories of humanity at large – memories that crush the child-woman, *ekphonesis V*, the new work, is based on lanza's memories of his family and his childhood in Argentina. His text uses both Spanish and English words but the emphasis is on Spanish. In the work lanza revisits the small village of his youth. The singer tells us of a woman – "abuela siempre vestida de negro y gris" [a grandmother always dressed in black and grey] – a man – "only he could read in town" – and a child – "un niño ilusorio que se aleja en la niebla" [an illusory child who drifts into the mist].

Each of these figures represents a member of lanza's family.[10] The woman in black and grey is his grandmother, whom he remembers with long flowing black hair and dark clothes. lanza grew up in a

large extended family, but everyone except his widowed grandmother left the house each morning to go to work or school, so she
was alone for much of the day. lanza had a feeling that the old
woman was lonely, or, more astutely, that she was alone, even when
in company, with her memories.

The man who could read is lanza's grandfather, Don Ramón, a
tailor by profession, who had learned to read and write, a skill that
set him apart from the rest of the townsfolk. Whenever anyone received a letter, he would read it to them; whenever they needed to
write, he was the scribe. lanza has no personal memory of his
grandfather, who died when he was a baby, but his uncle Velmiro
had often described him and had used him as a character in one of
his novels.

The "niño ilusorio" disappearing into the mist is Pablo, lanza's
first child who was born severely handicapped and died at the age of
six. It is difficult to persuade lanza to admit that any of his works
have a connection with this tragic episode in his life. He is very reticent on the subject, but on one rare occasion, concerning this part of
ekphonesis V he said, "It became clear in my mind that ... I was trying to deal with my own memories of my first son, Pablo, Pablito,
who died when he was only six years old. So directly or indirectly,
subliminally or whatever, that's what [that part is] all about."[11]

It is difficult to know with certainty why an artist begins to re-
examine his youth. UNESCO had declared 1979 the Year of the
Child, and lanza wanted to bring children into his new work in
some way. The birth of a healthy son to lanza and Sheppard in
1978 may also have been significant. Perhaps holding his newborn
son in his arms triggered memories of his first-born child, memories
of sadness and also, no doubt, of joy. lanza at fifty may simply have
reached the age or the crossroads in life when one considers both
the past and the future; and part of mapping out the future is coming to terms with the past.

ekphonesis V opens in darkness. Over a span of six minutes a
woman sings long sustained vowels that evolve into syllables and
then groups of syllables, made up for the most part of the vowels
contained in the word *abuela* [grandmother]. The woman has her
back to the audience but she holds a flashlight under her chin so
that the shape of her head is vaguely outlined in the darkness. The
material in the tape component, which begins a few seconds before
the singer, is constructed mostly from Sheppard's voice, and is so

similar to her vocal part that the audience is unable to distinguish between what is sung in real time and what is on the tape.

Let us examine how lanza draws us into the drama. Example 5.4 shows the first two systems (the first two minutes) of the work. The singer begins gradually with a series of long held notes on the vowels O–A–O–U–A, all expressed quietly on the D above middle C. Here lanza uses trigram notation, but he indicates the exact pitch with letter names in parentheses. In the second "bar" of the second system we hear a hint of the word "abuela" minus the letter "b" (a ... u ... e ... [l] ... a), again on the note D.[12] The separate vowels at the beginning hover around *pp* to *mp* (dynamics 3, 4, 5), but the quasi-word "a ... uela" that finally emerges is sung *mp* to *f* (dynamics 5, 6, 7). There is only one voice on the tape during the separate vowels, but two voices are introduced as the crucial word "abuela" is suggested. Up to now, everything in the singer's part is sung on the note D. At the end of the first page other notes begin to appear, eventually coalescing into brief melodic motives framed in rectangles; example 5.5 shows the first two rectangles, with Sheppard's interpretation of the passage transcribed in traditional notation below.

lanza is creating a quiet, introspective, dreamlike ambience: out in the darkness a woman is humming to herself, unaware that we are listening. She begins with a few tentative vowels, then gradually works up to brief diatonic motives that expand and contract, as if she is searching her memory for a particular musical phrase. It is as if the audience is eavesdropping on her. Eventually she turns to face the audience and sings the words "mira" [look] and "niño" [child]; these first complete words alert us that a story has begun.

A spotlight now appears on the singer, and she introduces the dramatis personae, singing a brief motive with the introduction of each character. The lilting phrase, "Tell me something," sung in a childish voice, like a child asking for a story, acts as a refrain that begins each new section of the piece. Example 5.6 shows this phrase in lanza's graphic notation along with a transcription of Sheppard's interpretation. "Tell me something," the singer asks, and we are introduced to three personae: a woman ("her long days alone"), books ("books are also memories"), and a man ("only he could read in town"). When the refrain returns with the words, "Tell me something, tell me," we meet "un niño ilusorio que se aleja en la niebla" [an illusory child who disappears in the mist], and the old grandmother who is alone ("la vieja abuela estará sola"). The

Example 5.4.
ekphonesis V, opening.

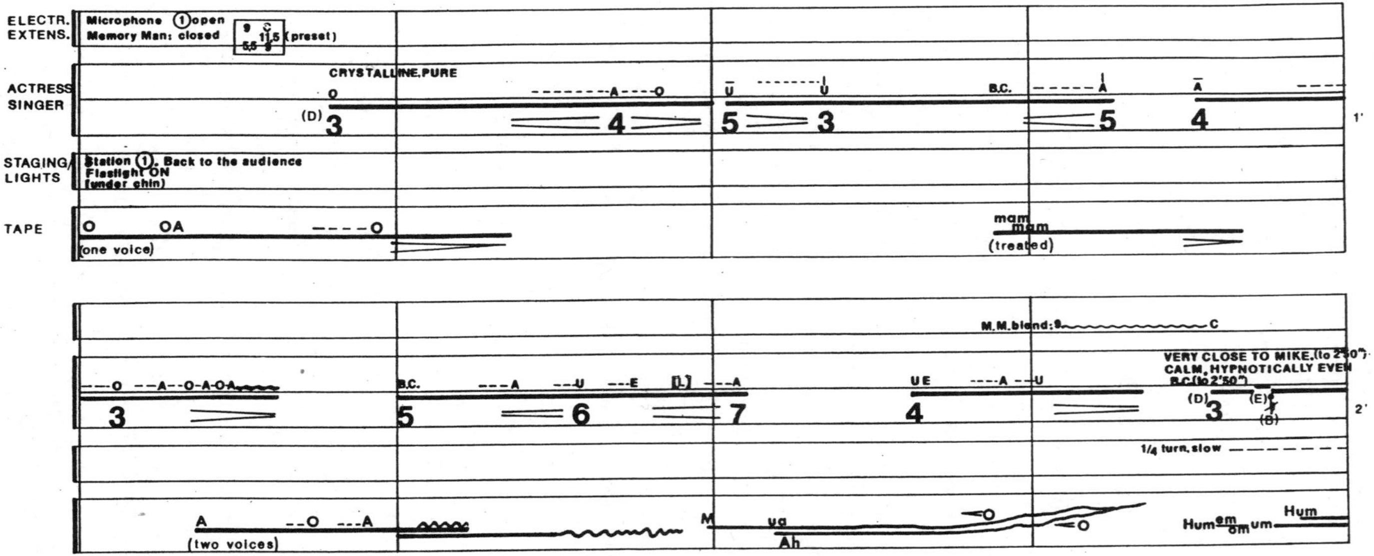

Example 5.5.
ekphonesis V, excerpt from p. 2 showing notation in score and
a transcription in conventional notation.

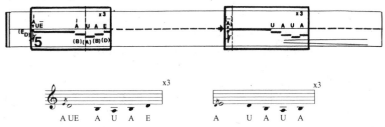

Example 5.6.
ekphonesis V, excerpt from p. 3 showing notation in score and a
transcription of Meg Sheppard's interpretation.

refrain is heard once again – "Tell me something, mami" – and, as
though she were answering a question from a child, the singer provides several vignettes about the characters. She tells us that the
grandmother "on misty days ... was always rather triste," and that
the child is "a dreamchild" who lives in an "imaginario mundo interior" [an imaginary interior world].

As the piece gradually builds to a gentle climax the tape part su-
perimposes what sounds like a group of voices (consisting mainly of
superimposed layers of Sheppard's voice) speaking simultaneously
of "historias, ghosts, remembrances, a dreamchild," and much
more. The voices fade into silence and, in a touching moment, the
singer says "Dadi." The refrain – now truncated to only "Tell me"
– is followed by a final intense reminder of the old grandmother's
solitude. Her isolation thus reinforced, the singer returns once again
into darkness, punctuated by the sustained vowels of "abuela." The
grandmother has returned to her world of memories.

lanza believes that the recurring question, "tell me something,"
probably came out of two experiences.[13] The first is a childhood
memory of asking this question when he was bedridden at home

recuperating from nephritis. The second is a memory of his uncle Velmiro Ayala Gauna, the writer of the family, who often asked his mother (lanza's grandmother) to tell him about their ancestors. She would oblige with stories of their family history, and Velmiro used the characters and incidents in his novels. Thus, in *ekphonesis V* all questions are addressed to the grandmother; sometimes it is her grandson alcides asking, sometimes it is her son Velmiro. It is fitting that the work opens and closes with a vocalise on the word *abuela*. lanza is acknowledging her as the shaman, the storyteller, the keeper of the family history.

But *ekphonesis V* is far more than a straightforward narrative; lanza has coloured the grandmother's stories: they are his memories of her memories, blended with personal memories of Pablo that belong to him alone. The listener is awash in a sea of intersecting memories fading in and out like a dream.

When I asked lanza why the piece begins and ends in darkness, his answer was striking: "I asked myself, what if a singer were inside my brain – it's dark in there – with a flashlight? It would be like being inside a library full of different books of memories. That's the image I had in mind: Meg is walking inside my brain and [she sings about] what she finds there."[14] Commenting on her role, Sheppard said, "I enter his brain and wander around in the dark, and stub my toes on all of his memories ... It's a very strange experience ... to bump up against other people's memories, and to try to translate them into a universal that people will relate to."

lanza was worried that the subject matter was so personal that audiences might not relate to it, but to his surprise, the premiere in San Diego was wildly successful. He wondered how the audience, in spite of a brief program note, could understand and relate to a work with so much Spanish, and concluded that there must have been a number of Mexican Americans who understood the language, but this conclusion proved erroneous when the piece was equally successful in Norway and Sweden. It seems that *ekphonesis V* is a work that triggers a response in everyone; we all have memories of childhood, we all have grandmothers and grandfathers, we all have libraries of memories inside our heads. *ekphonesis V* touches a deep chord. Sheppard explained the work's appeal in a moment of insight: "Everybody's got this in their past," she said, and then after a moment's hesitation added, "or wants to. Yes, perhaps that's it."

Victorina Figueroa de Ayala Gauna, the grandmother in *ekphonesis V*. Photograph from the
personal collection of alcides lanza.

Style Change

The nostalgically evocative nature of *ekphonesis V* is enhanced by
an audacious change in lanza's compositional style, the most striking feature of which is a reliance on equal temperament. The appearance of diatonic and modal elements is a remarkable shift,
considering lanza's previous abhorrence of equal temperament. Underlying much of his previous music was a desire to saturate the
acoustic space by using complex textures spanning a wide range,
with a multitude of microtones and glissandi. In the new work, he
pares down his resources to a minimum: most notable to the ear is a
focus on simple melodic fragments with a narrow range, repeated
over and over again. For example, from minute 3 to minute 6 of
ekphonesis V, a motivic fragment is repeated at least forty times in
various permutations, like miniature variations: example 5.7 shows
the first eighteen of these modal fragments followed by a transcription in conventional notation. What is significant here is that these

Example 5.7.
ekphonesis V, excerpt from p. 2 showing notation in score and
a transcription in conventional notation.

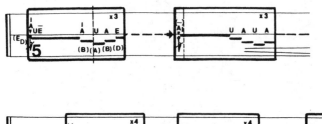

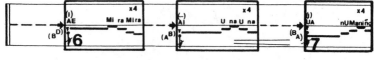

Example 5.8.
ekphonesis V, excerpt from p. 3 showing notation in score and
a transcription in conventional notation.

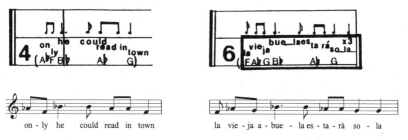

modal motives are not just passing allusions or isolated fragments
inserted here and there, but are instead a central element of the
work. It is also significant that two of the main characters – the
grandfather and the grandmother – share a lilting diatonic motive
(see example 5.8). In addition, several of the vignettes are sung to
diatonic melodies (see example 5.9). It is unthinkable that such
"folklike" phrases could have occurred in earlier works such as
cuarteto IV or *eidesis II*. We hear something like this in the blues
improvisation of *penetrations VI/VII* (1972), but there the diatonic

Example 5.9.
ekphonesis V, excerpt from p. 4 showing notation in score and a
transcription in conventional notation.

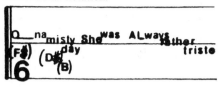

O—na mist - y day She was AL - ways rath - er triste

motives sound "foreign" to the overall style of the piece; in *ekphonesis V* they are integral. *ekphonesis V* has a harmonic language unlike anything lanza had used previously. In addition, the continuous
circular repetition of motives creates a sense of regular rhythmic
pulsation, which is also foreign to lanza's style up to this point. *ekphonesis V* was a surprise not only to listeners who knew lanza's
previous compositions, but also to the composer himself. He had
not expected to write a work with this character and colouring, but
had simply followed the inspiration of the moment. At the time of
composition, these repetitive modal and diatonic fragments might
have appeared to be a simple expression of programmatic elements,
but lanza continued to use motives of this type in several pieces
through the 1980s and 1990s. After *ekphonesis V* he added diatonicism to works or sections of works whenever he wanted to create a
specific – and usually evocative – atmosphere. It became part of his
compositional bag of tricks; although it does not appear in every
piece, he uses it unabashedly when he feels the need.

It is important to note, however, that lanza did not reject his
atonal, microtonal, thick-textured style. As will be seen below, he
continued to create works in that style. But something has changed.
The repetitions, expansions, and contractions of small cells found in
ekphonesis V also began to influence the way he composed nontonal music. Thus *ekphonesis V* is a watershed in lanza's career, a
breakthrough work which added new dimensions to his style.

lanza's change of style can be related to a worldwide shift in musical language that has come to be called postmodernism. As noted above, lanza is an indefatigable concert-goer and participated in numerous new music festivals in Europe and the Americas. He was well aware of the new developments in advanced musical circles that replaced the conventional postwar ideal of continuous unpredictability with the reintroduction of such previously scorned features as diatonic melody, triadic harmony, and regular rhythmic pulsation. With its multilevel concern for "memories," *ekphonesis V* can definitely be understood as part of this new tradition. While lanza did not follow it up with other works in such a purified tonal style, he did continue to adapt the concepts of easily recognizable repetition and recollection introduced in *ekphonesis V* to new musical contexts. Some of the ways in which he did this will be examined in chapter 6, in the discussion of *sensors III* (1982). But first we must return to *trilogy*.

ekphonesis VI (1988)

lanza had now composed two pieces for Sheppard. *penetrations VII* and *ekphonesis V* could be performed separately or together. Eventually lanza decided that when they are performed together, *ekphonesis V* should come first, reversing the order of composition, creating a scenario that proceeds from personal memories to the memories of humanity, with the music shifting from the mellow to the stringent, and the character from the tender to the violent – an introspective movement followed by an aggressive, nerve-wracking assault.

For about ten years Sheppard performed the pieces either separately or as a two-movement work, but both she and lanza felt that a third movement was needed, something that would resolve the agonized tensions of *penetrations VII*. They wanted the new piece to be healing and redemptive, and searched for a "theme" that would tie the previous ideas in the work together. After much discussion, they decided that the third piece, later entitled *ekphonesis VI*, should be based on their shared experiences with their children and, in a larger sense, with the listener's experiences of children.

By 1988, the year lanza decided to write the third part of *trilogy*, the lanzas had three children, aged fourteen, ten, and six – their last child, Emily Elizabeth Sheppard-Lanza, had been born on 2 November

1982. Theirs was a typical middle-class Canadian household with everyone pursuing a range of activities: piano lessons, tap dancing, tennis, homework, and so forth. As Ianza and Sheppard watched their children grow, they began to consider what it was like to be a child at this time and place and what the future of their children would hold.

As soon as they decided on the theme of the new movement, Ianza began to consider the text. As is so often the case with creative enterprises, a fortuitous event caused the work to fall into place. In the autumn of 1987 Sheppard sang a concert in Vancouver. At the reception following the performance she met the Canadian poet Norbert Ruebsaat who gave her a copy of his poem *The Children like Marbles Tumble into Life*."[15] As she read the poem during the flight home she knew instantly that this hauntingly beautiful poem about mothers and children was the text she wanted for the third part of *trilogy*. Up to that time, however, with the exception of some juvenilia, Ianza had written all his own texts. Sheppard knew it would not be easy to convince Ianza to use Ruebsaat's poem, and when she broached the subject, his initial reaction was negative: "No," he replied, "I never use other people's poems." Undaunted, she sat him down in his study and said, "Your problem with poetry is that you always read it to yourself. But poetry has to be experienced as sound. You have to hear it."[16] She recited the poem in her deep-throated voice, and as she spoke, the rhythms, colours, and nuances of the text came to life. Ianza agreed to set the poem – a significant precedent that would affect many future vocal works. Once he had accepted the Ruebsaat text, it was easy for Sheppard to persuade him to use two other texts she admired: Robert Frost's poem, "Fire and Ice," and a few lines by W.B. Yeats.

ekphonesis VI does not really have a score. Musical decisions about the vocal part, which consists of improvisation and quotations from the two previous movements of *trilogy*, are often left to the performer's discretion. Ianza's "score" supplies only an outline of a few key elements. The following description of the work is taken from the recording made by Meg Sheppard in 1992[17] and from my experience of seeing her perform the work on numerous occasions.

ekphonesis VI opens with a loud crash followed by a prolonged solo tape section. According to Sheppard, "[It] is really based on pop music. I happen to like the music of Billy Joel. His song, 'You May Be Right,'[18] opens with a sound like a million glasses crashing to the ground, and I said to alcides: 'That's the kind of sound we need to wake the audience up after *penetrations VII* leaves them in such a state of shock: they are sitting there with their mouths open; they almost can't breathe. So this [opening] crash is like a slap across the face.'"[19] The opening tape music, a sort of symphonic prelude, contains multiple layers of energetic rhythms that slide in and out of the foreground. This is one of lanza's common techniques seen in sections of previous works, but something is different here. The individual rhythmic layers are made up of continuously throbbing regular pulses, as opposed to the irregular random-sounding rhythms he preferred in the 1950s and 1960s. This feature correlates with his use of outright diatonic material; his style change is both harmonic and rhythmic.

At the end of the symphonic prelude a woman enters tap dancing. During the year before lanza composed *ekphonesis VI*, Sheppard and one of their daughters had been taking tap dance lessons at a local dance studio; although neither was particularly good or had any real ambition as a dancer, they had enjoyed the classes and it had been a happy family experience. The dancer in *ekphonesis VI* is supposed to be an amateur; we hear fragments of "Tea for Two" and watch as she awkwardly tries to master a tap sequence, like a student who can't quite get it right. This light-hearted moment lifts the audience out of the dark and ominous mood of *penetrations VII*.

Slowly the work begins to move toward more serious material dealing with motherhood, children's expectations, and our responsibilities to our children. The singer recites Ruebsaat's remarkable poem:

The children,
like marbles,
tumble into life

play tug-of-war,
spring!
as if they were robins

all bodies,
all hands,
all fingers and worms

and the earth consists
entirely of ropes
attaching the things to their names

and children's eyes are stories
with little magnets attached,
things creeping into life

and sorting it,
sand,
or stardust

and the body is far away,
like a planet.

At night the mothers come out of their shadows
to collect the eyes that the children have left
like objects all over the block.

The children's eyes,
the things
and the hands

and somewhere a little altar,
close by a bedside,
where a song is asleep.

lanza creates a moment of magic by accompanying this sad and tender poem with sustained modal harmonies that have a distant, plaintive, and otherworldly sound. This "distant planet" music acts as a major unifying device throughout *ekphonesis VI*. lanza uses this serene and eerie music at the close of each improvisational section, to introduce a new section and new text. With the line, "The body is far away, / like a planet," we, the audience, feel that we have been transported outside our world; we are the narrator looking down on the protagonists of the drama; the children, the mothers, and all of humanity. At the lines, "At night the mothers come out of their shadows / to collect the eyes that the children have left / like objects all over the block," lanza subtly adds the sound of children's voices babbling quietly in the background, and the singer intersperses brief snatches of the jazz improvisation from *penetrations VII*, a telling reminder of the child-woman of that piece, and of the child in all of us. At the line, "the children's eyes are stories," the spell is broken, and the singer embarks on an improvisation in which she reflects on all the stories of *trilogy*, the characters we have met, and the pictures painted. We hear passing verbal and musical references to the previous two movements and to ideas introduced in this section. We are reminded of the dreamchild, of the woman that no one listens to, of the books that are also memories, and of children's searching eyes. This moment of reflection reaches a climax when the singer focuses on her own children: we hear them on the tape practising the piano, tap dancing, asking questions, giggling and squealing as they play, while she watches and reminds us that "Nobody listens." This improvisation section comes to a conclusion with the return of the "distant planet" music first heard in the introduction to the Ruebsaat poem. Here it underpins the recitation of Robert Frost's well-known poem about desire, hatred, and the end of the world: "Some say the world will end in fire, Some say in ice ..."[20]

The singer's recitation is interspersed with brief fragments of the texts by Ruebsaat and lanza; a momentary focus on the words "ice" and "eyes" linking the Ruebsaat and Frost texts is accompanied by a sound akin to an Arctic wind, as if the singer were standing in a cold, desolate place. Throughout this section Sheppard's voice in real time is accompanied by distant echoes of her voice on tape that build into multiple layers of sound, all constructed from her speaking and singing. lanza gradually adds other voices (his own, his children's, and those of his friends) creating a wave of voices that gathers momentum, becoming louder and louder and eventually blocking out all other sounds. Suddenly the singer screams and, as if a switch has been thrown, the voices stop instantly in mid-speech. After a brief silence the "distant planet" music returns. In a sense, it establishes tonal stability after the chaos, hope after despair, redemption after the fall. In a quiet voice, exuding peace and fulfilment, the singer reassures us with words based on a quotation from W. B. Yeats: "Let us go forth the teller of tales and have no fear."[21] lanza adds a bell-like, quasi-Tibetan ostinato as the music shifts to an F-sharp pentatonic mode. As this key of transcendence envelops us, the singer whirls round and round like a Dervish in spiritual ecstasy, in the end, leaving us, our children, and the world in the lap of the gods.

The form of *ekphonesis VI*, as shown in the following outline, has a comfortable predictability:

Introduction   Symphonic prelude
"verse 1"   Improvisation

	Modal "distant planet" music
	Ruebsaat poem recitation
"verse 2"	Improvisation
	Modal "distant planet" music
	Frost poem recitation
"verse 3"	Improvisation
	Modal "distant planet" music
	Yeats quotation recitation
Coda	Pentatonic ostinato

The work opens and closes with symphonic tape music (Introduction and Coda), and all three verses have the same three elements: improvisation, modal tape music, and a recitation.

ekphonesis VI leaves a great deal to the discretion of the singer-actress. *trilogy* is a work about memories, and in this final movement lanza allows Sheppard the freedom to choose the characters, memories, musical phrases, poems, and texts she will quote in the improvisational sections. Because these sections are equal in weight to the more "composed" passages, lanza acknowledges Sheppard as more than just a performer by listing her name in the score of *ekphonesis VI* as a collaborator.

It is rare for a composer to write a work over a sixteen-year period with a major style change in the middle; Wagner's *Ring* cycle and Stravinsky's opera *The Nightingale* are notable examples. lanza's *trilogy*, one of his finest works, is satisfying to hear and watch because it is so musically convincing. Despite a major change in style, lanza creates a feeling of unity over the span of an hour. How does he achieve this?

On the simple level of form, lanza sandwiches *penetrations VII*, the oldest movement, between the two newer ones. Because we hear it as a contrasting second movement, the effect of the style difference is blunted. There is also a textural evolution: *ekphonesis V* is minimalist, *penetrations VII* is maximalist, and *ekphonesis VI* reconciles this seeming opposition. Even the proportions of the movements support this reconciliation: the length of the *ekphonesis VI* is equal to that of the other two movements combined.

The similarity of subject matter also connects the three movements. *trilogy* is an exploration of memories, particularly memories associated with childhood and children. In *ekphonesis V* lanza remembers his own childhood and the child he lost to illness; in *penetrations VII* a woman reverts to childhood after she is overwhelmed by the memories of humanity; in *ekphonesis VI*, through lanza's and Sheppard's portraits of their children, we remember our own childhood and all the children of the world. lanza builds up the listeners' memories by having his cast of characters and their musical associations travel from movement to movement. For example, the dreamchild and the books of memories from *ekphonesis V* and the woman nobody listens to from *penetrations VII* reappear in *ekphonesis VI* as familiar characters. It is significant that, in her improvisation sections, Sheppard brings back not only the dramatis personae but also the musical motives associated with these characters; in this way she creates a group of musical references that make the work easy to absorb and give it a satisfying rootedness.

I believe that while each of the three movements can stand on its own, the full magic of the work emerges only when it is heard as a trilogy. This is especially true if we consider *ekphonesis VI*, where all the ideas of the previous two movements are combined, sifted, rearranged, and expanded. Hearing *ekphonesis VI* without the other two parts is like hearing the development and coda of a work without the exposition – it can be an entertaining experience, but the music makes more sense, and is so much more convincing and satisfying when we hear the whole evolution. This, after all, is the nature of memory.

But the real link between the three parts, the soul of the work, is Sheppard's voice. What does lanza do with her voice in *trilogy*? First, direct sound (her singing in real time) is fed through a microphone and played to the audience. A second copy of the signal is processed through various machines to produce electronic modifications of the voice – echo, delay, and different types of distortion. lanza uses these colourations not as isolated special effects but as integral elements of the whole. They highlight the drama; indeed they do much to create the distinctive atmosphere of each part. During the sixteen-year period over which *trilogy* was composed it became easier to manipulate audio signals because more sophisticated and affordable technical equipment was developed for the pop music industry. lanza, like many other avant-garde composers, was quick to seize upon such equipment and exploit it for expressive purposes.

More than 85 per cent of the tape part underlying the three movements of *trilogy* consists of electronic processing of Sheppard's

Meg Sheppard and alcides lanza in Ottawa, 2006. Photograph by Alexander Somma, reproduced by kind permission.

voice. In *penetrations VII*, for the most part, we can distinguish between the live performer and the tape, but in *ekphonesis V*, the second piece to be composed, lanza begins to blur the line with great subtlety. Phrases in the voice and tape parts are very similar, and there is a certain amount of overlapping: a sustained note in the tape may be taken over by the singer, a phrase begun by the singer completed on the tape, and multiple choral layers of her singing on the tape accompany her singing in real time. It is often difficult, particularly when the singer is in darkness, to distinguish live sounds from tape sounds or from electronic colouration of live sound. It is all Sheppard's voice.

On the surface *trilogy* appears to be about lanza – certainly the depiction of his youth in the first movement is very personal – but as the piece moves on, it becomes increasingly focused on Sheppard's personae as wife, mother, thinker, performer, and muse. All three movements are dedicated to her, and in a very concrete sense, the piece is an aural and physical representation of her inner self. The work is constructed from her voice on the tape, her voice in real time, her voice in all manner of colourations, her dancing, her choice of poetry, and most importantly the huge improvisation sections left to her discretion. *trilogy* has a number of profound and moving "themes," but it could be said that these themes are merely the picture frame, and Sheppard is the painting. In an astute review of *trilogy* Argentinean critic Federico Monjeau writes:

> It is inevitable to associate [Sheppard] with Cathy Berberian, not only for her tremendous sensuality but also for her particular relation with the work: Luciano Berio wrote for Berberian just as lanza does for Sheppard. lanza's work draws a great dramatic curve ... which culminates with some questions on the fate of the planet ... But it is not the importance of these questions that confers strength and profundity to lanza's piece, but rather its unique corporealization: in [*trilogy*] it is impossible to separate the voice and body of Sheppard from the work.[22]

Monjeau understands that at its core *trilogy* is Sheppard. As such, it is a timeless and intimate gift of love from the composer to his wife.

6

Early Years in Montreal, 1971–1982

lanza and Sheppard moved to Montreal in the summer of 1971. lanza was delighted; for him the move meant an opportunity to teach electronic music, to be responsible for a major electronic music studio, and to enjoy a considerable increase in income. The move was less welcome for Sheppard, who wanted to pursue a career in music theatre; she felt there would have been more performance opportunities for her in New York. When she first arrived in Montreal she considered the city as something of a backwater because there was hardly any English theatre and few contemporary music concerts. lanza, however, instantly fell in love with the city: "After living in New York, Montreal reminded me in a way of Buenos Aires. Both are cities of the New World but have a strong European atmosphere."[1]

Avant-garde Music in Quebec

Osvaldo Budón, one of lanza's former students, once remarked that lanza was a lucky man because he always seemed to be in the right place at the right time. This is certainly true of his move to Montreal. He arrived during a period of prosperity, civic pride, and enormous expansion in the arts. With the children of the baby boomers reaching university age, universities and other institutions of higher learning across North America enjoyed large increases in enrolment and an ever-expanding need for more teachers and facilities. Montreal's music schools shared in this expansion; between 1965 and 1979 new programs – including ethnomusicology, musical semiotics, electronic music, early music, and sound recording – were introduced, and the possibilities seemed endless.

In spite of the rise of nationalism among francophone Quebecers, the new music scene in Montreal was predominantly "internationalist" in orientation. Montreal's music institutions were full of teachers from Europe and the Americas; in the 1970s the music faculty at McGill included teachers from Argentina, Sweden, the United States, Italy, Great Britain, Germany, France, Hungary, and Korea, and from many parts of Canada. This rich stew of musical cultures greatly enriched both faculty and students alike. The period of internationalism, however, was brief. By the end of the 1970s the world economy had taken a downturn: money and jobs became scarcer and Canada's postsecondary institutions began to produce enough artists, composers, and researchers to fill the home job market. lanza was fortunate to have arrived on the scene just before the doors began to close.

Through the 1950s and early 1960s the instruction of conservative tonal music was entrenched in Quebec's institutions of higher learning. Two composers of very different stylistic and aesthetic orientations challenged this conservative heritage. The young Serge Garant (1929–1986) travelled to Paris in 1951 to study with Olivier Messiaen. In Paris he met Pierre Boulez and Karlheinz Stockhausen, both of whom were also students of Messiaen. Boulez believed that the late works of Anton Webern pointed the way toward an extension of serialism beyond pitch organization to include serial control of rhythm, dynamics, and sound colour. Garant came under the influence of Boulez and returned to Montreal a committed serialist.

Pierre Mercure (1927–1966), another young Quebec composer, came under the influence of Quebec avant-garde visual artists in the late 1940s. (In Quebec the visual arts entered the modernist stream long before the musical arts.) Armed with a fierce passion to learn more about musical modernism, Mercure went to France in 1949 to study with Nadia Boulanger. That he could have considered Boulanger in the forefront of musical modernism demonstrates how provincial the Quebec musical scene was. While Boulanger was a brilliant teacher, it was not long before Mercure realized that she was not the person to guide him in his exploration of new musical frontiers.

By the late 1950s Mercure was writing atonal music, but unlike Garant, he was not interested in serialism, a technique he had already rejected as incompatible with his personality. Indeed, it is difficult to pigeonhole Mercure: he seems to fall between the cracks of most stylistic labels. His *Structures métalliques I et II* (1961), in which a performer explores the sounds achieved by striking metal sculptures, comes out of the experimental line, but his tape music – for example, the extraordinary *Incandescence* (1961) – is atmospherically "romantic." Mercure studied *musique concrète* in the late 1950s with the Groupe de recherches musicales in Paris; later he studied in Darmstadt, Germany, and worked at the Bell Laboratories in the United States.

Above all, Mercure was interested in mixed media. He wrote a number of works combining electronic music with dance, and several involving live musicians, tape, dance, and visual arts. His desire to use electronics to create special effects and to enhance mood was related to the aesthetics of French *musique concrète* composers such as Pierre Schaeffer, but whereas the French composers tended toward a rigidly systematic approach, Mercure and later Quebec composers were much freer.[2] Nevertheless, Schaeffer and his associates had an enormous influence on Quebec attitudes to electroacoustic music. For decades many Quebec composers working with either pre-recorded or electronically synthesized sounds used the medium expressionistically.

In 1961 Mercure organized the Semaine internationale de musique actuelle in Montreal; this seven-day festival of contemporary music was a watershed event in Quebec's musical history. Performances of music by leading composers in a wide range of advanced musical styles included works by Cage, Feldman, Kagel, Babbitt, Stockhausen, and Xenakis, along with Canadian composers R. Murray Schafer, Serge Garant, and Pierre Mercure. The festival also commissioned and premiered Cage's *Atlas Eclipticalis* (conducted by dancer and choreographer Merce Cunningham). Cage and Feldman attended the festival and Kagel conducted the premiere of Garant's *Anerca*. The Semaine internationale de musique actuelle introduced Quebec composers and audiences to the world of the cutting-edge avant-garde, and it was also one of the main catalysts for the founding of the Société de musique contemporaine du Québec (SMCQ) in 1966. Today Montreal is a city with more festivals than days of the year, so it is hard to imagine the excitement generated by this festival, but according to Garant, it was a "week that can only be described as delirious, literally delirious."[3]

By the early 1960s the avant-garde musical scene in Quebec was beginning to fracture along the same aesthetic and stylistic fault

lines that existed elsewhere: doctrinaire atonal serialists were opposed by atonal experimentalists who rejected serialism. In Quebec, however, the opposing groups did not manifest as much
hostility as those in New York or even Argentina. In a number of
other centres, Garant the rational serialist and Mercure the intuitive expressionist might not have been on such good terms. In fact
one of the astounding aspects of Mercure's Semaine actuelle was
that both Cage and Garant appeared together; it is unlikely that,
for example, Cage and Babbitt would have appeared on the same
program in New York in the early 1960s. The reason for this lack
of hostility is perhaps because in Quebec both groups faced a
highly entrenched tonal-oriented establishment. They needed each
other to survive. In other countries the battle to establish nontonal
and experimental music as legitimate had begun decades earlier.
The fact that the struggle in Quebec began relatively late may also
explain the initial hostility to the neotonal postmodernist movement during the 1980s. The atonal composers, by then establishment figures themselves, had only managed to achieve a secure
foothold in the late 1960s; just fifteen years later neotonal music
was being touted as the new avant-garde. To many of Garant's
generation it seemed like a betrayal.

Mercure died in 1966 in a car accident at the age of thirty-nine. Of
the young Quebec composers working in the late 1960s and early
1970s, one could say that Micheline Coulombe Saint-Marcoux
(1938–1985) inherited his interests. She too was vitally interested in
mixed media and the expressionistic use of electronics. In 1972 she
founded a rudimentary electronic music studio at the Conservatoire de musique de Québec à Montréal. Her compositions include
works for tape, percussion, and modern dance, and she was also a
gifted organizer of music festivals. lanza had a close friendship
with Saint-Marcoux, who, like Mercure, unfortunately died
young.[4] The other Quebec-born composer of this period who must
be mentioned is Gilles Tremblay (b. 1932). While he was not interested in electronics to any great degree, he was fascinated with the
exploration of sonority: to this effect he used instruments unconventionally and sometimes tuned them to produce sounds outside
the tempered system. Although his influences were mainly European, while lanza's were New World, the two composers share a
common obsession. lanza greatly admires Tremblay's compositions, and has referred to him as a "terrific composer, a real poet."[5]

With Saint-Marcoux's love of mixed media and Tremblay's explorations of timbre, lanza felt very much at home in Quebec, and sensed that his new fellow composers would not greet his style of music with hostility.

Quebec composers in the late 1960s were also lucky in that history was on their side. In 1967 Canada celebrated its centennial as a nation and Montreal was host to the world's fair, Expo 67. Countries from all over the world sent their best musicians to perform in Montreal, and many of them played music by their own country's contemporary composers. The Canadian government, the Quebec provincial government, and the Montreal municipal government were determined to show that Canada too had extraordinary composers and performers. A wide spectrum of Canadian composers, ranging from the most conservative to the most radical, was commissioned to produce new works, and an impressive amount of money was awarded in grants. In the frenzy surrounding the centennial celebrations, Montreal's civic pride in Expo 67, and Quebec's growing sense of nationalism, many projects that had been in the works for years finally crystallized. In 1966 the SMCQ began its first season of concerts, in 1967 the Montreal Métro opened and two new theatres were added to Place des Arts, and 1968 marked the establishment of the Université de Québec à Montréal. Montreal was abuzz with construction on both material and artistic planes. It was a good time to be in Quebec.

Mercure was to have been the first director of the Société de musique contemporaine du Québec, but after his death in 1966 Garant inherited the position. The Société, as is evident from its name, has a mandate to perform contemporary music, but in reality was interested primarily in nontonal contemporary music; many tonally-oriented Quebec composers were ignored. In those early years, however, the SMCQ did perform an impressive number of nontonal works with an almost healthy disregard for stylistic difference. Audiences enthusiastically applauded everything they heard. It was all "modern"; it was all welcomed.

It could be said that the SMCQ and other contemporary music groups that followed in their wake during the 1970s and 1980s were so successful that Montreal today has become a city obsessed with being *au courant*, almost to the detriment of its heritage: works by composers of Garant's and Mercure's generation are rarely played, and are almost forgotten in a ceaseless quest for newness.

The McGill Electronic Music Studio

One of the most important contributors to electronic music in Canada was the brilliant scientist, inventor, and composer Hugh Le Caine (1917–1977). He had worked on the development of the first radar systems during the Second World War and was later a researcher in atomic physics, but his "hobby" was researching the electronic production and manipulation of sound. Around 1945 he built an electronic music studio in his home, the first such studio in Canada. In 1954 he persuaded his employer, the National Research Council of Canada, to allow him to turn his hobby into a full-time area of research. That they agreed to this during the cold war – a time when physicists were in great demand as researchers on defence systems and rocket programs – is remarkable. His studio became known as the Electronic Music Laboratory of the National Research Council of Canada. Between 1948, when he made the first prototype of the Electronic Sackbut, and 1964, Le Caine built an impressive series of electronic instruments that became the basis of the first two university electronic music studios established in Canada (at the University of Toronto in 1959, and at McGill in 1964). Le Caine continued to develop new instruments, many of which were added to the university studios. His major inventions include the Special Purpose Tape Recorder or Multi-Track Tape Recorder (1955),[6] the Oscillator Bank (1959), the Spectrogram (1959), the Level Control Amplifier (1962), the Adjustable Filter (1964), the Printed Circuit Keyboard (1962), a ring modulator (1964), an envelope shaper (1965), the Serial Sound Structure Generator (1966), and the Polyphonic Synthesizer (1970).

Composer István Anhalt (b. 1919) had been teaching composition at McGill since 1949. In the late 1950s he developed an interest in electronic music and spent several summers in Ottawa working in Le Caine's studio at the National Research Council. In 1959 Anhalt presented a concert of electronic music at McGill. This event, probably the first public concert of electronic music in Canada, included Le Caine's *Dripsody* (1955) and Anhalt's *Electronic Composition no. 1* (1959). It was Anhalt who invited Le Caine to supply electronic instruments for a studio at McGill in 1964. Anhalt was director of the McGill Electronic Music Studio until 1971, when he accepted a position at Queen's University in Kingston. After Anhalt's departure, lanza shared the directorship of the studio with Bengt Hambraeus. In 1974 lanza became the sole director, a position he held until 2003, a period of twenty-nine years.

At first the McGill studio had been restricted to composers on staff and invited visiting composers, but when the faculty of music instituted a master of musical arts degree in composition in 1968 the studio expanded into a teaching centre. From then on McGill rejected the closed-door policy common to so many European studios, a situation that made it difficult for even highly trained professional composers to gain access to the equipment they needed. In addition, the directors were convinced that students could only learn to compose electronic music from a hands-on approach, a practice that differed from some other studios. When lanza visited the University of Toronto studio in 1971 he was surprised by its pristine appearance, and asked how they managed to keep it so clean; the director replied that students were rarely allowed to touch the equipment. lanza's studio, on the other hand, was always packed with students and professionals experimenting on the machines. It looked very busy and vibrantly messy! Throughout his career as a teacher, lanza has always believed that students learn first and foremost by doing.

lanza felt very much at home in the electroacoustic community of Montreal. Because a number of Quebec's francophone composers had studied with *musique concrète* composers in France, they tended to use electroacoustics in an expressionistic manner, as sounding materials to create atmosphere. This was exactly the way lanza used electronics. In the pitch-centred, serial-dominated Columbia-Princeton Electronic Music Center lanza had felt like a fish out of water. In Montreal, his aesthetic approach to electronics was more the norm – he was in the right place. By this I do not mean simply that in Montreal he met a group of like-minded composers, such as Saint-Marcoux, Tremblay, and Mather. Composers in many cities focused on mixed media, expressionistic use of electronics, experimental exploration of unusual sonorities, and so forth; in New York all these things existed in abundance. The difference lies in the fact that in Montreal there was still a somewhat united front among the "modern" composers – a pact that unfortunately did not survive into the 1980s. lanza has commented that in the late 1960s and early 1970s it was possible to attend almost every event involving new music. There were so few that all were treasured, all were important. In Montreal lanza was accepted by the composer community, embraced as one of the tribe.

First Compositions in Montreal

For the most part, this book presents lanza's life and career chronologically. I veered from this path in chapter 5 in order to discuss the three movements of *trilogy*, composed over a sixteen-year span (1972–88). Two movements of *trilogy* exhibit a change in lanza's style, a change that incorporates repetitive diatonic motives and recognizable rhythmic patterns. We now go back to 1971, eight years before this style change: lanza had just moved to Montreal and brought with him the interests he had in New York in the late 1960s. He was committed to composing electronic music that centred on the intuitive and expressionistic use of sound to enhance mood and character, with no reference whatsoever either to serialist technique or to any style rooted in equal temperament. He was interested in all types of sounds, real or synthesized, lyrical or noisy, pleasant or unpleasant. In fact, lanza's music often sounds like *musique concrète* even when the sounds are entirely electronically produced.

This interest in expressionistic electronic music went hand in hand with a desire to compose works that incorporate theatrical elements. Both *strobo I* (for double bass and tape, 1967) and *ekphonesis II* (for opera diva, pianist, and tape, 1968) include acting, costumes, sets, special lighting, and a visually enacted narrative, all layered on top of a tape part that creates the initial atmosphere and changes it at crucial moments in the drama. lanza's tape parts function somewhat like an "orchestra" that accompanies, enhances, and guides the soloists. And what are the soloists doing? Often they make unusual sounds by tuning and playing their instruments unconventionally, or by using ordinary objects as instruments. These instrumental sounds frequently have an "electronic" feel. This is especially true of *eidesis II* (1967), a chamber work that is entirely instrumental but sounds as if it has an electronic component.

During the late 1960s and early 1970s lanza went through a brief period in which he notated several works for tape and instruments solely as graphic drawings. These works are moody, atmospheric pieces in which the tape part creates the atmosphere and form, while the live musicians, playing in the dark, react to the tape in a sort of parallel improvisation. Let us now examine one of these works.

plectros III (1971)

plectros III,[7] for piano and tape, was the first composition lanza wrote in Canada, but the genesis of the work goes back to 1965 when lanza was living in New York. At that time soft, bouncy superballs, a popular new toy, were all the rage. lanza bought several for his son Guillermo, but before long he was experimenting with them himself, dragging a ball along the strings and the wooden frame of the piano. He liked the eerie timbral quality this produced; his next step was to cut a small hole in the ball and insert a wooden stick, creating a superball mallet. lanza was not the only musician to see the musical possibilities of superballs; a number of composers and percussionists came up with the same idea at about the same time. lanza used superball mallets in several works of the late 1960s, but it was not until plectros III that its possibilities became the primary focus of a piece.

In plectros III the pianist plays on the inside of the piano and on the wooden frame, only touching the keys to help elicit harmonics from the strings. The work is performed in the dark with the only light on stage coming from a tiny flashlight placed inside the piano (so that the pianist can see what he is doing). The audience sees only the shadowy outline of the performer and is never really aware of what is going on inside the piano, or even which sounds come from the piano and which from the tape.

The piano part is written in pure graphic notation. lanza uses graphic images and verbal instructions to give the performer general indications of what to do and when to do it. In the preface he writes: "The general idea of the piece is to match, precede and follow the tape sounds in an improvisatory manner." lanza stipulates that the pianist must have two superball mallets, a glass ashtray, a set of metal keys, and a short metallic chain, and he indicates how to use these objects to create the timbral effects that enhance the tape music.

During the first four minutes of plectros III, we hear long, sustained, low-pitched rumbling sounds on the tape. The pianist drags the superball mallet along the wood of the piano frame while holding the damper pedal down; this produces low "moaning" sounds in keeping with the dark atmospheric music on the tape. The superball sounds and the electronics fade in and out with no sense of attack;

lanza has described these seamless flowing layers of sound as his "oozing magma" style.[8] Over the next three minutes, the tape part increases in activity adding a dramatic, new timbral quality: we hear short staccato bursts, sharp sounds with abrupt attacks. The pianist reacts to this change of mood by creating percussive effects on the piano, dropping and dragging the various metal and glass objects on the strings to create a series of buzzing, pinging, thumping, scraping, and wailing sounds. Toward the end of the work, the mood changes. The tape part returns to the long low continuous rumblings heard in the opening, and the pianist once again uses the superball mallets to produce sad and eerie moans. Then the pianist dangles a car key against a vibrating bass string to add a distant, soft buzzing. Gradually the music fades into silence.

In the preface lanza supplies a legend explaining a series of symbols, each representing a specific timbral effect; four of these symbols are shown in example 6.1. How are these symbols used in the score? Example 6.2 shows the final four minutes of the piano part (indicated as 8', 9', 10', 11', 12'), the section in which the music returns to the low eerie sounds of the opening. The letters in square brackets indicate the part of the score under discussion. At 8' (8 minutes into the work) the performer drags two superball mallets along the lower strings [a]; a little after the ten-minute mark the pianist elicits harmonic tones from the low strings [b] and creates a buzzing sound by plucking a low string and suspending the car key against the vibrating string [c]; at about 11' the pianist drags the superball mallets along the lid of the piano, in a decrescendo gradually fading away to nothingness [d]. While the graphic score might appear puzzling at first, once the pianist has read lanza's prefatory instructions and studied the legend of symbols, the music is amazingly easy to read and is quite clear as to when and how to produce the different timbres.

In a sense the pure graphic score of *plectros III*, which is entirely focused on the production of shifting but controlled soundscapes, is the child of *plectros I*, which, although it has pitches, is focused on the same concept. In *plectros I* five contrasting soundscapes are explored in five miniature movements. *plectros III* is a single-movement work consisting of three soundscapes (ABA). Both compositions are essentially the same type of work. Although lanza reintroduced some form of standard notation in later works, when actual or relative pitch is required, he nevertheless tends to compose works that concentrate on a sonic plan rather than a pitch-centred plan.

Example 6.1.
plectros III, excerpt from prefatory instructions.

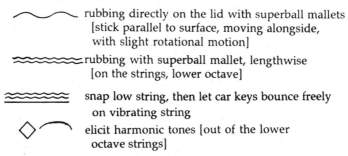

rubbing directly on the lid with superball mallets
[stick parallel to surface, moving alongside,
with slight rotational motion]

rubbing with superball mallet, lengthwise
[on the strings, lower octave]

snap low string, then let car keys bounce freely
on vibrating string

elicit harmonic tones [out of the lower
octave strings]

Example 6.2.
plectros III, p. 3, final system of piano part.

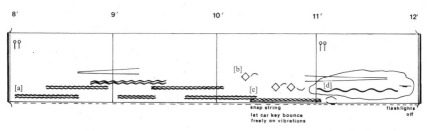

A performer can look at a score written in traditional notation and have a fairly good idea about how the music will sound. This is not always the case with a graphic score. Of course, performers who specialize in experimental music – who are used to piano works in which they drag superball mallets and drop metal objects on vibrating strings – can "read" the piano part of *plectros III* and know, with a certain confidence, what it will sound like. However, many performers who do not have a background in contemporary music are baffled by scores that seem to tell them very little. In addition, even performers with experience in working with graphic scores cannot know what the overall sound of the piece will be without listening to the tape part. In this respect, performers approaching a pure graphic score need to have an open mind. They must say to themselves, "Let's follow the composer's instructions and see what sounds emerge." There are a few musicians in most major centres who have the curiosity to do this, but not many; most performers have an extreme aversion to experimental notation.

In the history of western music there have been times when experimental notation was more in fashion: the fourteenth century comes to mind, and certainly the late 1960s. However, the notations of the late 1960s are now definitely out of fashion. Today lanza is more likely to hear a performance of *plectros II*, a piano work focused on pitch organization, than one of *plectros III*, a work centred on the creation of atmospheric sounds. This is not because *plectros II* is more innately appealing than *plectros III*, but rather because, for an average musician, it is less frightening to read notes on a staff than to interpret drawings. Ironically, *plectros II* is a technically demanding work requiring a lot of practice, while *plectros III* is easy to prepare and perform. The player need not even be a trained pianist to follow a stopwatch, listen to the tape, and apply the superball mallets and various glass and metal objects at the appropriate moments. Moreover, *plectros III* is always a success with audiences, who enjoy the dark atmospheric oozing sounds and the mystery of seeing only vague shadows of the performer and guessing how the sounds are produced.

ekphonesis IV (1974)

The second work lanza wrote in Montreal is also performed in the dark. *ekphonesis IV*[9] has an overtly political message, something rare for lanza who usually avoids anything to do with politics. One meaning of the word "ekphonesis" is "to speak out loud." In this work lanza is "speaking out" about an atrocity of war. The inspiration for *ekphonesis IV* goes back to lanza's time in New York. One of the paintings on permanent exhibition at the Museum of Modern Art was Picasso's *Guernica*. This massive canvas (370 x 790 cm), one of the greatest antiwar statements in art, is the artist's harrowing response to the bombing and burning of the city of Guernica during the Spanish Civil War. On 26 April 1937 Guernica, a Basque city with no anti-aircraft defence weapons, was firebombed for more than three hours by German and Spanish fighter planes commanded by the forces of General Franco and his German allies. The planes were also ordered to fly low over the city in order to shoot at civilians trying to escape the blazing inferno. Picasso's painting juxtaposes various visual motives – a terrified horse, a woman screaming, arms extended upward, a dead child. lanza was overwhelmed by this work, and he particularly identified with the stark colour scheme (tones of black, white, and grey) and the collage-like interspersing and intersecting of motives. lanza wanted to animate the painting in some way. He considered writing music to accompany an avant-garde film, and even went as far as discussing the project with film director Jerome Ducrôt, for whom he had previously composed a film score.[10] The project never got off the ground because of a lack of financial backing, but lanza shelved the idea in his brain.

In late 1971 he returned to the idea of a composition based on Picasso's masterpiece. The resulting work, *ekphonesis IV*, is a fifteen-minute electroacoustic composition designed to be played in a darkened auditorium with slides of details from the painting projected on a screen. There are also optional parts (drawn in graphic notation) for unspecified instruments. As in *plectros III* the performers, again playing in the dark, imitate the sounds on the tape.

Although *ekphonesis IV* is not, strictly speaking, a theatre work, it is organized so as to present the implicit narrative of the painting as an unfolding drama. Taking his cue from Picasso, lanza divides the work into visual themes: the hands held upward, the woman with the open mouth, the horse, the dead child. The slide projections present these themes in isolation from each other, as small images surrounded by blackness, distanced from each other in space and time. Gradually the images become larger. It is only near the midpoint of the work that the complete painting is shown; it first appears as a tiny image in the centre of the huge screen, and gradually expands to fill the entire screen. As the full picture emerges, lanza supports Picasso's message of the terror of war by building the music to an emotional climax in a hair-raising crescendo. At this point both the images and the music "decompose" into fragments: we see fleeting images of newspaper articles followed by the well-known anonymous news photograph of the city of Guernica in flames. These images are shown first as seen from far away – as the pilots who bombed the city might first have seen it – and then as large-scale blow-ups of sections of the photograph, emphasizing the burning buildings. At the conclusion of the work the photograph of the city in flames fills the entire screen; gradually this terrifying image drifts out of focus and disintegrates, leaving the audience stunned and disturbed.

The presentation has a realistic immediacy that is gut wrenching. lanza presents the story of Guernica in the manner of an abstract film documentary, using both faraway images (the viewpoint of the attackers) and harrowing close-ups (the viewpoint of the victims). Even the disintegration of the final image gives the audience the sense that they are watching a newsreel that has broken down. The accompanying electronic music is typical of lanza's work of this period: long slow pedal points of sustained sound punctuated, at crucial times, by frantic activity. If we were to hear this music on its own, with no visual imagery and no idea of the subject, we would not hear anything particularly programmatic. lanza's accompaniment is never obvious, but the music takes on a new life in combination with the projections: we cannot help but hear the long droning pedal points as approaching warplanes, and the frantic activity as screams, bombs, and gunfire.

ekphonesis IV is extremely effective, so much so that when it was performed in Madrid in 1971, the audience did not applaud: the performance was followed by total silence. After the concert many people approached lanza to say that they were so moved that they could not clap. One said, "You see, Señor lanza, it almost seemed sacrilegious to clap, for in some way applause is a manifestation of enjoyment. This is our story; it happened to us, and only recently. We are still in mourning."[11]

plectros IV (1974)

In 1974 the Société de Musique Contemporaine du Québec, with the aid of a grant from the Canada Council, commissioned a new work from lanza for Bruce Mather and Pierrette Lepage, a husband-and-wife piano duo specializing in the performance of contemporary music. Mather had been instrumental in bringing lanza to McGill, and lanza was only too happy to have an opportunity to thank him with a new work. Those who have met Mather know him to be knowledgeable and cultured man, but at times he is engagingly awkward; Lepage is more of an extrovert. When lanza considered their contrasting but charmingly compatible personalities, he was inspired to compose a theatre work about the mystery of love.

plectros IV is scored for "two pianists of opposite sex" and tape.[12] The stage setting is an antique shop of the distant future. A large sign reading "Antiquitäten" hangs on the wall. The shop is full of "ancient" musical instruments: brass and wind instruments hang on the walls, and two grand pianos face each other surrounded by a large assortment of percussion instruments. The protagonists of the drama are two robots of opposite sex: the female robot is a customer, the male is the salesman. The performers walk in a rigid, awkward manner and raise their arms or turn their heads in abrupt, jerky movements. The tape part, which is full of mechanical ticking noises, reinforces the notion that the protagonists are cold-blooded machines. Each robot wears a blinking red light around the area of the heart (appropriate for a work about love) that flashes on and off.

The scene begins as the beautiful young robot woman enters the antique store and the robot salesman rises to greet her. She is "just looking," so to speak, and hits one percussion instrument after another, as if to find out what they sound like. The salesman, after showing her some of the instruments, settles down at one of the pianos, and she eventually settles at the other. For the next seven minutes they play on their separate pianos and various percussion instruments within reach. The two robots, both absorbed in their own noisemaking, eventually work up to a frenzy of sound. The effort overwhelms the woman robot. She collapses on the keyboard with her long flowing hair dangling over the edge. The salesman, unaware of her predicament, continues to play for a while, and then suddenly notices that his customer has collapsed. He rushes to her side in jerky robot-like motions, but has no idea how to revive her. He sits down beside the woman and begins to shuffle through some dusty old sheet music. One piece catches his eye, and he begins to play an excerpt from the third movement of Schumann's *Phantasie*, op. 17 (a piece in which Schumann sends cryptic love messages to his beloved Clara). The moment the woman hears the lush, romantic sounds, she revives, places her hands on top of his, and joins in the *Phantasie*.

The tape part, which until this moment has been full of mechanical noises, now takes over the *Phantasie*, and as the romantic music soars through the room, the robots stare into each other's eyes, rise from the keyboard, and walk slowly off the stage with their arms linked about each other. The stage is empty for a moment while ticking clock-like sounds are heard on the tape. Then a baby robot about 45 cm tall waddles across the stage – a sight that never fails to bring a smile to the audience.

For much of this piece the robots, playing at their separate pianos in their separate worlds, seem dramatically oblivious to each other, but they are certainly not musically oblivious. Throughout the work they pass distinctive musical ideas back and forth. Most of the time

Example 6.3.
plectros IV, excerpt from p. 4, first system.

it is the female robot who initiates new musical ideas that are closely followed by the male. It is only at the end, when the male robot discovers Schumann – that is, Romanticism – that he takes the lead. It is music that unites the couple.

Throughout the work there is a gradual buildup of musical material from the minimal to the maximal. At first the pianists pass only isolated single notes back and forth, then a lonely dissonant minor second, followed by a brief wide-ranging atonal motive. As the tape music becomes increasingly louder, they play active flourishes of dense chromatic clusters (see example 6.3). At about the midpoint of the work, these dissonant clusters suddenly coalesce into rapid quasi-diatonic flourishes, emphasizing perfect fourths and minor thirds (see example 6.4). lanza's choice of intervals is telling, for these intervals are important in the closing Schumann excerpt (see example 6.5). Rhythmic motives in the robot music are also related to the Schumann work. These intervallic and rhythmic references are subtle and few, but they are significant. lanza's point is both psychological and musical: the robots, without realizing it, are already falling in love, and our ears, without realizing it, are being prepared for Schumann. Closely

Example 6.4.
plectros IV, excerpt from p. 4, second system, with a reduction
in conventional notation.

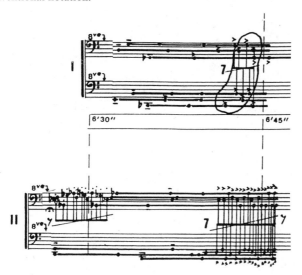

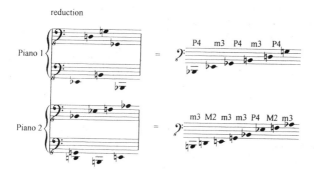

following these quasi-diatonic passages is a return to highly dissonant
flourishes, which now cover the whole range of the keyboards. As the
piece reaches its climax, where the robots play with such abandon
that the woman collapses, lanza characteristically drops staff notation
and specific pitches to move into graphics, freeing his performers to
flail away at their instruments without restraint (see example 6.6).
Thus the level of dissonance is at its most extreme just before the
Schumann quotations begin.

Example 6.5.
plectros IV, excerpt from p. 6, second system.

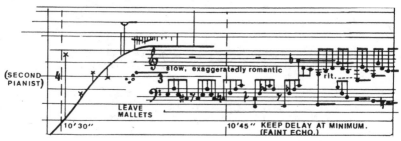

Example 6.6.
plectros IV, excerpt from p. 6, first system.

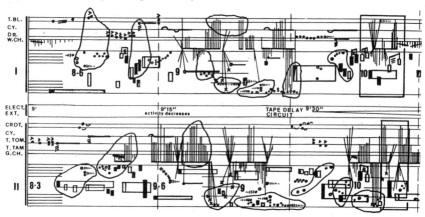

There are two anecdotes – one naughty and one tender – associated with *plectros IV*. lanza's program note for the première informs readers that the baby robot is named Eric. What he did not mention in the note – but did share with a number of individuals – is that he named the baby robot after Montreal music critic Eric Maclean. When lanza first moved to Montreal he felt that Maclean, robot-like, always gave him and many other contemporary composers negative reviews. According to lanza, "Eric," is an acronym for "Embryonic-Reiseführer-Information-Caduca," so lanza was surreptitiously calling Maclean "an infantile tour-guide of obsolete information." Maclean somehow heard about this, and naturally was insulted. It was some time before he forgave lanza for labelling him in this way. Several years later the two met at a contemporary music concert. Maclean had a fearsome headache and confided to lanza that he didn't know how he could get through the evening. lanza reached into his pocket and produced two Argentinean aspirin tablets, warning Maclean that they were far stronger than the Canadian variety. After the concert Maclean approached lanza with a broad smile: the Argentinean cocktail had worked, and the two men were again on speaking terms.

The other anecdote associated with the baby robot is more endearing. Nine years after the premiere of *plectros IV*, Mather and Lepage had a baby boy, who they named Eric, but both insist the name has nothing to do with their robot offspring in *plectros IV*!

lanza received support from many performers associated with McGill. Directors of a number of McGill performance ensembles commissioned works, including *sensors I* (1976, commissioned by Pierre Béluse and the McGill Percussion Ensemble), *eidesis IV* (1977, commissioned by Robert Gibson and the McGill Wind Ensemble), *sensors IV* (1983, commissioned by Christopher Reynolds and the McGill Concert Choir), *sensors V* (1985, Pierre Béluse), *un mundo imaginario* (1989, commissioned by Iwan Edwards and the McGill Concert Choir), *in … visible* (1994, commissioned by Iwan Edwards and the McGill Chamber Singers).

But not everything went so smoothly during lanza's first years in Montreal. A number of Montreal music critics were consistently hostile to his concerts. In 1974, in a review of a piano recital, Jacob Sisskind of the Montreal *Gazette* wrote: "This sort of concert is fun, of course, and perhaps it is most amusing because everyone takes the music so seriously. Of course one must take the performers and the performances seriously, but the music?"[13] It should be noted that Montreal critics were not singling lanza out; at the time they tended to be hostile to all forms of experimental music. lanza, however, was accustomed to musical journalism in Buenos Aires and New York, where there were some knowledgeable and appreciative critics of experimental music, and he found the constant barrage of insult disconcerting. It is not easy to be a composer of experimental music in some places: some critics associate experimental music with anarchism or downright silliness, while others find it intellectually suspect. Performers also can be hostile; some are much less willing than their audiences to accept new music. The audience is free just to enjoy the sensations of the moment, but performers are always part critic, and in addition are terrified of looking like fools. For these and perhaps other reasons, lanza's next commission resulted in a fiasco.

kron'ikelz 75 (1975)

New Music Concerts, a contemporary music organization based in Toronto, performed *eidesis II* in 1974 during their third season. In 1975 they commissioned a new work from lanza. At the time of the commission they were planning their first European tour, and composer and flutist Robert Aitken, one of the co-directors of New Music Concerts, specifically asked lanza to compose a theatre piece. Aitken had noticed that most of the works they were taking on tour were relatively conservative and he wanted to balance out the program with an avant-garde piece involving theatrics that would add some spice and controversy. lanza was given a list of the performers on the tour and asked to write for this ensemble.

The resulting work, *kron'ikelz 75*, is scored for two actor-singers (one male, one female), flute, English horn, mandolin, cello, horn, harp, piano, double bass, and two percussionists. It is a fifteen-minute theatre work about old age. An elderly man, who is carrying a heavy bag of groceries that he can't quite manage, meets an elderly woman friend. They try to cross a busy street, panic in the oncoming traffic, and shout for help, but the world, indifferent to their plight, ignores them. The text has no actual words, but rather is made up of a series of syllables: we cannot understand what the two actor-singers are saying but their grunts, moans, stuttering, and shrieks vividly convey their emotional state. The fact that we hear no recognizable words reinforces the message of the work: society does not hear, see, or understand the elderly. On a larger scale *kron'ikelz 75* is also a disturbing commentary on late twentieth-century alienation. In the forward to the score, lanza writes, "since this composition is related to incomprehension and individualistic attitudes, it would be advisable to perform it in [such] a way as to give the idea of several musicians accidentally within the same room who are playing their individual musics to themselves."

The alienation of the musicians from each other is underscored by the acting they are asked to do. For example, the mandolin player tries to show something to the pianist, but the pianist is too busy to look. Later the mandolin player tries to tell the English horn player something, but he too does not listen. The flute player attempts to conduct the ensemble, but the musicians, narrowly focused on their own agendas, completely ignore him. They are as indifferent to each other as they are to the plight of the two elderly people caught in the traffic. The audience is not permitted to watch all of this from a safe distance. Toward the end of the work they are drawn directly into the drama. Several musicians don white masks and wander into the audience. They each select an individual at whom they stare, freezing in position until the music fades out. *kron'ikelz 75* is a disturbing piece for both audience and musicians; it is deliberately designed to make everyone uncomfortable. As lanza puts it, "this is a piece intended to hit you in the gut, intended to force [you] to think."[14]

New Music Concerts began rehearsals of the work in February 1976.[15] The singers had no objection to the cries and noises they were asked to make, and while some of the instrumentalists didn't "like" the work, they were willing to learn it. Unfortunately, harpist Erica Goodman was unable to attend the first two rehearsals. It is difficult to say whether or not this affected her attitude to the piece. She played the Toronto première, but found the work so objectionable that she drew up a petition demanding that the work be removed from the European tour; six of the thirteen musicians in the group added their signatures.[16] After a vigorous confrontation with co-directors Robert Aitken and Norma Beecroft, the other musicians backed down, but Goodman threatened to resign if she were forced to play *kron'ikelz 75* on the upcoming tour.

The various people I consulted had quite different memories of this minidrama. Aitken was under the impression that Goodman objected to the piece because it was "ugly" and because she considered it insulting to the elderly. Goodman, however, said that although she didn't like the piece, she did not think it was insulting to old people; instead, she felt it was insulting to the musicians. "My job is to play the harp. I have no training in theatrical things. Music is my bag. I don't like being asked to do degrading things on stage. I felt like a fool."

When lanza was informed of Goodman's refusal, he was puzzled by the feeble reaction of the administration. He reasoned that his music could not have been that much of a surprise to them, since they had performed *eidesis II* the year before. Moreover, he had been specifically commissioned to write a work involving theatrics. Why then had they hired a musician who was so uncomfortable with theatrical demands? But lanza is eminently practical when it comes to performance. He did not try to persuade Goodman to change her mind, or to embarrass the directors by forcing them into a showdown. Instead, he merely said, "Just leave out the harp part. The piece will be fine without it." This pragmatic and reasonable response ought to have resolved the situation, but Goodman, for reasons she cannot recall today, insisted that if *kron'ikelz 75* was programmed on even one concert in Europe, she would not play any of the other pieces on the tour. This put the administration of New Music Concerts in a quandary. Since a harp was required for several other works on the tour, they either had to replace Goodman at the last minute or give in to her demand. They chose the latter, and *kron'ikelz 75* was dropped from the tour. In the long term, neither Goodman nor lanza seem to have suffered any ill consequences: Goodman continued to be hired by various groups in Canada, and lanza went on to a successful career, particularly in the field of music theatre. In the short term, however, lanza lost royalty payments because of the cancelled European performances and broadcasts.[17]

Today it is difficult to understand what all the fuss was about. Regardless of its subject matter and gut-wrenching, even ugly sounds, *kron'ikelz 75* can be seen as somewhat tame in comparison to the extremes of the experimental music-theatre scene of the late 1960s and early 1970s. *eidesis II*, which New Music Concerts had played the year before, contains the same type of improvisation and graphic notation, but the instrumentalists are not required to act. I suspect, however, that this was not the reason why it was accepted and even enjoyed, while *kron'ikelz 75* was rejected. My impression, after interviewing many of the individuals involved, is that the rebellion was more than an objection to theatrics. *eidesis II* is an energetic, youthful, positive work in which the musicians perform very much as an ensemble. In *kron'ikelz 75* the tone is oppressive and the musicians play as isolated individuals; they are widely separated from each other on stage and deprived of the feeling of safety in numbers. While some musicians may well have been uncomfortable with the few theatrical gestures required, it is equally true that the work is written in such a way as to make the players feel ill at ease because they are not only making strange, ugly sounds, but they are also totally exposed; they are by themselves with no connection to each other or to the actor-singers. The piece *is* nerve wracking – intentionally so. I don't think the musicians were really aware of what the work was about. They didn't understand that they were supposed to feel uncomfortable, and consequently to project their discomfort onto the audience.

kron'ikelz 75 marks the close of a period when lanza was focusing almost entirely on grim subjects. We, the audience, are given disturbing close-ups of a bombing raid (*ekphonesis IV*, 1971), a woman having a nervous breakdown (*penetrations VI/VII*, 1972), lonely robot-people (*plectros IV*, 1974), and an elderly couple trying to survive in a hostile environment (*kron'ikelz 75*). These are all pieces about alienation. The robots find their salvation through music, but for the other protagonists there is no way out. When we consider the works he wrote during his first five years in Canada, we might well ask if lanza, as an immigrant, felt as though he were an alien in a new land. lanza denies any conscious awareness of this, but one wonders what was going on subconsciously.

New Directions

The present chapter traces lanza's career from 1971 to 1982. In the late 1970s, as noted above, a crucial style change appeared in lanza's music. To oversimplify, a typical early work consists of a constantly changing soundscape, a constant succession of one new gesture after another, with only lanza's flair for dramatic shape and timing to provide a satisfactory sense of coherence. No individual pitches, chords, motives, or rhythms achieve a sense of structural significance. *ekphonesis V*, as we saw in chapter 5, marks a radical break with this style. lanza's concern with the concept of "memories" led to a score full of repetition at many different levels. Simple vocal motives with associated syllables and words are subjected to frequent literal and varied repetitions. Sustained notes acting as drones create a sense of pitch centricity. Most importantly, the work evolves through a mixture of new material and recollection of things previously heard. The discussion of *ekphonesis VI* in chapter 5 draws a connection between the new stylistic elements and postmodernist musical tendencies in the air at the time. Eric Salzman, in his discussion of postmodernism as applied to music, has observed that the term is typically used to refer "to the revival or renewal of tonality in new music – usually in close association with the revival of metricality (rhythmic regularity), repetition, and recollection as basic, structural elements."[18]

While the "revival of tonality" is not a significant factor in lanza's work (except for quotations and allusions, such as the Schumann excerpt in *plectros IV*), the latter elements of Salzman's definition – metricality, repetition, and recollection – do assume significant roles in lanza's later works. It did not take him long to realize that the lessons of *ekphonesis V* could be applied just as easily to atonal compositions. These works, prominently concerned with the structural use of repetition and recollection, contrast strongly with nearly all of lanza's previous work. We turn now to *sensors III* (1982) to see how lanza has incorporated these postmodern features into his style.

sensors III (1982)

sensors III, commissioned by New York organist Leonard Raver, is scored for organ and two percussionists playing a large array of percussion instruments. lanza composed the work with the reverberant acoustics of a large church in mind, and stipulates that the percussionists must be placed in the two corners at the opposite end of the space from the organ. This arrangement allows lanza to explore antiphonal effects between the organ and the two percussion setups. If the work is performed in a concert hall rather than a church, the triangular placement must be maintained, with the players separated as widely as the available space permits.

sensors III is concerned primarily with the creation of atmosphere through instrumental colour and spatial effects. The title is derived from the Latin *sensus*, meaning "to feel" or "to perceive." lanza asks the musicians to sense or feel their entrances and nuances – in other words, to make chamber music – through an inner awareness of the pulse and direction of the music, rather than through visual cues on the page. In a work with no real bar lines or specific rhythms, the ability to listen and react to one another is essential. There is no authority here but the musical ear and the acoustics of the building.

As noted above, *sensors III* incorporates several "postmodern" elements – rhythmic regularity, repetition, and recollection – that lanza first explored in a significant way in *ekphonesis V*. The two works, however, have a strikingly different sound: in *ekphonesis V* much of the repeated material is based on simple modal melodic patterns with a perceptible tonal centre; in *sensors III* the musical

Example 6.7.
sensors III, p. 1.

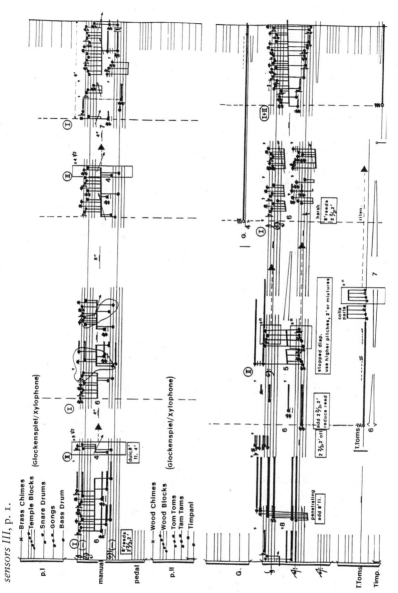

Example 6.8.
sensors III, reduction of opening flourish.

material is atonal. Although this difference of vocabulary gives the
two pieces highly contrasting musical features – a contrast emphasized by the predominantly quiet and mellow character of *ekphonesis V* and the exuberantly loud and aggressive character of much of
sensors III, it is remarkable that the structural use of repetition and
recollection is so similar in these two works, and so different from
lanza's previous practice. Symptomatic of lanza's concern with repetition and recollection is the fact that virtually the entire organ part
is notated in exact pitches on traditional staves.

The work opens with a series of flourishes for the organ manuals,
separated by silences of varied lengths (see example 6.7). The first
flourish introduces several building blocks that are repeated and recalled throughout the piece; three of these are identified in example 6.8
and described below. (The following discussion will be easier to follow
in example 6.8, a reduction of the pitches from lanza's score into conventional notation, but readers should refer to example 6.7 for important non-pitch elements – such as rhythm, tempo, dynamics, organ
registration – that are omitted in the reduction.)

mordent: the melodic figure, E-flat–D–E-flat, occurs fairly frequently in *sensors III*, both at the original pitch level and transposed. Its appearance at the opening helps to establish a pitch
hierarchy in which E-flat has a sense of centricity and D sounds
like a lower neighbour. When the final note of the figure is omitted (as happens several times later in the piece) there is a sense of
unfinished business; we are left hanging, awaiting resolution. I
have labelled these incomplete occurrences "mord ...".

doodle: This figure, like the mordent, recurs frequently. The notes are
often heard in scrambled re-orderings. All the fast, narrow-range,
chromatic running passages can be traced back to this figure.

Example 6.9.
sensors III, annotated transcription of the opening organ solo.

Example 6.10.
sensors III, summary of bass progression in opening organ solo.

atonal triad (A.T.): The useful term "atonal triad" is borrowed from Richard Taruskin.[19] This three-note sonority, one of the most popular pitch-class cells of the early twentieth-century atonalists, acts as perhaps the most significant reference sonority for *sensors III*.[20] It often recurs in its initial configuration as a minor ninth (or augmented octave) filled in with a tritone above the lower note. It also appears frequently as a major seventh filled in with a tritone; in more abstract transformations the notes are compressed to a narrower range or expanded to a wider range. This cell permeates *sensors III*, beginning with the first four notes of the right hand of the organ part.

Example 6.9 is my annotated transcription of the first one and a half systems of the organ part. The opening flourish ends with a five-note sustained chord (labelled "[1]" in example 6.9) containing the atonal triad in the left hand plus C (the lowest note of the doodle motive) and A-flat in the right hand. The A-flat is part of an alternation between A-natural and A-flat in the upper register that acts as an out-of-phase parallel to the E-flat–D–E-flat motion established by the mordent motive. The five-note chord is followed by a five-note wide-ranging melodic figure that is repeated quietly five and a half times like an echo, using four of the five notes of the previous chord. After a four-second silence the organ plays a variation of the opening flourish, ending on another five-note chord (labelled "[2]").

Chords [1] and [2] have their three middle notes in common (the atonal triad B–F-sharp–C) but the outer notes are different. In the top voice, the A-flat moves up to an A-natural (part of the oscillation between these two notes mentioned above); in the lowest register the F of chord [1] moves down to D. This movement is also part of a slowly evolving melodic process, an alternation of the pitches F and D, embellished by neighbour notes. (This process is indicated by comments below the music in example 6.9, and is summarized in example 6.10.

The six-note chord near the end of the passage (marked "[3]" in example 6.9) has obvious connections with what has come before. It includes the atonal triad G–C–F-sharp,[21] and its two lowest notes are the important bass-line notes D and F moved up two octaves. This six-note chord also has important echoes later in the piece: there is a literal repetition as the culminating sonority of a gradual buildup of intensity on p. 3 of the score (see chord "[4]" in example 6.11), and a number of chordal passages on pages 2, 7, and 8 of the score can be heard as based on it.

A later passage from the piece demonstrates how lanza re-uses ideas presented in the opening organ solo. The passage shown in example 6.11 opens with a typical incremental buildup. The organ plays two notes (F, B), pauses briefly, then repeats them and adds three more notes (E-flat, D, B). After a second brief pause, these

Example 6.11.
sensors III, p. 3, reduction of organ part.

five notes are repeated with a sixth note, A, added at the end. After a third brief pause the A is taken up as the beginning of a four-note gesture sweeping downward. Following a fourth pause, the downward gesture is repeated, prefaced by the note B that preceded it, introducing a running passage that incorporates the mordent and elements of the doodle figuration. A comparison of this passage with figure 6.9 reveals that everything in the present passage comes from the opening solo, though not in any systematic way. (The most extended example of exact repetition is the sequence of eight notes that ends the first system of example 6.11; it is a repetition of the first eight notes in the fourth system of example 6.9.)

The second system of example 6.11 continues the process. Once again, motives from the opening solo are strung together in new arrangements. At [2] there is an "almost repetition" of a passage from the previous system (compare [2] with the sequence of notes beginning at [1]). At [3] this flourish is repeated with further changes, leading to a repetition of the eight notes that concluded the first system (taken, we recall, from the opening solo). The changes made in the second system of example 6.11 (notably the addition of F-sharp in the figure beginning at [2] that brings in the atonal triad) serve to relate the passage more closely with the opening of the work. The culminating chord [4] of example 6.11 is identical to chord [3] of figure 6.9, where it has a similar climactic function. A comparison of examples 6.9 and 6.11 reveals that the latter passage can be understood as a fantastic free "improvisation" on the opening solo, using the same melodic and harmonic ideas and having the same general shape. Because the opening solo is itself so improvisatory, the overall effect is somewhat mobile-like, with clearly recognizable motives and harmonies blowing in the wind, creating unpredictable yet logical designs.

When I first began to examine works such as *ekphonesis V* and *sensors III*, I saw a great difference of style on the surface: the former is so modal, simplistic, and obviously repetitive; the latter is atonal, complex, and builds motives incrementally but not in a systematic fashion. My initial conclusion was that *ekphonesis V* was an anomaly – a piece that had been influenced by postmodernism – but that lanza had immediately abandoned this style in subsequent works. It took me some time to realize that the fundamental basis of lanza's "new style" is not simply the use of tonal or modal motives and harmonies, but rather the repetitive use of small-range blocks of sound, whether modal, tonal, or atonal, to establish networks of memories in the mind of the listener. We can conclude, therefore, that postmodernism influenced lanza's atonal writing – the predominant musical language of his works – just as much as his tonal or modal writing. It changed the way he put his pieces together. I suspect that a hundred years from now tonal and atonal works of the end of the twentieth century will no longer be considered as far apart stylistically as they are seen today, and historians will realize that postmodernism affected most composers of the late twentieth century, regardless of their harmonic language.

7

In Memoriam ...

As anyone who has ever lost a loved one knows, our reactions to grief are unpredictable. In some cases the loss can be faced immediately; although our reactions may be intense, we are at least able to react. In other cases, however, the pain may be so unbearable that we become frozen with grief, and cannot even begin the process of healing. It can take a lifetime to come to terms with this kind of grief.

Two of lanza's works written in the late 1980s are expressions of grief. *bour-drones* was an immediate response to the death of his close friend and colleague Micheline Coulombe Saint-Marcoux in 1985 at the age of forty-six after a long struggle with cancer. *un mundo imaginario* is a long delayed response to the tragic life and early death of his first son, Pablo.

Contemporary Music Festivals

Early in 1971 lanza and Sheppard travelled to a number of European cities performing in concerts of contemporary music. While in Paris they were introduced to the young Quebec composer Micheline Coulombe Saint-Marcoux (1938–1985).[1] lanza had just applied for a position at McGill University but had not yet heard whether he had got the job. Since it was possible that he would be living in Montreal the following September, he was full of questions about the contemporary music scene there. Saint-Marcoux did her best to reassure him that it was an interesting place.

lanza and Saint-Marcoux both began teaching in Montreal in the fall of 1971 – lanza at McGill, and Saint-Marcoux at the Conservatoire – and they soon realized that they shared a common grievance:

the paucity of concerts of contemporary music in the city. Although the McGill music faculty had a student ensemble devoted to performing "classic" twentieth-century music – works by composers such as Stravinsky, Bartók, Milhaud, and Schoenberg – there was no forum for more recent or avant-garde compositions. For a variety of reasons, most other performing groups in Montreal programmed few works of experimental or avant-garde music. The exception was the Société de musique contemporaine du Québec, which presented a series of about six concerts a year – hardly enough to make Montreal a flourishing centre of new music.

From 1972 to 1974 lanza had repeatedly asked Helmut Blume, the dean of the McGill faculty of music, to let him organize a festival of experimental music. Blume was sympathetic but always refused, claiming that McGill could not afford to sponsor such a large-scale event. Finally, in the fall of 1974, Blume invited lanza to his office to meet Hugh Davidson, an officer of the Canada Council. lanza asked Davidson if the Council would consider a grant for either McGill or himself to sponsor a festival. Davidson explained that Council policy in the area of contemporary music was to support only one group in each major city. In Montreal that group was the SMCQ.[2] lanza admired much of the work of the SMCQ; he had a good rapport with them, and he did not begrudge them their substantial grant. Nevertheless, he felt that the Canada Council policy was short sighted. He explained to Davidson that in a situation where one group has all the money and all the power, the aesthetic of that group may come to dominate the city to the point that it becomes culturally stagnant. He emphasized that it takes a lot of different ideas bouncing off one another to keep a place culturally healthy. lanza's reasoning, however, carried no weight, and Davidson again said that it was unlikely lanza's proposed festival would receive Council funding.

lanza was somewhat discouraged by this conversation, but he was more than ever determined to organize a festival. Shortly after the meeting lanza and Sheppard had lunch with Saint-Marcoux, who sympathized with lanza's dilemma. In 1971 she had mounted the Carrefour électroacoustique, a minifestival of electronic music at the Montreal Conservatoire, so she had had some experience in this area; she also had contacts who knew how to "work the system." She suggested that she, lanza, and Sheppard organize a joint McGill-Conservatoire festival. Saint-Marcoux also mentioned the project to her close friend Maryvonne Kendergi, who taught at the Université de Montréal and was on the board of directors of the SMCQ. Kendergi contacted lanza and offered to join the team, creating a triple alliance of McGill, the Conservatoire, and the Université de Montréal. Before long two more institutions got wind of the project and asked if they too could be part of the festival; as a result, Concordia University and the Bibliothèque Nationale du Québec were invited to participate. This city-wide festival of contemporary music, La Semaine de musiques nouvelles, took place on 12–19 February 1975.

In the end, funding proved quite easy to obtain: a number of agencies were impressed by the fact that academic communities from across the city were uniting on a project, and the festival received grants from the Quebec Ministry of Cultural Affairs, the various academic institutions involved, the composers and publishers associations of Canada, a France-Quebec exchange program, and even the Canada Council. Three composers from the Groupe de recherches musicales in Paris – Bernard Parmegiani, Michel Chion, and Guy Reibel – were invited as guest composers, and the festival featured a rich variety of events: in addition to nine concerts there were lecture-demonstrations by the composers, films with avant-garde music, a workshop for children, and an exposition of scores with avant-garde notation.

It is hard for readers today to understand the excitement generated by the Semaine de musiques nouvelles. There were few large-scale contemporary music events during the 1960s and early 1970s. Pierre Mercure's Semaine internationale de musique actuelle in 1961 and the Montreal world's fair in 1967 had both featured an impressive amount of recent music of the highest international stature, but since 1967 there had been nothing to generate the kind of excitement that comes from a concentrated dose of avant-garde art. The Semaine de musiques nouvelles was an event that audiences were eager to experience.

In 1976, the year after the festival, Saint-Marcoux composed a work especially for Sheppard and lanza. *Arksalalartôq* was originally written in 1971 as a tape piece, but now she created a new version, adding a voice part for Sheppard and piano, synthesizer, and percussion parts for lanza. The title is the Inuit word for "games." *Arksalalartôq* is a joyful piece with a number of improvisational sections in which the two live performers spontaneously react to the tape and to each other's inspiration of the moment. lanza and Sheppard enjoyed the piece so much that they performed it all over Canada, Europe, and South America; they also recorded it for their 1996 CD, *transmutations*.[3]

In 1979 Saint-Marcoux visited Brazil to attend a conference on the contemporary music of Latin America, and returned to Montreal full of enthusiasm about the new music she had heard there.[4] Interest in Latin America was somewhat rare in Montreal. lanza has always maintained that while communication between Europe and the Americas (for example, between Spain and Latin America, or France and Quebec) is vibrant, there is little dialogue on the north-south axis. Saint-Marcoux's interest in Latin American music gave her yet another interest in common with lanza. They both thought that the Quebec music scene would be enriched by exposure to this music, and with this in mind decided to collaborate on a second festival devoted entirely to the music of Latin America. The Journées de musiques nouvelles d'Amérique Latine, held on 15–19 February 1982, included four concerts of recent music from Mexico, Argentina, Brazil, and Venezuela as well as conferences and interviews with Mexican composer Mario Lavista.

bour-drones (1985)

During the planning of the Latin American festival, lanza discovered that Saint-Marcoux was battling cancer. For the next few years she appeared to be winning the fight, but in February 1985, after a courageous three-year struggle, she died of a brain tumour. lanza was deeply upset by the news. He spent the two and a half months following Saint-Marcoux's death composing a work for the Montreal Chamber Orchestra. The work, *bour-drones*, is dedicated to the orchestra but lanza added the words "... micheline, a tu memoria ..." above the title.

bour-drones is scored for thirteen strings divided into a main group of ten players (six violins, one viola, two cellos, and double bass) and a trio (two violins and a viola) labelled "separata." Each group has its own score. The larger ensemble plays intense, often active, and resolutely atonal material depicting a fierce struggle. The trio begins with pitches and musical gestures related to the music of the main ensemble but, as the piece progresses, the players begin to separate themselves more and more from the

Example 7.1.
bour-drones, conclusion of "burden."

larger body. During the final four and a half minutes of the approximately thirteen-minute piece, the trio plays a plaintive, serene, almost baroque tune in G minor, labelled "burden (dou-loureux)" over and over again following its own expressive path, totally oblivious to the intense struggle of the larger group (see example 7.1). Eventually this small, serene ensemble manages to persuade the larger group to join it: the main orchestra imitates a motive of the G-minor "burden," and its fierce atonality resolves to the tonic note G, a resolution that represents both the musical and the philosophical point of the piece.

Ianza had just begun to compose *bour-drones* when the G-minor "burden" kept running through his head. At first, it seemed so incongruously out of place with the atonal character of the work that he simply ignored it, but one day, with this sad tune forcing itself on his psyche, he realized that it had something to do with Saint-Marcoux. He yielded to its presence and let it flow into the work. He also came to understand that the entire piece was related, in some way, to her passing.

The dramatic character of *bour-drones* has a certain resemblance to the second movement of Beethoven's Piano Concerto no. 4. For much of that movement the orchestra is rigid while the piano part is mellow and lyrical, but eventually the piano succeeds in subduing the orchestra. (Liszt is said to have described this movement as "Orpheus taming the wild beasts.") In *bour-drones* the beasts of death are tamed into serenity. The point is quite spiritual: the serenity has been present all along, but ignored. It is only when it is acknowledged and embraced that the struggles stop.

un mundo imaginario (1989)

lanza did not deliberately set out to make a philosophical point in *bour-drones*. He began work with no preconceived musical metaphor in mind, and simply followed the inspiration of the moment. Artists are not always aware of all that is going on in their heads and hearts, and indeed it took lanza some time to understand why this piece was evolving as it was. His second "in memoriam" work was quite different in this respect. With *un mundo imaginario* he knew from the outset that he was writing to exorcize a ghost that had been haunting him for years.[5] In order to understand what generated this piece, we need to look back at an earlier work.

ekphonesis V, the opening movement of *trilogy*, is an autobiographical work about lanza's family and youth in Argentina. One of the characters in this drama is his first child, Pablo, who was born with a crippling degenerative illness. Although his parents tried desperately to keep him well, his condition gradually deteriorated until his death at the age of six. lanza was emotionally shattered by the experience. He wanted to express his feelings in music, but for many years was unable. Finally in 1979, some fifteen years after Pablo's death, he found the courage to include a brief section on the child among the cast of characters of *ekphonesis V*. lanza's haunting words, beginning in Spanish and ending in English, go to the heart of the matter: "un niño ilusorio que se aleja en la niebla ... and vanishes" [an illusory child who drifts into the mist ... and vanishes]. These simple heart-wrenching words tell us of an illusory child who gradually drifts away into another world.

In *ekphonesis V* Pablo is only one of a cast of several characters, but in 1989 lanza found the emotional strength to write *un mundo imaginario*, a work entirely about his son, based on an expanded version of the same text: "un mundo imaginario interior; / un niño ilusorio que se aleja en la niebla ... and vanishes" [an imaginary interior world; / an illusory child who drifts into the mist ... and vanishes].

un mundo imaginario was commissioned by Iwan Edwards for the McGill Concert Choir, and is scored for mixed choir and optional tape. In the course of the work, which lasts about fourteen minutes,

Example 7.2.
un mundo imaginario, opening.

the text is presented somewhat like a mystery; we are given only one clue at a time, so that we do not grasp the full story until the end.

The work begins with the sopranos and altos singing a simple diatonic tune in parallel tritones, set to the words, "mundo imaginario" (see example 7.2). The melody resembles the sort of tune that children sing to themselves while playing. lanza has written, "like children" above the music, but these children inhabit a strange world; although they sing a childlike melody, the parallel tritones are faintly disturbing. This phrase is followed immediately by childlike babbling on the words, "un imaginario mundo interior," this time mostly in parallel fourths. The tritones of the first phrase and the perfect fourths of the second underlie many of the harmonies of the work. By placing them so conspicuously near the opening, lanza primes our ears for the harmonies to follow, but all we really know at this point is that the children are singing of an imaginary world; as yet we know nothing about that world.

Next, lanza begins to fragment the words "mundo imaginario" by rearranging or omitting letters to produce new or made-up words (see example 7.3). The tenors and basses sing in chromatic motives of a "mundo mudo mudo" interspersed with groups of spoken words constructed from letters of "mundo imaginario." By removing the "n" from "mundo" lanza turns the word into "mudo," which is Spanish for "mute" – a reference to Pablo's inability to speak. The word is repeated so often that listeners who understand Spanish cannot help but notice it, but they will probably be just as baffled as their English counterparts about what it means. All we are likely aware of at this point is that we are moving still further into an imaginary world.

Example 7.3.
un mundo imaginario, excerpt from p. 2.

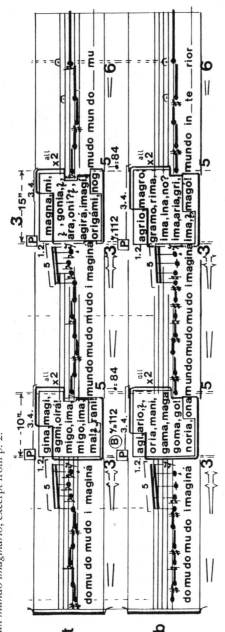

The first section of the piece is centred on the text "mundo imagi-nario." The opening words of the second section, "interior, mundo interior, interiormente," give us another piece of the puzzle. We now know that we are not dealing with a physical world but an imaginary, interior one. At the bottom of page 3 of the score, the male voices sing a text based on the words "interiormente interior," repeatedly and obsessively, like a moto perpetuo, sometimes emphasizing "inte-rior" and other times "tero" (little bird). As they become louder and louder, the female voices focus on the word "terror" (which is the same word in English and Spanish), sung first in tritones and then in fourths, echoing the sonorities of the opening children's song (see ex-ample 7.4). But here the text speaks of terror; and each note of the fourths begins to expand and contract repeatedly in tense microtonal clusters entirely negating a sense of anything childish. The microtonal texture reinforces the sensation that this terror is something other-worldly, something from another dimension.

The terror builds to a climax, at which point the entire choir cries out "niño, niño" [child, child] in dense block chords. To achieve the required intensity lanza asks the choristers to choose their own pitches within a general range; it is the gut-wrenching cry rather than the specific harmony that matters. Up to this point there has been so much obsessive repetition, so many complexly layered textures of real words, made-up words, isolated syllables, and microtonal clusters, that the stark block chords in rhythmic unison on the words "niño, niño" jump out at the listener. We now know that this imaginary inte-rior world is a terrible world, a terrifying world, and that it is the world of a child. When I asked lanza *who* is in terror – the parent who watches the child, or the child who inhabits this isolated world – he replied, "I don't know. I had been thinking about this piece for twenty-five years; so when I was finally able to sit down and write it, it flowed out of me as easily as breathing. When the terror section came to me, I just followed the inspiration without questioning it."

This striking introduction to the *niño* is followed by a quiet, lov-ing, and tender section in which lanza tells us that the child is "un niño ilusorio que se aleja en la niebla" [an illusory child who drifts into the mist]. The music at this point is quite programmatic. The text is set to a series of simple motives that circle back on them-selves so effectively and repeatedly that we get the impression of something lost and drifting, unable to find a beginning or end. At the climax of this drifting, in a moment of great poignancy, a few high female voices cry out "niño, niño," four times, as if calling to the lost child (see example 7.5). The rhythm of their cry is natural, as if they were calling out for someone who is lost, instinctively lengthening the first syllable in a desperate hope that this emphasis will carry the sound further.

While the choir sings this drifting lullaby, a few sopranos and al-tos separate themselves from the larger ensemble to form two small circles; the separata begin a plaintive, wordless vocalise in a minor mode, barely discernable in the overall texture. The illusory child has drifted into the mist and is lost. Will he be found? Will he be saved? In the final section our questions are answered. During the final moments of the work (see example 7.6), we hear voices on the tape and in the choir, whispering "vanishes and vanishes and van-ishes." As the larger ensemble gradually fades out, the separata con-tinue their evocative, ancient, otherworldly vocalise until they too fade into silence. The *niño* has drifted into another dimension.

bour-drones and *un mundo imaginario* are connected both in a spiritual sense and in the technical method lanza chose to present his images. In both works there is an intense physical, emotional,

Example 7.4.
un mundo imaginario, excerpt from pp. 3–4.

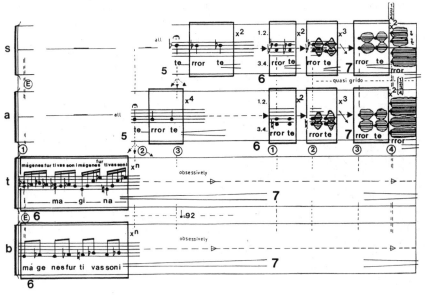

Example 7.4 (cont.)

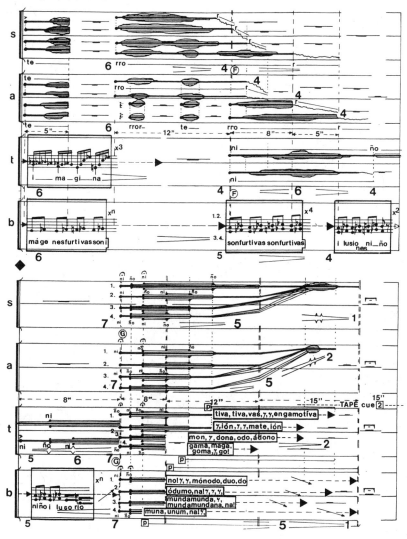

Example 7.5.
un mundo imaginario, excerpt from p. 7.

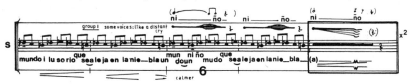

Example 7.6.
un mundo imaginario, conclusion.

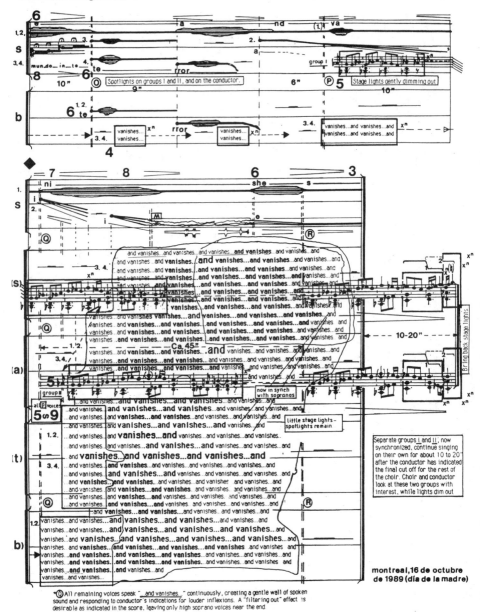

*All remaining voices speak "...and vanishes..." continuously, creating a gentle wall of spoken sound and responding to conductor's indications for louder inflexions. A "filtering out" effect is desirable as indicated in the score, leaving only high soprano voices near the end.

and spiritual struggle in the main performing group. Both pieces also have a small second ensemble that is physically and musically separate from the larger group. These separata play or sing a repetitive, haunting, interior tune, like air from another planet, a music that at first goes unnoticed by the larger ensemble, but eventually becomes the focus of the piece.

Both works are in the tradition of Ives's *The Unanswered Question*, a piece in which a serene string ensemble is totally oblivious to the other musicians who struggle with a question that has no answer. In lanza's "in memoriam" works the separata do not become involved in the struggles of life, for to struggle is earthbound; the separata are celestial. To me, they are the angels that lead our loved ones on their final journey. Needless to say, lanza, the atheist, would never admit to any such analogy.

un mundo imaginario flows like a dream. It has a clarity of expression that is direct and honest. This kind of honesty can come only from the heart; otherwise it would be banal. lanza's piece sounds real, so real, in fact, that at the time of the premiere, several women in the McGill choir asked lanza if the lost child was related to him. "No," he replied, in a barefaced lie. Even after twenty-five years he was still unable to speak about it. But the music says all that need be said. Sometimes the world cannot bear to humanize a child such as Pablo, a child who could not move or speak. lanza's glimpse into the mysterious uncharted world of his son, the child who left an indelible mark on his soul, makes real the humanity, spirit, and history of the little boy who lived on this earth for six years.

8

Mcgill: Bouquets and Brickbats

In addition to his achievements as a composer, lanza has also had an extensive career as a performer and an organizer of contemporary music events. This chapter will examine some of the exceptional contributions he made in these areas. As will be seen, the thread that links most of his concerts, recordings, and festivals is his love and single-minded promotion of music of the Americas.

The McGill Contemporary Music Festivals

During lanza's first years at McGill University he repeatedly tried to persuade his colleagues and the administration of the music faculty to allow him to organize a contemporary music festival sponsored by the school. He proposed two different events: one devoted entirely to experimental music, and the other (co-directed with his colleague Robert F. Jones) to the music of John Cage. Both proposals were rejected. McGill had never sponsored a contemporary music festival. The administration feared the expense, and were uneasy with the idea of an entire festival devoted to Cage's music. It was not until 1975 that lanza finally was able to organize a contemporary music festival in Montreal: La Semaine de musiques nouvelles was a collaborative event organized by lanza (representing McGill University), Micheline Coulombe Saint-Marcoux (from the Conservatoire), Maryvonne Kendergi (from the Université de Montréal) and Meg Sheppard. lanza and Saint-Marcoux mounted a second festival, Les Journées de musiques nouvelles d'Amérique Latine, in February 1982.

In both these festivals, lanza worked in collaboration with members of other institutions, but he continued to believe that McGill was capable of producing an annual contemporary music festival on its own. In 1982, supported by his composer colleagues on the faculty, he proposed a series of annual festivals, and this time the administration gave him the green light. lanza is uncertain why this particular proposal was accepted: "I had been trying to have a contemporary music festival at McGill for a number of years. Eventually I had this idea for a series of festivals. It was approved. I cannot tell why there was a change in atmosphere, but all of a sudden [the proposal] landed well."[1]

lanza suggested that each festival should have at least two directors, with one director replaced by a new person each year: "I felt it was wrong for all the energies and decisions to be in only one pair of hands. By having co-directors I hoped to ensure that the tastes and prejudices of only one person would not dominate from year to year. But I felt that one of the directors should remain in order to pass on the experience of how the previous festival had been organized." lanza shared the directorship of five out of the six festivals; other McGill composers who served as co-directors were Brian Cherney, Bruce Mather, John Rea, and Donald Steven.

According to the original proposal each festival was to highlight a particular family of instruments. The organizers planned to involve as many performers as possible from McGill; over the course of six festivals the directors managed to marshal most of the performing groups of the university – including the Chamber Singers, the Concert Choir, the Wind and Percussion Ensembles, the Gerald Danovich Saxophone Quartet, the Contemporary Music Ensemble, the Group of the Electronic Music Studio (GEMS), and the McGill Symphony Orchestra – as well as a number of soloists, both student and faculty. Such an ambitious enterprise required substantial cooperation between the composition and performance departments. Space in the present study does not permit a complete description of these eclectic and dense events, but the following discussion will provide at least the flavour of each, in the context of lanza's role.

The First McGill Contemporary Music Festival (1982)

lanza has said that the first festival was the most difficult to organize because there was no system in place to provide funding: "We put it together with ingenuity rather than tons of money." lanza and his co-director John Rea decided that the festival would feature keyboard instruments. The decision, lanza remembers, was in part a practical one: "We thought that a festival around keyboards wouldn't cost too much because we already had plenty of keyboard instruments and keyboard players at McGill."

lanza and Rea invited the Spanish composer-pianist Carles Santos as the guest composer. Santos had lived in New York between 1968 and 1970 and had performed with the Composers/Performers Group on several occasions, so lanza was well aware that his personality and works were extremely extrovert and exuberantly theatrical. He was counting on Santos to jumpstart the entire festival series with an explosion of energy and imagination. Santos called his concert a "one-man show" with the subtitle "concert spectacle," and in keeping with this theme he opened the event by pushing a grand piano onto a darkened stage by himself. He then showed four avant-garde films that he accompanied at the keyboard with his own compositions. In his program notes for the concert he says of these pieces: "Surprise and humour (often tender, often blunt, often subtle, often shocking) constantly play an important role and are always associated with the spirit of my country." Santos carried off the evening with great panache and established a theatrical tone for the entire festival.

The other guest composer at the first festival was John Beckwith of Toronto. Beckwith's *Keyboard Practice*, a work scored for ten keyboard instruments (regal, harpsichord, clavichord, grand piano, upright piano, celesta, harmonium, electronic piano, a practice keyboard, and a dummy keyboard) was commissioned by New Music Concerts in 1979. The work consists of fifteen variations that explore the range of timbres available on keyboard instruments throughout the centuries. Each of the four performers is given an historical quotation to play on the appropriate instrument: seventeenth-century music for the clavichord, eighteenth-century music for the harpsichord, nineteenth-century music for the grand piano, and twentieth-century music for the upright piano. In a festival focused on keyboard music Beckwith's composition served as a reminder that although keyboard instruments share a common "user interface," the sound-producing elements – reed pipes, flute pipes, struck strings, plucked strings, percussion, electronic synthesis, and so on – are incredibly diverse.

Another fascinating work for multiple keyboards was Jocy de Oliveira's *One Player and Four Keyboards*. lanza, the soloist for the

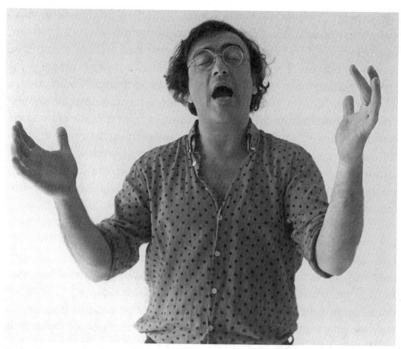

Carles Santos at the first McGill Contemporary Music Festival, 1982. Photograph from the personal collection of alcides lanza.

work, recalls, "I had performed it already in Rio de Janeiro on only three days' notice when someone got sick. The work requires four keyboards placed in a quadrangular arrangement: a piano, harmonium, harpsichord, and celesta. On each keyboard there is a score; but between the keyboards there are also four music stands with scores. So the performer is surrounded by instruments and eight scores. Of course my eyes were younger then. It's a challenge." De Oliveira stipulates that the work should have something of a circus atmosphere. The pianist at the centre of the drama, surrounded by instruments and scores, makes quick turns and gestures while moving from one keyboard to the other. lanza's visually flamboyant performance continued the theatrical theme established by Santos's one-man show.

The Second McGill Contemporary Music Festival (1983)

The second festival, which featured string instruments, turned out to be extraordinarily interesting. Rea suggested commissioning a work from Alexina Louie, a young Canadian composer who in 1983 was relatively unknown. The commission was a significant one that helped to launch her career. Louie had been moved by the recent death of Glenn Gould and decided to write a work for string orchestra honouring his memory. O *Magnum Mysterium: In Memoriam Glenn Gould* was premiered at the festival by the string section of the McGill Symphony Orchestra conducted by Antoine Padilla. Louie attended the concert and was appreciative of work the students had put into her piece. Looking back, lanza commented that the work "was so successful that I felt it was enough to justify all the efforts we had made. What a good result, something positive to remember."

Two international artists were highlighted at this festival. By a happy coincidence the extraordinary contrabassist Bertram Turetzky was scheduled to play a concert in Maine just before the McGill festival, and he was able to swing by Montreal on his way home to California. Turetzky gave a master class and played a concert demonstrating the use of the contrabass as a percussion instrument. Anyone privileged to hear Turetzky play can testify to his enormous creativity; both students and faculty were amazed at the percussion-like sounds and colours he produced. The other invited artist was the Mexican composer-violinist Manuel Enriquez who, in a sense, was doing for the violin what Turetzky was doing for the double bass. Some avant-garde composers of the time felt that traditional instruments were so limited that they would soon be replaced by electronic machines. Artists such as Turetzky and Enriquez took up this challenge and proved that traditional instruments, in the right hands, were well suited to express the musical ideas of the late twentieth century.

The Third McGill Contemporary Music Festival (1984)

The third festival centred around pipes and reeds. Co-directors lanza and Brian Cherney invited Joseph Petric, a noted concert accordionist who performs a great deal of contemporary music, as guest artist. Most of the audience attending the festival had never before heard art music played on the accordion. While they found it strange, Petric's performances were so vital that many could not help but soften their attitudes toward the instrument. This was also lanza's experience. For some time Petric had been trying to persuade lanza to write a piece for him. lanza had been hesitant, but after hearing

Petric's performances of music by Teorbjörn Lundquist, Mauricio Kagel, Mariano Etkin, and Richard Romiti, he began to think seriously about the project. Two of lanza's works for accordion, both commissioned by Petric, are discussed in chapter 9. The other featured instrument at the festival was the organ. John Grew played excerpts from Bengt Hambraeus's *Livres d'orgue* (1980–81) and Brian Cherney's *Gothic Scenes and Interludes* (1984); Réjean Poirier played Bruce Mather's *Three Etudes* (1982) and his own *Arcane* (1977); Alison Riseley-Brown played Hambraeus's *Constellations V* (1982); and Leonard Raver played lanza's *sensors III* (1982), Alan Belkin's *Fantasy and Fugue* (1981), and François Morel's *Alleluia* (1964–68).

The Fourth McGill Contemporary Music Festival (1985)

The use of conventional instruments in unconventional ways had always been part of lanza's aesthetic, and the McGill festivals reflect this obsession. Invited artists were often chosen because they played their instruments in non-conventional manners. The fourth festival highlighted wind instruments, with Spanish composer and clarinettist Jesús Villa Rojo as the guest artist. Villa Rojo specialized in the performance of avant-garde music for the clarinet, and in his book, *El clarinete y sus posibilidades*,[2] he explores and catalogues unconventional clarinet techniques. He had come to McGill for several months on a visiting composers grant. In his classes at the university he introduced students to a fascinating repertoire they had little idea existed and demonstrated avant-garde sounds, mainly multiphonics and microtones, that could be produced on the clarinet. At the festival concerts, Villa Rojo and his students performed a wide array of contemporary music for both solo and multiple clarinets.

Although the fourth festival was devoted to winds, it had a strong subtext: a large part of the festival focused on composers who were also inventors. The other guest artist that year was American composer Jon Appleton, co-inventor of the Synclavier,[3] a computer synthesizer that the McGill Electronic Music Studio had purchased in 1981. Appleton gave a master class on the instrument and three of his works for Synclavier – *Sashasonjon* (1981), *Degitaru Ongaku* (1983), and *Soviet-American Dances* (1984) – were performed. Other concerts included a retrospective of music by Canadian electronic music pioneer Hugh Le Caine. Several works by Le Caine dating from 1957 though 1971 were performed, and Gayle Young gave a lecture on the instruments Le Caine invented between 1945 and 1975.

The Fifth McGill Contemporary Music Festival (1986)

The fifth festival, centred on percussion instruments, was the one closest to lanza's heart. The guest composer, French composer-percussionist Jean-Charles François, gave a lecture-demonstration on his percussion music, and several of his pieces were performed. The main performers were two Montreal ensembles, the McGill Percussion Ensemble and the Atelier des percussions de l'Université de Montréal.

On the opening night the McGill Percussion Ensemble, conducted by Pierre Béluse, gave the Quebec premiere of Alberto Ginastera's *Cantata para América mágica* (1960), an extraordinary work for dramatic soprano and percussion orchestra in which the composer paints a musical picture of ancient Inca, Maya, and Aztec civilizations. The soprano, who sings pre-Columbian poetry set in strikingly angular phrases, is accompanied by an ensemble of fifty-four mainly unpitched percussion instruments, some of which are indigenous aboriginal instruments. Ginastera links us to the distant past in an almost spiritual way: it is as if the singer is a shaman telling her people the ancient stories of her tribe, and foretelling the sad demise of their culture with the arrival of the *conquistadores*. (The tone of this composition was a strong, though distant, influence on lanza's *vôo*, a work that expresses a similar concern for the demise of indigenous Latin American culture.) Although we can analyse the sophisticated serial techniques in *Cantata*, it is not the pitches that haunt us but rather Ginastera's use of percussion to create an atmosphere that is ancient, mysterious, and magical.

lanza did not attend the world premiere of *Cantata* in Washington, D.C., in 1961, but he was involved with the Argentinean premiere the following year. At that time he had studied privately with Ginastera and was about to become his student at the Di Tella Institute. He was present at all the rehearsals, and the work has had an enormous influence on him. lanza's percussion music focuses on the creation of atmosphere through instrumental colour; and it is the colour that we notice, not the pitches and form. There is something primitive and quasi-aboriginal about lanza's percussion music; this he has inherited from Ginastera. lanza has passed on this approach, this almost primordial sound, to his Argentinean student Osvaldo Budón, who is now the third generation inheritor of the percussion mantle of Ginastera.

In 1997 lanza produced a CD of Ginastera's *Cantata para América mágica* with soprano Elise Bédard and the McGill Percussion Ensemble conducted by Pierre Béluse.[4] This recording represents his tribute to the man who did so much for him, and to the work that changed his life. The CD also includes lanza's *sensors V* (1985) and Budón's *Amorçage* (1994), bringing together three generations of Argentinean percussion composers.

The Sixth McGill Contemporary Music Festival (1988–89)

It was Bruce Mather's idea to turn the sixth festival into a homage to two McGill composers – Bengt Hambraeus and alcides lanza – both of whom were celebrating their sixtieth birthdays (Hambraeus in 1988, lanza in 1989). Mather had first met lanza at the Festival de Música de América y España in Madrid in 1970, and Hambraeus at the Festival of the International Society of Contemporary Music in London in 1971. Since Mather had played a significant role in bringing both composers to Montreal as professors at McGill, it was fitting that he was the organizer of this festival. His introduction to the program book for the festival pays tribute to the two men.

They have both enormously enriched the musical environment of Montreal and Canada. They trained a generation of Québec composers in electronic music. Their strong personalities so evident in their music have been equally evident in their activities at the university.

Bengt is the Renaissance man, organist, composer, scholar, a walking encyclopedia. His key work is "scope." An opponent of narrow specialization he constantly searches for interrelationships between disciplines ...

Alcides is the irrepressible concert organizer, the force behind all the festivals at McGill. A true composer-performer, an excellent pianist and conductor, and the creator of the G.E.M.S. ensemble of performers and composers.

Both composers were consulted about the choice of works to be programmed in the five concerts devoted entirely to their music. Hambraeus chose to present a retrospective of his work over four decades from the early 1950s to the late 1980s. During the course of the five evenings audiences gained an awareness of the depth of this composer's knowledge and creativity by listening to some of his early electronic compositions, his Concerto for Organ and Harpsichord (1951), his deeply moving choral work *Constellations V* (1982), and his *Night Music* for guitar and percussion (1988).

lanza approached the event quite differently from his colleague. He decided to saturate the audience with his newest ideas by choosing only works he had written during the past decade (1977–88): *acúfenos III* for flute, piano, and tape (1977); *eidesis IV* for wind ensemble and tape (1977); *eidesis V* for chamber orchestra (1981); *sensors III* for organ and percussion (1982); *sensors IV* for choir (1983); *arghanum I* for accordion and chamber ensemble (1986); *sensors VI* for percussion (1986); *ektenes II* for oboe and percussion (1987); and *ekphonesis VI* (the third part of *trilogy*) for voice and tape (1988). The concerts highlighted two recent developments in his style: the introduction of diatonic material and periodic rhythms into his predominately atonal and aperiodic style, as heard in *ekphonesis VI*, and the use of Argentinean style features, such as the imitation of indigenous ensembles and the quotation of tango rhythms and melodies, as heard in *acúfenos III* and *arghanum I*. This latter feature, one of the most important developments of his later career, is discussed in chapter 9.

The Lanza–Hambraeus festival was full of contrasts. Although both composers are uncompromisingly modern, their aesthetics and approaches to composition are very different – Hambraeus has the systematic exactness of a European, lanza the more impulsive spontaneity of a Latin American – and the juxtaposition of their works brought out an Old vs New World contrast. The spiritual tone of much of Hambraeus's music and the more secular explorations of noise in much of lanza's music made for four fascinating evenings. In a review of one concert, the habitually acerbic Claude Gingras concluded, "the final impression: Hambraeus makes music, Lanza makes noise."[5] Fortunately both composers took this statement as a compliment. Much of the music was performed by McGill ensembles including the Chamber Singers, the Concert Choir, the Group of the Electronic Music Studio, the Percussion Ensemble, and the

Contemporary Music Ensemble. Hambraeus and lanza were appreciative of the efforts made on their behalf and were deeply moved that their university had chosen to honour them in this way. Each also knew that he owed a debt of gratitude to Bruce Mather.

Other Festivals

In the early 1990s lanza and composer and computer-music specialist Bruce Pennycook co-directed two festivals at McGill that were not part of the original series. The year 1990 marked the twenty-fifth anniversary of the McGill Electronic Music Studio, and lanza had been director or co-director since 1971. He and Pennycook organized a festival that included guided tours of the studio, lecture-demonstrations of the machines, and five concerts of electroacoustic music. Former directors István Anhalt, Paul Pedersen, and Bengt Hambraeus were invited to attend, and the festival co-directors also let it be widely known that they wanted all Canadian electroacoustic composers to "come and celebrate with McGill." Since the festival programs presented a survey of music produced at the studio from 1964 to 1990, the concerts were historically as well as artistically interesting. In the following year McGill hosted the International Computer Music Conference, a truly international event attended by 250 composers. lanza and Pennycook organized a festival of sixteen concerts of computer music, tape works, and music-theatre compositions presented during the conference.

The Impact of the Festivals

During the nine years between 1982 and 1991, there were eight large-scale festivals of contemporary music at McGill: the six Contemporary Music Festivals, the twenty-fifth anniversary celebration of the Electronic Music Studio, and the International Computer Music Conference. McGill can look back on these festivals with pride. The festivals included at least eleven world premieres and more than forty Canadian premieres of works by composers from thirteen countries: Spain, Italy, France, Poland, Sweden, Mexico, Ecuador, Argentina, Cuba, Brazil, the United States, Canada, and Japan. The impressively wide ranging programming was due, in large part, to the democratic way each festival was organized. The co-directors endeavoured to consult composers on staff, who often suggested guest composers. The festivals also reflected the different backgrounds and tastes of the composers on the faculty. Thus, for example, it was lanza's idea to invite Carles Santos and Manuel Enriquez, John Rea who suggested Alexina Louie and Michel-Georges Brégent, Bruce Mather who invited John Burke, and Brian Cherney who suggested Stephen Gellman and John Beckwith. Students at the faculty during these nine years were exposed to a vast array of different contemporary styles. There was something positive about the way the entire faculty – students and teachers in both large and small ensembles, backed by an active and helpful administration – pulled together to make each festival memorable.

With the exception of the festival honouring his and Hambraeus's sixtieth birthdays, lanza was the driving force that propelled these festivals. He did not merely propose ideas, but was willing to get into the trenches and deal with the nuts and bolts at every stage of the planning and production. It takes someone with this type of willingness and dogged determination to get a festival off the ground.

In 1996 lanza travelled to Buenos Aires as a judge for the Second Alberto Ginastera International Composition Competition. While in Buenos Aires, Aurora Ginastera, the composer's widow and the chief organizer of the competition, invited lanza to ask McGill to host the next competition. lanza expected the university to give serious consideration to the offer to sponsor such a prestigious event, but the music faculty had a new administration. With no serious exploration of how the competition could have been funded by grants, the request was denied on the grounds that it would be too expensive and would place too much strain on the publicity department! The political, social, and economic climate that had enabled McGill to produce eight large-scale contemporary music festivals between 1982 and 1991 had changed: composers on the faculty had aged, retired, or died; the administration was focused on other projects and was faced with daunting annual government cutbacks; and the performance department had become so successful, with so many commitments of its own, that there was little time to support the composers' projects. It is fitting, however, to look back with respect to a time not so long ago when the music faculty was able to marshal resources from every department to mount ambitious festivals of contemporary music.[6]

When lanza was hired by McGill University in 1971, the contemporary music ensemble at the music faculty was under the direction of a performer rather than a composer. This ensemble played standard twentieth-century repertoire by composers such as Honegger, Ravel, and Stravinsky, but rarely performed works by McGill student composers, or for that matter, works by any living composers. During the 1970s most of the chamber ensembles at McGill were exploring eighteenth- and nineteenth-century repertoire, so the contemporary music ensemble's exploration of "classical" twentieth-century repertoire fulfilled a need that lanza well understood. During his time as a student in Buenos Aires he had attended five or six concerts a week to hear this repertoire, and he had played a great deal of it earlier in his career. He felt, however, that students should also be exposed to more contemporary styles, and that a university renowned for its electronic music studio and for the high calibre of its composition students ought to have a forum for performing the music of those composers. lanza had painful memories of the frustrations he and his fellow student composers at Columbia had experienced when their works were not performed at their own faculty. As a teacher lanza was also convinced that student composers were not receiving a pedagogically complete education if they did not have the opportunity to learn from hearing their compositions rehearsed and performed.

Although the McGill music faculty was teeming with performers, as matters stood, lanza and the other composition teachers had to beg the administration for money to hire musicians from outside the school to perform their students' works. By the 1980s they had had enough. Bruce Mather had been appointed co-director of the Contemporary Music Ensemble in 1980, which entitled him to conduct about two concerts a year. This was a step in the right direction, but with so many composition students at McGill, it was not enough to fulfil the students' needs.

In September 1983 two graduate composition students, Claude Schryer and John Oliver, approached lanza to discuss what they could do to get their music performed at McGill. lanza had been giving serious thought to the matter for a long time, and was convinced that McGill should have a new ensemble directed by a composer that would program about four or five concerts a year

Preparations for the first GEMS concert, Pollack Hall, McGill University, Montreal, 1984; *on stage*: Richard Lloyd, Bernard Savoie; *in pit*: GEMS co-founders John Oliver and Claude Schryer. Photograph from the personal collection of alcides lanza.

devoted entirely to recent music. Since lanza was the director of the McGill Electronic Music Studio, he suggested that the new group be associated with the Studio. This way, he could make sure that the ensemble maintained a focus on living composers. That same day Claude Schryer, John Oliver, and lanza founded the Group of the Electronic Music Studio (GEMS).[7] lanza realized that such a group would succeed only if the administration provided access to instruments, equipment, concert halls, rehearsal space and time, and some funding. To the administration's credit, they willingly embraced the idea and provided modest but adequate resources.

The founders decided that no academic credit would be granted for work involved with GEMS; there would be no marks and no examinations. The participants would be volunteers. What seemed a risky decision at the time – basing so much work on volunteerism – turned out to be the core strength of the group. Over the years GEMS tended to attract only the purposeful, ambitious, and willing. GEMS was organized along the lines of an apprentice system. The group presented four or five concerts per year and the students, with minimal guidance from lanza, were expected to arrange everything from A to Z

associated with these concerts: choosing repertoire, finding performers, getting parts to musicians, arranging rehearsal space and times,
obtaining instruments, writing program notes, supplying publicity,
setting up and operating electronic equipment, stage managing, and
often playing and conducting as well.

Certainly students had struggled to arrange concerts at McGill
before GEMS, but now there was a system in place to direct and enhance these efforts: doors that were once difficult to open a crack
were now open wide, and there was a faculty member to advise and
oversee the nuts and bolts. After 1986 Bruce Pennycook joined
lanza as a co-director of GEMS, bringing his expertise on computer
music and interactive works. The GEMS "do-it-yourself" system
proved to be a golden opportunity for many students, who graduated with knowledge that cannot be easily learned in a classroom,
knowledge that indeed, is best learned through experience.

When GEMS was first founded no one could have predicted how
artistically important it would become. During the twenty years of
its existence the group premiered more than one hundred compositions by Canadian composers from across the country and several
works from other countries. It is perhaps too soon to say what
long-term effect this has had on the contemporary music scene in
Quebec, but at the very least GEMS has enriched the cultural tapes-
try of the province. Today at McGill there is no question that student composers need to hear live performances of their own music
and the music of other living composers. That this is now considered so obvious is due largely to the efforts of lanza and Mather.
Furthermore, in 1983, the year GEMS was founded, Mather became
the full director of the Contemporary Music Ensemble; Quebec
composer Denys Bouliane took over the position in 1997. Thus, for
more than two decades McGill had two active forums for living
composers – few music faculties could boast as much. lanza retired
from McGill University in July 2003, and in March 2004 GEMS presented its final concert.

The Piano Wars

Over the thirty years that lanza has worked at McGill he has been
given commendable support for his work performing, recording, and
disseminating contemporary music, involving marathon concerts, the
formation and direction of GEMS, the invitation of Canadian and

international performers and composers to present lectures and appear in festivals, and the production of recordings in the faculty's concert halls and recording studios. All of these activities have taken considerable time, money, and energy on the part of the faculty. This overwhelming support should be emphasized before examining the single area where there has been significant friction.[8]

In the fall of 1977 Lloyd Wagner, the piano technician at the McGill faculty of music informed the dean, Paul Pedersen, that considerable damage had occurred when the school's pianos had been used as prepared pianos. Pedersen expressed his concern in a general memo to the piano and composition teachers.[9] lanza, one of the few faculty members who played music requiring piano preparation, saw the memo as a direct challenge to his professionalism. He met with Pedersen and informed him that Wagner's claims were unfounded, and that the performance of new music caused only normal wear and tear on a piano. Pedersen proposed a Solomonic compromise: one piano in each of the major concert halls at McGill would be designated for use as a prepared piano, the others could not be prepared. In addition, no piano could be prepared without the piano technician's supervision. lanza and the other composers agreed to the compromise, even though it meant that there would be no venue for the performance of music requiring two prepared pianos. The composers saw the agreement simply as a way to avoid controversy, but in hindsight it is easy to see that this decision was unwise. Some pianists and technicians at McGill interpreted the agreement as an acknowledgement that damage does indeed occur during performances of avant-garde piano music; if this were not the case, they argued, such a compromise would have been unnecessary. The composers' acceptance of the new regulations without a challenge would haunt them for many years.

McGill was not the only institution in which there was friction between piano teachers and technicians on one side and composers on the other. Such confrontations were widespread through the 1960s and early 1970s, as performance of compositions for prepared piano left the domain of dance studios, art galleries, and esoteric environments and began to appear more regularly in established concert halls. Institutional administrators, unsure whether or not preparation caused damage, usually asked piano technicians, who nearly always categorically condemned it, regardless of the growing number of professional articles and books indicating that preparation could be accomplished safely.[10] Some pianists took rather ingenious precautions to assuage a technician's fear. Margaret Leng Tan, a specialist in the prepared piano music of John Cage, has said, "Even today I have to convince tuners and piano technicians to allow me to do what I do ... Steinway have written me a letter, a seal of approval, and that's often enough to convince them. I do not damage pianos, I do [preparation] carefully and I am sensible about it."[11]

The committee formed in the early 1980s to oversee the maintenance of all the faculty pianos has had various names over the years; in the following discussion I will use the current name, Piano Maintenance Committee. When reading the various memoranda dealing with this area of friction it becomes clear that the pianists and the composers had a different understanding of the term "prepared piano." The *New Grove* defines a prepared piano as "a piano in which the pitches, timbres, and dynamic responses of individual notes have been altered by means of bolts, screws, mutes, rubber erasers and/or other objects inserted between or placed on the strings."[12] This was also the composers' understanding of the term. The pianists and the technicians, on the other hand, used the term to cover anything other than conventional playing on the keyboard, including pizzicato, muting, and harmonics. This difference of interpretation created much misunderstanding and miscommunication between the pianists and the composers.

Matters came to head late in 1986, when a series of misunderstandings and exaggerations surrounding two concerts led to a bitter confrontation. A concert of new music organized and performed by lanza on 12 November required one piano with extensive preparation, one with light preparation (moved in from another hall), and one requiring no preparation. Unfortunately, due to a miscommunication, the piano technician came to supervise the preparation of the pianos in the morning, while the performers thought he would be there in the afternoon. Later that day, however, the technician inspected the prepared pianos, agreed that the work had been done properly, and expressed no misgivings or reservations. During the rehearsal – after the piano technician had left – a string on the piano that had had no preparation broke when the pianist was playing a fortissimo trill in the highest octave. Two days after the concert the piano technician sent a memo to the Piano Maintenance Committee, stating that the Steinway piano had two broken strings and six malfunctioning dampers.[13] The head of the committee, Eugene Plawutsky, passed the memo on to

John Rea, the dean of the music faculty, who asked Maria Jerabek, head of the concert office, to investigate the matter; in her report Jerabek rightly referred to the information she received as "recent piano rumours."[14] By this time (two days after the concert) reports of the damage had escalated to four or six broken strings, many twisted dampers, and a broken hammer. lanza kept telling anyone who would listen that only one string had been broken, and this had occurred during the execution of a normal trill on the keyboard of a completely unprepared piano, but exaggeration and rumour had taken over.

On 18 November there was a second concert of new music directed by Bruce Mather at Pollack Hall. On 21 November the technician sent a memo to the Piano Maintenance Committee in which he accused performers of adding more preparation following his inspection, of leaving rosin residue on the strings, and of possibly removing an iron brace from the frame of the instrument. (It is not clear from his statement whether he was referring to lanza's concert or Mather's concert.) At this point, Plawutsky circulated a petition to nearly all the piano teachers in the faculty, expressing concern about the "abuse" of pianos in Pollack Hall, and requesting a meeting before the forthcoming GEMS concert "to establish regulations governing the use of the Faculty of Music pianos."[15] Most of the teachers signed. lanza found the whole idea of a petition confrontational, and he was disturbed that the document started from the assumption that the abuse had indeed taken place, rather than requesting a meeting to look into the allegations concerning the abuse of pianos.

On 24 January 1987, he sent his response to John Rea, with copies to Maria Jerabek and the signatories of the petition, in which he discusses the issue in firm yet reasonable terms.[16] He notes surprise that the musicians who play new music were still held responsible for abuse of pianos, pointing out a previous compromise made during Helmut Blume's tenure as dean that only the "old 'red' piano" would be used for preparation. He expresses disappointment that the protest had taken the form of a petition rather than a meeting to discuss concerns, noting that McGill was noted for its tolerance of differing musical aesthetics among staff members. He felt that "differences of opinion should be the subject of frank discussion among colleagues," and commented that he was offended by such questioning of his competency and professionalism.

lanza also pointed out that most of the individuals who signed the petition were not present when the pianos were played, and moreover that the piano tuner had approved the preparation. lanza had been amazed to read the tuner's comments after the fact, and asks why those concerns were not expressed at the time. In answer to the specific charges, lanza answered that the broken string had occurred on one of the pianos that was not prepared, while playing on the keyboard, and pointed out that strings also break during performances of nineteenth-century works. He noted that the twisted dampers he was accused of causing can also result from normal wear and tear on a piano. The third point – that a metal brace had been removed – he categorically denied: "who had the tools? the time? the need?" Finally, lanza pointed out that that the greatest cause of deterioration in pianos is overuse, and that the pianos at Pollack Hall were in almost constant use for rehearsals, workshops, recitals and concerts. Since the musicians who played contemporary music only played about ten concerts a year, they did not contribute significantly to the deterioration of the pianos.

lanza closed his letter with an offer to address further concerns about piano preparation and its potential for damage by presenting a master class demonstration to all interested staff, to "give the lie once and for all to this source of seemingly perpetual discord," and addressing Rea directly, writes, "we have worked together for too many years for you to consider me some sort of musical vandal. my reputation must speak for me. i am a little long in the tooth to submit to any supervision of my professional conduct by those who are uninformed in the contemporary keyboard techniques and whose motives are questionable."

When Rea confronted the pianists who had signed the petition, they admitted that none of them had attended either the rehearsal or the concert, that no one had spoken to lanza to verify the accusations, and that no one had considered other explanations for the wear and tear on the pianos. They had taken the information they were given at face value and did not suspect that there might be inaccuracies or faulty conclusions. At this point, most of the pianists backed away from the controversy, sensing that it had shifted from the realm of professionalism to the murky area of rumour, innuendo, and personality conflict. A few apologized to lanza.

The issue quieted down only to erupt again in 1997. lanza was teaching a graduate seminar on performance practice in twentieth-century music. The course requirements included a recital in which each student performed a piece of avant-garde music. Pianist Christine

Vanderkooy, one of the students, chose to play lanza's *plectros II*. The recital was to take place at Clara Lichtenstein Hall, a small recital hall at McGill. *plectros II* requires no piano preparation in the strict sense of the word – that is, no added material is placed between the strings – but it does contain some plucked notes and a few muted notes. Both Vanderkooy and lanza were surprised when the Piano Maintenance Committee vetoed *plectros II*. After negotiations with lanza, the Committee agreed to have a piano transported from another hall so that *plectros II* could be performed as written – at a cost of about $400. Vanderkooy, however, was so fearful of offending the Committee and being accused of damaging a piano that she withdrew from the performance.

That she deemed this necessary was a sign of the times. I have limited the present discussion to accusations levelled against lanza, but the Piano Maintenance Committee also had a habit of blaming students for "damage" to pianos, and a number of such accusations had been made, particularly after performances of contemporary music or jazz. It goes without saying that students were in a far more vulnerable position than lanza. Clearly Vanderkooy had good reason to worry. When she withdrew from the performance, lanza agreed to take her place so that *plectros II* could be heard as programmed.

In an effort to bring some sanity to the situation lanza and Denys Bouliane, another composition teacher, made an appointment to see François Robitaille, McGill's new piano technician. lanza was concerned that his reputation as something of an *enfant terrible* was confusing the debate. Over the years he had written a number of works that stretch traditional instruments far beyond their normal use, but *plectros II* is not one of those pieces. The few interior effects required for the work are quite innocuous. lanza played *plectros II* for Robitaille, who sensibly concluded that a few gently plucked strings and harmonics would not cause damage. Six days later, however, on the day of the recital, Robitaille withdrew his approval in a curious memo, stating that if piano strings are touched, the performer's fingers leave a greasy residue that causes the strings to rust.[17] With this complete about-face, lanza wondered if the technician had been pressured into changing his mind, and began to suspect that the piano technicians at McGill were not free agents. In a time of job insecurity and massive budgetary problems, with their jobs dependant on the good will of the piano department, their statements might be influenced.

Now that the technician's approval was withdrawn, the Piano Maintenance Committee stated again that they would order a grand piano moved from Pollack Hall to Clara Lichtenstein Hall, but to add insult to injury, just before the performance, the piano technician refused to authorize moving the piano in question because it had a broken leg. lanza had to play *plectros II* without the pizzicatos and harmonics, and before the performance read the following statement:

Tonight you will hear a new "sanitized" version of *plectros II*. A new policy concerning use of pianos during performance has created some controversy about the effect on pianos of contemporary piano performance practices. Tonight I will comply with the new policy, and play only on the keyboard. I do so under protest, and hope that the ongoing discussion concerning this policy will result in a revision of the policy which satisfies the need to preserve pianos with the need to ensure artistic freedom. It would be nice to resolve once and for all the conflicts arising from twentieth-century contemporary performance practices before we enter the twenty-first century.[18]

Soon after, this controversy reached the ears of the press. On 28 January 1998 Mike Somerville published a well-meaning but somewhat inaccurate article in the *McGill Daily*. Referring to lanza as "the man who holds the golden key to McGill's electronic music studio," he describes the incident as a "struggle between the establishment and the vanguard in musical academia" revolving around *plectros II* (for which he gives a composition date of 1996).[19] He writes that the "higher administration" found lanza's piece to be "too aggressive for the expensive Yamaha grand pianos in Lichtenstein Hall," and were "afraid that he might damage a string, or detune it." Unfortunately Somerville's article misses the central point: *plectros II* had been written thirty years ago in 1966, and is neither a particularly modern nor a particularly aggressive composition. It would probably cause less detuning and wear and tear than a performance of a Liszt Hungarian Rhapsody or a Prokofiev sonata. The drama resumed several months later when lanza again programmed *plectros II* at Clara Lichtenstein Hall, hoping that this time the audience might hear it as written. Since the work was still "banned" from the Clara Lichtenstein piano, another grand piano was moved, at a cost of $400, into the hall. One is taken aback that in a faculty, and indeed a university, which had been suffering profoundly from years of underfunding, such a sum of money was spent in order to protect the piano in Clara Lichtenstein Hall from having its strings touched a few times.

It is a fact that pianos do deteriorate with use, particularly heavy use. The Piano Guild of America has stated that the pianos in conservatories and university music faculties, "receive extended hours of use, typically eight to twelve hours daily. This is the primary cause of deterioration."[20] The Guild warns music faculties and technicians to expect "almost daily mechanical failures" and recommends that pianos undergo at least partial rebuilding about every five years. During the 1980s the music faculty at McGill was suffering from a severe shortage of funds. Even routine piano maintenance was cut back, and pianos in the concert halls began to deteriorate more quickly, exhibiting the kind of mechanical failures associated with overuse and lack of adequate maintenance. Scapegoats are often blamed in difficult times when money is in short supply. No one wanted to take responsibility for the poor condition of the pianos. The technicians, fearful for their jobs, and of accusations that their work was inadequate, preferred to blame a few performers. The pianists preferred to believe rumours rather than face the fact that constant use of the pianos can and will cause such significant wear and tear. The administration was only too glad to have someone else blamed for the problem. It seems that during the 1980s and 1990s the Piano Maintenance Committee suffered from what might be described as "dead cow syndrome." In seventeenth-century Scotland, the last person who happened to pass a cow that dropped dead soon afterward could be accused of witchcraft, ignoring the fact that the cow had been starved and overworked for years. Similarly, the pianos in the McGill concert halls are used almost constantly for rehearsals, recording sessions, and performances. These dying cows are overworked and, because of budget restraints, undermaintained. Surely it is time to look at the overuse and neglect squarely in the eye and stop looking for easy scapegoats.

By the end of the twentieth century composers had produced a large repertoire of important piano music that requires direct contact with the strings of the instrument. lanza feels that piano teachers today can no longer realistically ignore eighty years of repertoire. The time has come when it should be a normal part of a pianist's education to be introduced to this repertoire and to learn how to do it properly. With this in mind, and also with a view to defending his reputation, lanza planned an elaborate and spectacular reply.

The Piano Marathons

lanza is the type of person who tends to go on the offensive when his professionalism is attacked. He was upset when the faculty pianists signed Plawutsky's petition without looking into the matter, but he suspected that many of them had done so because they had no information about the concerts in question and were genuinely misinformed about contemporary piano techniques. They had been drawn into the debate with scare tactics. With a view to reaching these people and dispelling the myths taking root in the faculty, lanza decided to present an ambitious five-hour marathon solo piano recital of works featuring an abundance of contemporary piano techniques.[21] The piano faculty was invited to attend the recital, and to examine the pianos afterward.

The concert was divided into five one-hour segments. At the end of each segment lanza would take a five-minute break, then proceed to the next. There was also one fifteen-minute intermission. lanza had devoted the twenty-five years of his career as a pianist to performing works of living composers, and his repertoire is immense. His marathon recital reflected his preference for music of the Americas over that of Europe. Canada was represented by composers spanning the century from Otto Joachim and Jean Papineau-Couture (both born in 1910) to Serge Perron (born in 1954), including Micheline Coulombe Saint-Marcoux, Bruce Mather, Brian Cherney, and Yves Daoust. The Latin American composers were Mariano Etkin and Oscar Bazán (Argentina), Manuel Enríquez (Mexico), Sergio Barroso (Cuba), Alberto Villalpando (Bolivia), and lanza himself. The composers from the United States were David Keane, Ann Silsbee, John Celona, Gitta Steiner, Richard Bunger, Charles Dodge, and John Cage. But mere lists of names cannot convey the abundant creativity of this program. Among its delights were John Cage's *Bacchanale*, his first work for prepared piano, an appropriate choice considering the controversy that triggered the marathon; Otto Joachim's *12-Tone Pieces for Children*; Charles Dodge's *Any Resemblance Is Purely Coincidental*, which contains a witty computer-synthesized reconstruction of Caruso's voice singing passages from

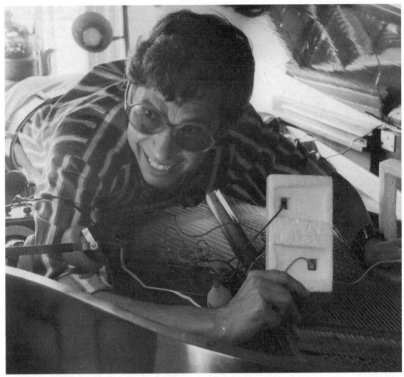

alcides lanza, New York, 1969. Photograph by Roberto Eyzaguire, reproduced by kind permission.

Leoncavallo's *I Pagliacci*; and Oscar Bazán's *Album de valses*, in which a (planted) member of the audience gets so upset at the seemingly endless repetitions of waltz music that she stomps on the stage and tears up the music. lanza's program also contained a number of ambitious and challenging piano works, among them Ann Silsbee's *Doors*, a masterpiece of tone clusters; Richard Bunger's *Mirrors*, with its intricate canonic writing between live performer and tape delays; and John Celona's *Player Piano I* with its mesmerizing minimalist moto perpetuo. One of the few exceptions to this stunning array of music of the Americas was Erik Satie's music for *Entr'acte*, the silent film by René Clair and Francis Picabia created for the 1924 ballet *Relâche*; the film was shown while lanza played Satie's original film score.

Listeners left the concert with the strong sensation that their musicality, imagination, and intellect had been challenged on many levels, and with the conviction that the piano was alive and well in the latter half of the twentieth century. The program included works that required piano preparation, plucked strings, harmonics, muting, glissandi on the strings, and a host of other contemporary techniques – and the pianos survived with no ill effects. This tour de force was a creative response to those who had challenged his professionalism, and indeed no better defence of lanza's playing and the music he champions could have been offered.

lanza's concert, however, failed to resolve any of the issues concerning the use of pianos for this repertoire. The personnel of the Piano Maintenance Committee remained the same, and their minds seemed closed. When further problems began to emerge, lanza decided to present a second marathon on 2 April 1992. In the program booklet for the concert he included a timetable explaining how he went about organizing the event. In December 1991 he read through fifty piano works and chose thirty-five for the concert. All but three – two works from Spain, and one from Portugal – were from the Americas. (lanza quotes a Spanish expression, "For Europeans, Europe stops at the Pyrenees.") That same month he established a practice schedule of three to four hours a day. In January he chose a silent film for the program – Man Ray's classic *Emak Bakia* (1926) – and prepared a sound track based on instructions left by Man Ray.[22] In February he increased his practice time to five or six hours a day, and began preparation of the tapes and material for the slides. On 15 March he gave up tennis! At this point he was able to play the complete marathon over three days; during the final weeks he played through half of the program each day.

lanza says that he planned the evening as if it were one long composition, with each hour as a movement. The program lists the five "movements," with their starting times and musical character:

18:00 Allegro
19:00 Andante
20:15 Scherzo – Allegro vivace
21:15 Rondo – Allegro non troppo
22:16 Allegro quasi presto

The program was arranged so that each segment would contain works that suited the character of the hour. lanza borrowed the rubrics from a work he admires, Beethoven's Piano Sonata in D major, op. 28.

The program for the first marathon had only two works requiring piano preparation. For the second concert, lanza began each segment with a prepared piano work by John Cage. He expanded the marathon into a teaching tool by training a team of students to prepare and de-prepare the piano set aside for the Cage pieces. During the five-minute break following each segment, this team was responsible for removing the preparations used that hour and installing the preparations for the work to follow. After some practice, the students were able to change the piano preparations safely, quietly, and efficiently in only a few minutes.

While the second piano marathon resembled the first in many ways (there were works using tape, film, slides, synthesizer, etc.), audiences left with the impression that this concert was somewhat darker than the first. Although there were fewer works involving humour, the heart of the difference lies in lanza's selection of a number of works that were introspective or stark in character. One such piece is Juan Carlos Paz's *Música 1946*, a work that lanza has championed for more than three decades. It is a single-movement twelve-tone composition of great dissonance and rhythmic complexity, lasting twenty-one minutes. Like other works of this type, it is not easily digested by audiences, but lanza had always felt this work was seminal to his generation of South American composers: "I think it is a very, very important piece. I know it's hard to swallow; it's not melodious and it's long – but there is so much food for thought. [Paz] is writing a dodecaphonic piece … using only the original form of the row and one inversion without transpositions, but he manages to keep [continual] interest. For 1946 that type of thinking was rare – it sounds like Boulez."[23] lanza has always felt it was important for the international musical community, many of whom narrowly associate Latin America of the forties with folklore and tangos, to know a composer in Argentina in 1946 was capable of writing a work of this calibre. lanza didn't study with Paz, but he admired him, and learned the work in the early 1950s. He had also played the composition for Paz in Buenos Aires, and received a number of suggestions from the composer about the its interpretation. lanza has always tried to remain faithful to Paz's wishes. As he puts it, "I do it the way he wanted it."[24]

The program included Micheline Roi's *Of Experiential Fruit*, a composition written when she was a graduate student at McGill, and dedicated to lanza. It is a serious study of the piano as a percussion instrument, in which the pianist creates percussive sounds by hitting the wooden parts of the piano (sides, lid, underbelly) while playing an intense and energetic keyboard part. lanza also programmed *Mutationen III*, by the Brazilian composer Claudio Santoro, a close friend who had died in 1986. Santoro had written a series of works for solo instrument and tape during the 1970s, but instead of supplying the tape, he wrote detailed instructions for the performer explaining how to produce the tape using amateur recording equipment. For example, the performer is asked to record a specific passage and play the recording at half speed, double speed, or backwards. lanza asked his student Osvaldo Budón to prepare the tape. Budón, respecting the composer's instructions, used several old analogue tape recorders that lanza still owned, but the tape he produced sounds quite sophisticated. Santoro's work fully explores percussion effects produced on the interior strings of the piano. The Roi and Santoro pieces made an effective juxtaposition, the one using the outside and the other the inside of the piano to produce percussive effects.

More than a thousand people attended the first marathon, and nearly 800 the second. When I asked lanza if the marathons had in any way ameliorated his relationship with the pianists on the staff, his response was positive. "Yes," he replied enthusiastically,

Students now consult me about repertoire, some teachers also: they have asked to borrow scores for their students. They also invite me to come and listen to their students play contemporary works or to demonstrate for them. There were hundreds of people [at the concerts]. Even today people still come up to me and confide, "I stayed for *all* of it, Mr lanza." There definitely was feedback. So slowly I am getting the pianists on my side.[25]

Ekphonesis – A Lifetime Achievement

No book on alcides lanza would be complete without a discussion of his significant contributions to the promotion of music of the Americas. He has noted, "The channels of communication between Europe and the Americas have been open for centuries, but the route between North and South America is less well travelled. We still know so little about each other's works."[26] lanza has made it his life work to open channels of communication on a north-south axis.

lanza's decision to promote his own music and that of his fellow South American composers was taken early in his career. As soon as he moved to New York he consciously enlarged this focus to include music of all the Americas. He has influenced every group he became involved with over the years – Agrupación Música Viva, the Krieger-lanza piano duo, the Group for International Performance, the Composers/Performers Group, and GEMS – to program this music: "I have nothing against European composers; but I think there are enough organizations, soloists, and conductors, that are performing their music. So whatever energies I have I prefer to devote to [those] who have less exposure: certainly Latin America, but also Canada." In a sense, this statement is somewhat misleading because it implies that lanza performs music of the Americas solely to fill in some sort of lacuna. In actual fact, he has devoted his life to this repertoire because he passionately loves this music and recognizes its individuality: "I am grateful to the composers of the Americas ... Their music is truly different from the European of the same generation ... There are certain colours, certain tendencies to use percussion in a different way, different use of rhythm. I am not saying it is better [than European music], just different: a sort of identity card."

There is no question that lanza carries this identity card with pride. Over the decades he has championed the music of the Americas with the regularity of a twenty-one-gun salute. In concert after concert, in lectures, master classes, festivals, radio broadcasts, recordings, and tours, lanza has played, analysed, discussed, recorded, and programmed music of the Americas. Moreover, he wants the communication to go both ways. He has performed Latin American music throughout Canada and the United States, and conversely, Canadian music in the United States and South America. The two piano marathons represent the culmination of this effort: ten hours of music, 95 per cent of which was music written in the Americas.

No other performer has devoted so much energy to the promotion of this music. In 1996 lanza's devotion to this cause was recognized by the Organization of American States and the Inter-American Music Council with a lifetime achievement award for "his exceptional contributions to the creation and promotion of music of the Americas." There was general recognition that the award was timely and well deserved.

As a musician who has spent her life in Montreal I can testify to the difference lanza has made in Quebec's perception of contemporary

alcides lanza and Lillian O'Connell de Alurralde (Argentinean ambassador to Canada) at the presentation to alcides lanza of the lifetime achievement award of the Organization of American States and the Inter-American Music Council, Montreal 1996. Reproduced by kind permission of the Concerts and Publicity Office, Schulich School of Music, McGill University.

Latin American music. Before he arrived, few recent works of Latin American origin were performed. We knew some names – Ginastera, Chávez, Villa Lobos – but had virtually no awareness of the amazing range of styles and creativity that existed in Latin America. Over the three decades lanza has lived in Montreal we have come to expect that, year after year, our musical scene will be enriched with the music of Latin American composers, and in fact we take it for granted. The same can be said for the Canadian music lanza has performed throughout the United States and South America. There is no doubt that through his choice of repertoire many Canadian composers have been heard in places that otherwise would never have known their music. lanza's former student Osvaldo Budón once commented that he first seriously considered coming to Canada to study with lanza after he attended a concert in Santa Fe in which lanza performed a work of one of his Montreal students.[27] Budón was impressed that lanza was willing to promote the music of his Canadian students in South America. This telling story reminds us that lanza has championed not only well-known composers but also lesser-known ones whose work he happens to like.

Over the years lanza has composed a series of works titled *ekpho-nesis*. One meaning of the word is "to speak out loud." But the word could be applied to the composer himself: as a spokesman, champion, and defender of music of the Americas, lanza "speaks out loud." This is lanza's ekphonesis. Composers who devote so much of their time to performing the music of other contemporary composers are rare. Liszt comes to mind in the nineteenth century, and lanza in the present. The work of these few individuals is of tremendous importance to the dissemination of the music of their time and its preservation into the next century and beyond.

9

The Soles of the Feet

For many years I [had been] writing music that I described as city, urban music – non-folkloric, non-nationalistic. Then, something prompted me to open the door and let some of those things enter my music ... I don't know what caused it. It just happened. I think it was there building up pressure inside me and finally it burst through.[1]

Thus lanza describes an evolution in his thinking. It is always interesting to a biographer when a subject does something wholly unexpected, especially when it is something he has previously opposed. For decades lanza had been determined to write music with an "international" sound, unconnected with his native Argentina, and bearing no trace of folkloric elements or nationalism, but during the late 1970s he broke with this practice and began to create works that have specific connections to Latin American culture. He does this in many ways: he might evoke the atmosphere of a place (such as a café in Buenos Aires), imitate the sound of indigenous instruments, include recognizable tango melodies and rhythms, or use a well-known tango as scaffolding for entire sections of a work.

Background

Before we enter into a discussion of lanza's works that contain overt quotations from traditional Latin American styles, it is important to consider the context in which these works were written. From the late 1960s through the 1980s composers from many different countries and from extremely varied backgrounds began to insert quotations from older tonal music into their compositions. What seems clear in retrospect is that this reinvestigation of mainly diatonic sounds was a first step taken by many atonal composers toward including significant diatonicism in their works, or even adopting a "neotonal" language. By the late 1970s a significant number of composers were writing some form of neotonal music. In North America – where most faculties, institutions, and award committees were dominated by composers who wrote and taught some brand of atonal music – it was a brave thing to do. There was a great deal of vitriolic and pointless invective between the atonal and neotonal camps, each arguing in favour of their own place in history. The debate drew together as allies composers who had little in common – for not all atonal composers respect each other's brand of atonalism, and the same is true of the tonal set. What many failed to grasp, however, was that for some time contemporary music had not been limited to one or even two universally accepted languages. Composers were now living in an era of multiplicity and idiosyncratic compositional languages. As an indefatigable concert-goer and participant in numerous contemporary music festivals world wide, lanza was cognizant of the different and overlapping trends, and was well aware of the outburst of quotation pieces, polystylistic pieces, and neotonal works.

In the 1970s lanza was not in favour of neotonal composition. He thought it "regressive" (and he still does). However, he was not vindictive about his opinion, and sometimes played the neotonal compositions of his friends and students in concerts. When it came to the use of tonal quotation, however, lanza was less hostile. He was not against quotation per se, and, as far as his own music was concerned, he believed that quotation had a place in theatre music for programmatic purposes.[2] But when it came to concert music, he felt that quotation was "something other composers did." He couldn't see himself doing it. lanza has said that if I had interviewed him in the early 1970s and asked if he would ever use extensive quotation or significant amounts of diatonicism in his atonal compositions, he would have replied with a resounding "No, never,"[3] – which only goes to show that composers, like everyone else, are often blissfully unaware of where they are heading.

By the late 1970s, it had been more than a decade since lanza had lived in Argentina. Although he loved his adopted country of Canada and had a successful career there, he began to feel nostalgic about his homeland. It was not the kind of nostalgia that makes one want to pack up and return home, but rather a realization that certain people, places, and sounds of the old country have left an indelible mark on one's character and art. *ekphonesis V* (1979) and *acúfenos III* (1977) both reflect this nostalgia. *ekphonesis V*, the opening movement of *trilogy*, is an intensely personal portrait of lanza's family in Argentina, and the singer's part consists of a series of tender vignettes about his grandmother, grandfather, and first son. None of the music, however, sounds particularly Latin American: the family could be anywhere. *acúfenos III*, for flute, piano, and tape, was inspired by an image of a native playing a *quena* (a native flute) on the wind-swept high mesas of the Andes. The tape component contains recordings of indigenous Latin-American flutes, while the solo flute and piano imitate the sounds of Andean folk instruments. It is important to note, however, that it is only the tone colours of the instruments that are recalled, not any specific indigenous musical style.

It is possible to listen to *ekphonesis V* and *acúfenos III* without recognizing any references to Argentina, but when we consider these two pieces, it is clear that lanza was reconnecting, however obliquely, with his cultural roots by recalling people, places, and instrumental colours. Some years later he went a step further and established a direct connection by using the actual music of his homeland in his works. *arghanum I* (1986) and *arghanum V* (1990) illustrate this change in musical focus.

arghanum I (1986)

lanza has said that the desire to use traditional Argentinean material in his music was ready to "burst out" of him, but it was not until 1986 that we get a vivid aural connection with Argentina. It took the right kind of commission from the right kind of performer to make this a reality. Joseph Petric, a first-rate Canadian concert accordionist, tirelessly champions the accordion as an instrument capable of interpreting serious music, and to this end, has commissioned a number of new works from Canadian composers. When he approached lanza about a commission in 1984, lanza replied that he wasn't interested; he has since admitted that at the time he had a rather low opinion of the accordion. Petric, who was quite used to negative reactions from composers on a first approach, sent lanza a few recordings of his previous commissions.[4]

Joseph Petric, photograph by Warren Beck. Reproduced by
kind permission of Joseph Petric.

After listening to them, lanza realized that Petric was an excellent
musician and that his own thinking vis-à-vis the accordion had been
limited: "I had been thinking of the piano accordion, *canzonetta
napolitana*, someone trying to accompany *O sole mio*. The tapes
made me realize that Petric was a concert musician."

   The timbral qualities of the accordion stirred old memories, and
lanza began to recall the sound of the bandoneon, a type of accordion
used in popular tango music in Argentina. With the link from accordion to bandoneon to tango to Argentina, he was more than happy,
even excited, to write for Petric. The result is *arghanum I*, scored for
accordion, clarinet, bass clarinet, vibraphone, and synthesizer.[5] In the

Example 9.1.
Angel Gregorio Villoldo, *El choclo,* opening.

Example 9.2.
arghanum I, accordion part, opening.

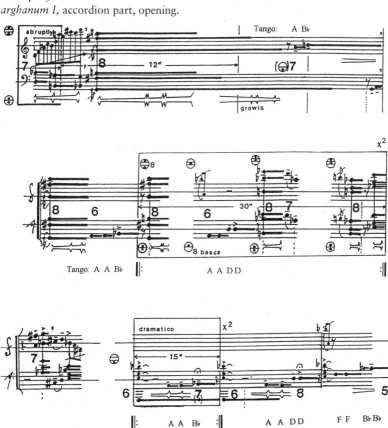

score, lanza indicates that the soloist can play either accordion or bandoneon: "What I'm actually doing is writing for bandoneon, but the bandoneon players haven't commissioned me." In Argentina, tango is ever present: in streets, restaurants, stores, dance halls, theatres, and most especially in cafés. lanza had vivid memories of the bandoneon players playing tangos in the cafés of Buenos Aires, and with this image in mind, chose a well-known tango melody – Angel

Example 9.3.
arghanum I, accordion part from figure *d*, p. 3.

Example 9.4.
arghanum I, accordion part from figure *e*, p. 3.

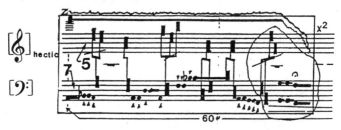

Example 9.5.
arghanum I, accordion part from figure *k*, p. 6.

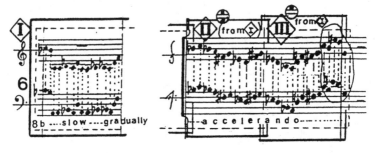

Gregorio Villoldo's *El choclo* [The Corncob] – to underpin his new composition (see example 9.1).

The accordion enters at the end of the first page of *arghanum I* and, after an brief flourish, immediately introduces the first twelve notes of *El choclo* in a version that is rhythmically spasmodic with stuttering repetitions and atonal interruptions. Example 9.2 shows the accordion part of this passage with the tango fragments indicated below. Here the tango melody is used somewhat like a cantus firmus. lanza has not hidden the tango references, and in fact takes care to thin out the texture when they appear so they can be easily recognized. For example, the initial two- and three-note motives in the accordion, which prepare the ear for the longer quotations to come, are played either solo or with light accompaniment. Without a program note, and with the frequent atonal interruptions, we may not yet be quite sure we are hearing snatches of tango, but because the instrument is an accordion and the tune is so well known, we surely suspect it. Our suspicions are confirmed a few moments later when, after so much teasing of our ears with brief glimpses of *El choclo*, lanza finally provides us with a full twelve-note phrase (see example 9.3). From this moment on our ears are primed to catch the tango quotes and rhythms that appear throughout the rest of the score. For example, on page 3 of the score motives of the tango are interspersed among a wild series of tone clusters (see example 9.4). The music is hectic, but now that our ears are sensitized to tango references, we recognize them in spite of the surrounding mayhem.

Toward the end of the work, after so much teasing of our ears with hints, allusions, and distortions, lanza finally shines a musical spotlight on *El choclo*. In a vivid cadenza passage, the accordionist plays an unadorned quotation of several phrases of the tango melody, but even here lanza cannot resist playing with us by removing the tango rhythm (see example 9.5).

The harmonic language of *arghanum I* is eclectic. In addition to the frequent embedding of tonal tango fragments in an overall atonal texture, there are a number of diatonic passages that have little or no relationship to tango. At the opening of the work (see example 9.6) every note is taken from the pitch collection of F minor (including both natural and raised sixth and seventh degrees) creating an impressionistic blur of sounds hinting at F minor. However, this and other diatonic passages do not really establish a key – they are not goal oriented – but instead give a certain harmonic colour to the music. In earlier works that contain tonal episodes, such as *ekphonesis V*, lanza keeps the tonal and atonal worlds quite separate: one does not intrude on the other. But in *arghanum I*, there is a constant blurring of boundaries. We shift back and forth between café and concert hall, between almost tonal and almost atonal, in a sort of dreamlike haze. lanza is playing with our perceptions. Schoenberg's *Pierrot Lunaire* has been described as "a Lieder recital that has taken the wrong turn."[6] In the same way, *arghanum I* sounds a little like a café concert heard through the ears of someone under the influence of a strong hallucinogenic.

Example 9.6.
arghanum I, opening, reduction showing pitches only.

arghanum V *(1990)*

Petric knew that in order to raise awareness of the accordion as a concert instrument, he needed a repertoire of strong solo works. With this in mind, he commissioned lanza to write a second accordion piece. This time he requested a solo. *arghanum* V (1990)[7] is a four-page work scored for accordion and tape. While the accordion plays throughout, the tape is heard only on the second and fourth pages. Petric was unhappy that performances of the work would require a technician to start, stop, and restart the tape at the appropriate moments – apparently he had had bad experiences when he had to rely on assistants – and he asked lanza to rework the piece so that the tape part would be continuous from beginning to end. lanza does not often rework a piece once it is finished, but Petric's argument must have been convincing. In the revised tape part, rather than simply splicing in blank tape to connect the two original sections, lanza added additional electroacoustic music.[8]

When Petric commissioned the work, he told lanza that it would be premiered at a sound symposium in Newfoundland. lanza had never visited the island, but he had seen photographs and films of Canada's rainy, wind-swept, maritime province. He felt that these images reminded him of a place back home in Argentina. At first he thought of Patagonia, but soon realized the two places were not really similar. Then, in a moment of inspiration, he thought of the Islas Malvinas (Falkland Islands), dramatically situated in the South Atlantic Ocean

Example 9.7.
arghanum V, excerpt from prefatory instructions.

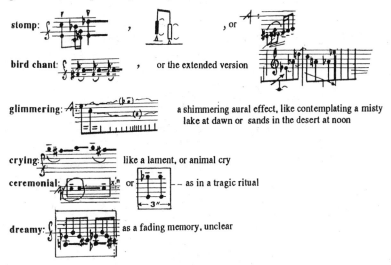

off the eastern coast of Argentina.[9] He immediately saw a similarity of climate, vegetation, and quirky national character. He knew the analogy could not be taken too far, but it served as an image, a connection between Canada and his homeland that made the new work more personal to him. lanza had been reading about industrial pollution in areas of Newfoundland. *arghanum* V reflects his feelings of frustration at the continuous destruction of nature by man. The work is subtitled "sobre la belleza de lo salvaje" [on the beauty of the wild], and the opening is marked, "agitated and wild, with repressed anger," a rubric that gives the flavour of the entire work. It is a piece of protest music: wild anger contrasting with lamentation.

arghanum V is made up of a series of programmatic gestures that are listed in the preface with explanations of their meaning (see example 9.7). Each gesture has its own distinctive rhythmic, melodic, registral, and timbral characteristics: the bird chant always has repeated notes with a chirping grace note upbeat; the glimmering lake is always a low tremolo; and the ceremonial ritual is a repeated gong-like low note or interval. lanza provides each gesture with an individual harmonic character: the "fading memory" gesture is essentially whole tone; the bird chant is usually accompanied by a pentatonic bass line; the glimmering lake always begins with suggestions of the dominant of F minor; and several gestures highlight diminished triads.

Example 9.8.
arghanum V, excerpt from p. 1, second system.

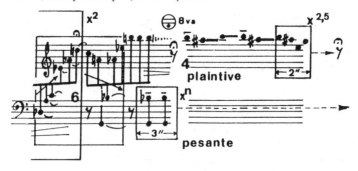

Example 9.9.
(a) *arghanum* V, opening ostinato.

(b) Julio de Caro, *El monito*, m. 1.

The language of *arghanum* V is eclectic, with atonal, diatonic, pentatonic, and whole tone passages appearing side by side, but the piece
most definitely does not sound like a bit of this and a bit of that; instead it is strikingly organic.[10] lanza has fashioned his family of sound
gestures so that one flows into another with deceptive ease. The extended bird chant ending on a high repeated B-natural leads easily
into the animal cry that begins on the same note (see example 9.8).
Similarly, the grace note of the bird chant, usually a major or minor

third, flows seamlessly into the low tremolo third that begins the glimmering lake motive. The most important feature uniting these disparate gestures, however, is the association with tango. In the preface lanza informs us that a number of the melodic, harmonic, and gestural features are derived from *El monito* [The Little Monkey], a popular Argentinean tango by Julio de Caro. These tango associations are seldom obvious; while there are places where almost everyone in the audience will recognize a tango quotation, the greater part of the piece exploits *El monito* in a more subtle manner. lanza uses melodic and harmonic fragments from the original piece but often strips them of their tango character, smoothing out a syncopated tango rhythm, or selecting a series of pitches from unrelated bars of *El monito*, so that the listener is unaware of the tango reference.

Let us examine a few of these references. *arghanum V* opens with two aggressive tone clusters (like gunshots setting the action in motion) followed by a repeating white key/black key (right hand/left hand) clustery ostinato (see example 9.9a, and note that both hands are notated on bass clef). The right-hand part outlines the diminished triad F–B–D–B–F with passing notes connecting the F and the B, a configuration of notes that corresponds to the opening measure of *El monito* (see example 9.9b). From the very beginning lanza takes his inspiration from the tango, but we would not likely have discovered this if he had not informed us.[11]

Example 9.10 shows a longer excerpt from the second system of the score featuring multiple associations with *El monito*. The passage opens with a repeated weeping semitone, B–A-sharp (labelled [a]) that is described in the preface as "an animal cry, like a lament." The descending semitone grows into a plaintive four-note motive, B–A-sharp–E–G (labelled [b]), that is repeated six and a half times before it initiates a sixteenth-note flourish [labelled c]. The four-note lament motive [b] is derived from measure 27 of *El monito* (see example 9.11; the arrows highlight the motive F–E–B-flat–D-flat that lanza transposes to begin on B so it can evolve out of the weeping animal cry, B–A-sharp. The continuation of the sixteenth-note flourish ([d] in figure 9.10) is also derived from bar 27 of the tango (see figure 9.12). The next gesture ([e] in example 9.10) is not a direct quotation from *El monito* but rather a conflation of bars 21–23 (see example 9.13). Its continuation ([g] in example 9.10) resoundingly reminds us of tango with a direct quotation of measure 22 of *El monito* (see example 9.14). To reinforce the gesture, lanza adds a

Example 9.10.
arghanum V, excerpt from p. 1, second system.

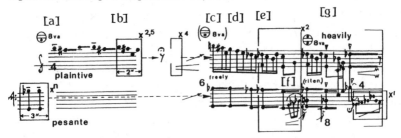

Example 9.11.
El monito, m. 27, and lament motive from *arghanum* V.

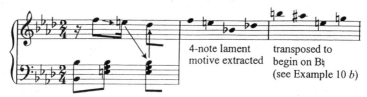

4-note lament transposed to
motive extracted begin on B♮
(see Example 10 *b*)

Example 9.12.
El monito, mm. 26–7, and excerpt from *arghanum* V (see example 9.10 "[d]")

Example 9.13.
El monito, mm. 21–3, and excerpt from *arghanum* V (see example 9.10 "[e]")

typical tango flourish in the left hand ([f] in example 9.10) and
heavy foot stomps by the accordionist (indicated by small triangles
in the score). Thus almost everything in example 9.10 is derived in
some way from passages of *El monito*.

In the previous paragraph we examined excerpts from the first
two systems of *arghanum V*. If we put the entire work under the
same magnifying glass we will find that more than 90 per cent of
the piece is connected either directly or obliquely to *El monito*.
With the exception of the closing dreamlike coda, practically no
new material is introduced in the remainder of the work. Instead,
lanza uses the motivic gestures introduced in the first page as building blocks, arranging and rearranging the various discrete components in different orders and combinations, as if he is shuffling a
deck of musical cards.

Example 9.15 shows an intimate passage about halfway through
the piece in which lanza recycles a number of gestures familiar to
the listener from their appearances earlier in the work: the "ceremonial ritual" interval (labelled [t]), the "animal cry" [u], the lament motive [v] accompanied by a tango flourish [w], a direct tango
quote [x], the lament motive once again [y], and finally several repetitions of the direct tango quote emphasized by foot stomps [z].
lanza follows the same process through almost the entire work, par-
ing down material to a few precise and strikingly recognizable gestures that are repeated and developed like leitmotivs. As a result,
arghanum V is an approachable work. Because of the network of
memories and associations, listeners become so familiar with the
components that they absorb the larger structure without struggle.
lanza also twists our heartstrings with plaintive, evocative echoes of
the past. Repetition and musical recall permeate this work thor-
oughly, leaving no doubt that it is connected both technically and
aesthetically to ideals of postmodernism.

Considering the amount of material derived from tango, we
would expect *arghanum V* to sound Argentinean. But does it? The
answer is both yes and no. While the accordion music sounds Latin
American in many places, the tape component has a somewhat
"northern" feel to it. The reason for this is that the tape part contains only minimal references to tango and is replete with realistic
sounds of nature: bird cries, icy winds blowing through vast empty
spaces, huge waves crashing against rocky shores – the sounds of
nature in Newfoundland. lanza took many of these "real" sounds

Example 9.14.
El monito, m. 22, and excerpt from *arghanum V* (see example 9.10 "[g]").
    El monito   *arghanum V*

Example 9.15.
arghanum V, end of p. 2 and beginning of p. 3.

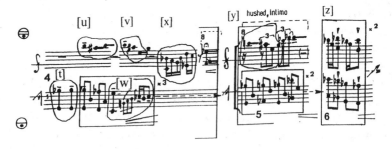

from special effects records. It seems to me, however, that the contrast between the accordion and tape parts is not "south" versus "north," but rather "humanity" versus "nature." The accordion part, with its tango fragments and "artificial" animal sounds, represents the human element; the tape depicts the real world of nature. As such, the tape component has no sense of musical development or emotional manipulation. Nature is simply there. It is the accordion that reacts and counter-reacts; it is humanity that experiences anger, regrets, and dreams.

lanza later made a piano version of *arghanum V* (entitled *arghanum Vπ*) that he recorded and performed extensively in concert.[12] At a performance of *arghanum Vπ* that I attended in Buenos Aires in October 1996 lanza was asked to speak briefly about his composition before the work was played. He explained that the work was essentially his protest against the destruction of nature in Newfoundland. He also said that the work contained a series of musical gestures depicting various aspects of nature, but did not explain the meaning of any of these gestures. I spoke with several members of the audience afterwards. Some had recognized the tango quotations, others had not. Each had felt the composer's anger and understood that nature was the main protagonist in the drama, but each had interpreted the musical gestures differently and were convinced of their own interpretations. One person heard the opening tone clusters and running ostinati as the composer's raging anger, while another heard animals fleeing the destruction of their habitat. The low "murmuring lake" tremolo was to some an anxious mother nature brooding over the loss of her domain. Some heard the "lament motive" as the composer's sense of loss, but to others, it was the despair of an animal that can endure no more. Of course, for an Argentinean audience, the subject matter of *arghanum V* touches a nerve, because so many of the natural habitats in Argentina are under attack from the corporate world. Nevertheless, the fact that people can have such different vivid images indicates to me that the work can cut through the consciousness to tap deep emotions.

lanza uses tango quite differently in *arghanum I* and *arghanum V*. In *arghanum I* we are meant to hear the quotations from *El choclo*. The melody is left relatively intact and lanza often gives us enough of the tune for our ears to grasp it easily. Also, the melody is so well known – it is almost a catchphrase for tango in the world at large – that we assume a programmatic intent. Fragments of this melody played on an accordion trigger certain associations even for listeners with no Argentinean background: we automatically think of cafés, tango, and Latin America. Even though lanza obscures the Latin flavour with atonal interruptions, other tonal passages, and general mayhem, the colourful programmatic effects are still easily perceived. In *Arghanum V*, on the other hand, lanza uses tango more as scaffolding than as a source of recognizable quotations. The tango he chose, *El monito*, is less well-known in North America than *El choclo*, and he takes as source material not only its melody but also its harmonies, rests, rhythms, and intervals. *El monito* serves as a quarry to furnish building material for large portions of the composition. Some quotations we recognize as tango, but most are so embedded in the texture that we are unaware of them. Why, then, does lanza use this material throughout the work? There may be purely musical reasons: in a work with such a plurality of harmonic languages, lanza may have sought an

underlying musical glue that would bind the disparate elements together. But it is an oversimplification to think that the tango quotations are there solely for technical reasons. In my opinion, there
are philosophical issues at play. Composers often use quotation extensively because the quoted music has a powerful personal significance. The medieval monks used Gregorian chant to underlie
polyphonic mass movements, not simply as abstract source material, but because the chant melodies connected them to their faith
and to their God. lanza chose tango for much the same reason: it
connects him to his essence – to the music of his youth, the dances
and dance songs of Argentina, to a symbol of his native land, to
both the soles of his feet and his inner soul.

Concerto for Midi Piano
and Orchestra (1993)

lanza used the *arghanum V* music in one other major work. In
1993 Argentinean pianist Hugo Goldenzweig commissioned him
to compose a piano concerto. lanza recalls, "Hugo specifically requested a piano concerto with electronics but stipulated that since
he knew nothing about electronics, everything would have to happen automatically."[13] lanza had in mind a piece with considerable
ebb and flow between pianist and orchestra, and wanted to avoid
situations where the musicians had to coordinate with a tape. With
this in mind he decided to score his concerto for MIDI piano. The
MIDI piano, first developed by Yamaha in the late 1980s, is a hybrid instrument, a normal grand piano with a keyboard modified
so that the keys activate not only the hammers that strike the
strings but also the triggers that send MIDI signals which can be
received and processed by synthesizers or other electronic devices.
In addition to the keyboard, there are a number of buttons that
can transmit other signals to the receiving devices. If the MIDI out-
puts are not connected to external devices, the instrument func-
tions as a conventional grand piano.

lanza could see the potential of this instrument. The electroacoustic elements of the work could be pre-programmed in synthesizer
modules that the pianist could trigger from the instrument. When
playing with a tape, performers have to synchronize their live music
with the predetermined and unvarying music on the tape. With the
MIDI piano, however, the performer can trigger the electronic effects

at exactly the right moment. This leaves the pianist free to "interpret" the music, vary the tempo, and introduce dramatic pauses, without worrying about coordination with an inflexible tape part. The live musician, rather than the electronics, controls the musical agenda.

When lanza received the commission in February 1993, the premiere with the Orquesta Municipal de Rosario was scheduled for December of that year. lanza was occupied with teaching, performing, and composing during the winter and early spring, so he planned to write the concerto in the summer after his university work was complete for the academic year. He had just begun work in June, believing he had ample time, when he received a telephone call from the conductor to say that the premiere had been advanced to October. lanza didn't panic – after all, October was four months away – but the next week he received a second call saying that the concerto was now scheduled for September. The pressure was beginning to mount when, like the third act in a comedy of errors, he received yet another call changing the date to August! At this point the premiere was in jeopardy: there were only six weeks for lanza to compose the work and for Goldenzweig to learn it.

After pondering his predicament for a few days, lanza suddenly saw a solution. Goldenzweig was a champion of *arghanum Vπ* (the version for piano and tape), and had performed the piece in several concerts. lanza decided to use the piano part of *arghanum Vπ* as the third movement of the concerto. It was an inspired idea. *arghanum Vπ* is a work of protest, replete with colourful programmatic and sonic images. Its energetic, fast moving, and rhythmically decisive character is much in keeping with the finales of classic piano concertos. But most importantly, Goldenzweig already knew the music, and he reacted positively to the idea.

lanza's MIDI piano concerto is scored for piano and a large chamber orchestra. When lanza reworked *arghanum V* as the third movement of the concerto, he made the important decision to retain only the piano part. In place of the unambiguous imitations of nature on the tape, he composed new orchestral music, drawing heavily on the intervals, motives, and harmonies of the piano part, with only minimal references to the original tape sounds. In *arghanum V* the sounds of nature on the tape sometimes soften the intensity of the piano part, but in the concerto both the solo and the orchestral parts have the passionate quality of protest. The concerto has a more universal character – it is a piece of protest music *per se* – but the nature of the protest is left to the imagination of the listeners.

Example 9.16.
arghanum V, excerpt from p. 1, second system,
and opening of piano part from lanza's *piano concerto*

(a)   *arghanum* V

(b)   *piano concerto*

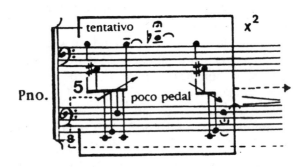

lanza composed the third movement of the concerto first. He then
linked the first and second movements to the third by quoting a few
musical gestures from *arghanum* V in the earlier movements. But
lanza often transforms the quotations to give them a new character.
For example, the high, lyrical, narrow-range lament motive is
stripped of its lamenting character to become the ominous and
threatening widely-spaced, low-register minor-ninth motive that
opens the concerto (see example 9.16). In *arghanum* V lanza used
El monito as a quarry for building material; in the concerto *arghanum* V itself is the quarry. Since listeners are introduced to elements
based on *arghanum* V before the third movement, the concerto is a
little like a musical detective story: the vivid, disparate "characters"
of the first two movements are only tied together when the listeners
hear the final movement, the music that generated so much of what
came before.

Each movement of the concerto has its own character and timbral quality but, it is important to note that the first two movements are carefully planned to lead to the final protest. We have the impression that an underlying drama is taking place, that we are experiencing a musical play. The piano part of the first movement contains a number of repeated melodic fragments in frame notation. These repetitions serve to establish pools of harmonic and melodic stability that are reinforced in the orchestra with repeated or sustained chords drawn from the piano part. At a certain point, all of this obsessive repetition becomes almost oppressive. Musically, the players exhibit a certain frustration, almost as if they are trying to break free of the confines of the frames. At two points a single cellist manages to escape and plays tender solos; lanza has described the solo that closes the movement as "a love duet between the cellist and the pianist."

The second movement, a strong contrast to the first, is scored for a small chamber ensemble (two flutes, two oboes, two clarinets, two bassoons, trombone, and solo piano). This movement is more improvisatory, with a certain amount of graphic notation, and is very unstructured. The musicians are quite independent of each other, and their mobile-like music creates a succession of seemingly random arrangements, like hanging objects turning in the wind. It is almost as if this small group, having broken free of the strictures of the first movement, escapes into aleatoric unpredictability and delicate special effects. The third movement breaks the spell; here the composer is angry. It doesn't really matter what he is angry about. The drama has evolved from oppression, to freedom, to rage, and this momentum is reinforced by the manner in which the orchestra supports the pianist: sometimes moving hand in hand at the pace of the soloist, other times pushing the pianist forward even more forcefully in his rage.

It is magical how lanza supports the drama of the moment in each movement with musical effects created by electronic processing of the MIDI piano. Sometimes the instrument sounds like a gamelan, giving the music a quasi-Oriental quality, other times, like a marimba. All of this adds subtle colour to the musical palate, but the MIDI "effects" represent a small proportion of the music, perhaps as little as 10 per cent. Knowing that few musicians or concert halls possess a MIDI piano, lanza composed the work so that it could be effectively played on a traditional piano. After the premiere in Rosario, the concerto was performed by the Orquesta Sinfónica Nacional (Buenos Aires), the Orquestra Simfónica de Ribeirão Preto (Brazil), the Orquestra de Cámara de Santos (Brazil), and the Aarhus Symphony Orchestra (Denmark). Of a total of ten performances, only the Danish performance used a MIDI piano; the soloist on that occasion was British pianist Philip Mead. lanza is the only Canadian ever to perform the concerto, but he has never played it in Canada, and no Canadian orchestra has ever programmed the work. On the other hand, when we consider how few contemporary experimental works are played by Canadian orchestras, lanza is in good company.

vôo (1992)

The tango-related works discussed above demonstrate lanza's deep connection to the culture of South America. It is embedded in the pores of his skin. His most moving work about this culture – and arguably the best work he has written – is *vôo*. Like *arghanum V* it is a work that cries out against man's destructive side, but in *vôo* it is not nature but peoples and cultures that are under attack. It is a work concerned with Columbus's discovery of America, and with the death of the New World at the hands of the Old.

In 1990 lanza was commissioned by the Centro para la promoción de la música Contemporánea of Madrid, Spain, to write a work commemorating the 500th anniversary of the first voyage of Christopher Columbus to the New World, to be premiered at the Festival de Alicante in 1992. The commission was controversial. In Spain Columbus is seen as a hero who ushered in a new and positive era in Spanish history, a courageous and farseeing individual who, against great odds, discovered a new land full of promise, space, and opportunity. But many in the New World, particularly First Peoples, have a negative view of Columbus, remembering the annihilation of millions through disease, exploitation, and slavery. lanza admired Columbus in the same way he admires discoverers of all types, knowing that such explorations require not only daring but also imagination, but he was equally aware of the horrors brought by the Old World to the New.[14] We should not forget that lanza is of mixed European and Native American ancestry.

lanza wanted to write a piece that would somehow heal the wounds between the Old and New Worlds, and as we shall see, the healing effect of *vôo* works in a way that he could not have imagined when he first thought about the work. In 1990 he began to look for a text that was poetic but economical, a text that would tell the tale simply and directly. He considered writing it himself, but then remembered *No olvido do tempo / No ouvido do tempo*[15] by the Brazilian composer-poet Gil Nuno Vaz. Ianza had attended the launch of this book three years previously in Brazil, and the author had inscribed a copy to him. This extraordinary work, written in Portuguese, relates the history of the world from the viewpoint of two imaginary poets, Raul and Leônidas. The two poets' work appears on facing pages of the printed book. Raul's text (printed on the right-hand pages) reads from the top to the bottom of the page, while Leônidas's text (printed on the left-hand pages) reads from bottom to top, so that the book can be turned either up or down. Readers can follow Raul's work from beginning to end, or turn the book upside down to read Leônidas's contribution. The two fictional poets confront each other on each set of facing pages, with each one's work upside down relative to the other's.

This poem fascinated Ianza. The text is replete with word games: Nuno Vaz is fond of words that when reversed spell a second word, and of the subtle associations of palindromes and anagrams. Ianza had pored over the poem for many days, and eventually put it away in his library. Three years later, when he received the commission from Spain, he took it down from the shelf, vaguely remembering that there was something in the work he could use. Soon his eyes fell on two facing pages that dealt with his subject matter. One page describes an Eden, a world where *columbinas* [doves] fly overhead; the facing page begins, "Os pés de Colombo pisam o Novo Mundo" [the feet of Columbus stepped onto the new world]. Ianza felt, however, that for the purpose of his composition, the Nuno Vaz poem was too uncritical of Columbus. He wanted to add a few lines of his own to address this issue, and contacted Nuno Vaz; the poet had no objection.

vôo,[16] scored for voice, tape, and electronic modification of the voice, was composed with the voice of Meg Sheppard in mind; she sang the premiere and has performed it more than forty times since. The title is a Portuguese word meaning "flight." The work opens with the sounds of wind, waves, and seabirds on the tape. The singer enters immediately with the words, "Asas Columbinas" [the wings of the dove]. It is a land at peace, where life is evolving at its own natural pace, a world replete with angels, reptiles, and a long flight

Example 9.17.
vôo, excerpt from p. 1.

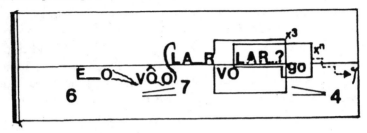

of eagles ("ser anjo, ser réptil e o vôo largo das águias"). At the line
"o vôo largo" [a long flight], lanza embarks on a series of word
games in which the text shifts between *ovo* [egg], *vôo* [flight], *volar*
[to fly], and *largo* [long] (see example 9.17). In the text, "E-
OVÔOLAR-VOLAR-GO," the palindromic word *ovo* becomes *vôo*
which elides into *vôolar*, followed by *volar*, which in turn elides into
largo. lanza chose the syllables for sonic reasons – he is always
thinking of timbral qualities (combining the same phonemes in different ways) – but he is also making a statement: he is telling us that
Columbus's voyage was not only a flight of imagination but also an
egg that would give birth to long-range (*largo*) consequences. At this
point the tape part introduces rhythmic drumming, telling the listener that this world now contains human beings. There is something heightened in the music, a feeling of suspense. Something is
about to happen. In the next line, "O ovo levanta o vôo: asas da
imaginação" [the egg lifts in flight: the wings of imagination], the
poet tells us of a flight – a voyage – of imagination. lanza accompanies the line with an ominous, dark cluster loop that becomes louder
and louder until the appearance of a disturbing G-minor ostinato
with the words, "Os pés de Colombo pisam o Novo Mundo" [the
feet of Columbus stepped onto the new world]. In a hushed voice the
singer whispers, "então" [then]. It is a fearful presentment.
    She proceeds to tell the tale of a world now surrounded by am-
bushes ["envolven-nos ciladas"], and we hear the words *oro* [gold],
prata [silver], *lanceros* [soldiers], *con crucis, con armas* [with
crosses, with weapons], all accompanied by ethnic percussion, cymbals, gongs, and deeply tolling church bells. Eventually the tension
subsides and the soloist, shadowed electronically in parallel lines,
sings plaintively of "A linha leviana" [the heedless path]. After a
five-second silence, lanza introduces a plaintive minor-mode melody

Example 9.18.
vôo, excerpt from p. 4.

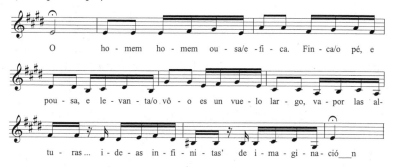

composed by the native-born Peruvian composer, José de Orejón y
Aparicio (1706–65), taken from his *Cantada a Sola Mariposa*, one
of the most beautiful works composed in the New World during the
eighteenth century.[17] Ianza has skilfully reworked the Baroque tune
to give it a more timeless flavour (see example 9.18), creating a melody to break the heart. To it he adds words of his own that speak of
the infinite ideas of imagination slowly disappearing ("largo, vapor-
las alturas ideas infinitas de imaginación"). The opening words of
the work, "asas columbinas," now return reminding us of what has
disappeared and how. As the music fades away we again hear the
gentle sound of seabirds and water, along with a half-whispered reminder, "asas – asas da imaginação" [wings – wings of imagination].

vôo is an overwhelmingly moving work that brings tears to the
eyes. Sheppard views the singer as a storyteller, a shaman relating the
story of her people around a campfire at night,[18] but like all shamans,
she is also a healer. When Ianza began to compose the work he had
an idea that he could somehow reconcile the opposing attitudes to
Columbus. *vôo* does not do this, but it achieves something better. It is
a cathartic work in which we relive the tragedy in order to heal from
within. Perhaps it is not surprising that *vôo* was not popular in Spain:
the subject matter is too incriminating. The New World, on the other
hand, has embraced the work wholeheartedly, recognizing its need to
relive the tragedy and be healed. Ianza, who has spent much of his career composing works about memory, instinctively understood that
the emotional scars of a nation can only be healed by accepting reality. As an old Jewish saying tells us, "Deliverance comes through
memory. Forgiveness is only possible through memory. And he who
suppresses, he who forgets, lengthens our imprisonment."

Closing Thoughts

vôo is essentially about memories, a theme that since 1972 has been ubiquitous in lanza's output, like a thread winding its way from one work to another. lanza remembers world history in *penetrations VII* with the woman crushed by memories of humanity; in *ekphonesis IV* with the bombing of Guernica; in *vôo* with the memories of genocide. He remembers South America in *acúfenos III* with the sounds of Andean instruments; in *arghanum I* and *arghanum V* with the memories of tango, cafés, and bandoneons. He remembers personal history in *ekphonesis V* with his family in Argentina; in *bour-drones* with a friend who has died; in *un mundo imaginario* with the life and death of a beloved son. It could be said that this exploration is part of lanza's approach to life. Some people remember through family photographs, letters, or knick-knacks; lanza remembers through sounds. And more importantly, he wants us, as listeners, to participate in the memory experience so that these people, events, and sounds will live again in our ears and minds.

It is lanza's good fortune that his focus on memories coincided with the period of postmodernism in which the use of musical memories was once again acceptable. He has often been able to link psychological and historical memories to musical memories, bringing back melodic motives associated with a specific person, or using the same passage of music to introduce each new section of a work. This is especially apparent in *ekphonesis VI*, the final movement of *trilogy*, where all the dramatis personae reappear with their musical tags.

The idea of musical recollection is present not only in lanza's programmatic works but also in his more abstract pieces, such as *sensors III* and the MIDI piano concerto. Since 1979 lanza has often constructed works out of small motivic cells that expand incrementally, contract, and then expand again to form cellular variations of the original motive. He also uses referential blocks of sound – melodic, motivic, intervallic, or harmonic – that keep returning. Whether the piece is completely atonal, partly tonal, or a mixture of musical languages, the building method is the same, and the result is strikingly different from works of the 1950s and 1960s, in which sonics come first and pitch is almost incidental. Since the 1950s lanza has travelled along a path from a music that sought unpredictability and instability at all costs to one full of musical recollection at many

alcides lanza at the Akademie der Kunste, Berlin, 1973. Photograph by Werner Berthsold, reproduced by kind permission.

levels – one of the major historical paths of the late twentieth century that a number of serialist and aleatoric composers have also followed.

When it comes to sonic exploration, however, lanza has never deviated from his original path. The sonic effects in *plectros I* (1962) – where two pianists explore the colours created by touching the strings of a piano with fingers and various objects – come out of the same mindframe as the timbral effects produced by the MIDI piano in his second piano concerto twenty years later. And indeed the waves of sonic energy in *eidesis II* (1967) – where thirteen instrumentalists create an ever-changing landscape of seemingly electronic sounds – are closely related to the rapidly changing textures of *un mundo imaginario* written in the late 1980s. Throughout his life, more than anything else, it has been instrumental colour and timbre that have directed lanza's musical decisions.

Some composers reflect a school of thought in which the actual physical sound of a musical work is, to a certain extent, considered to be of a lesser order of significance than the abstract relationships of pitches and rhythms, a position summed up in a jocular remark attributed to Schoenberg that great music is music that would sound great even played on a zither. lanza's philosophy is quite the opposite: for him the sound *is* the musical work. lanza's compositions would not make good zither solos; they would lose their identity. Each one is wholly connected to specific and carefully chosen sonic landscapes – it is this soundscape that is the soul of the composition.

When I began my research for this book I had the impression that lanza had been fortunate to live in interesting places in interesting times, but as my research progressed I began to realize that luck had little to do with it. I now believe that it is lanza's energetic, passionate, and outgoing personality that has enabled him to take advantage of each step, from Buenos Aires, to New York, to Berlin, to Quebec. In an address at the ceremony in which lanza was presented with the lifetime achievement award of the Organization of American States, Gilles Tremblay spoke of lanza's passionate nature: "His works with their evocative titles – *penetrations, eidesis, acúfenos, plectros* – testify to meticulous research and, at the same time, to a mode of thinking that is very intuitive, even frantic: a kind of organized frenzy. If I had to associate him with one of the four elements – earth, air, water, and fire – it is certainly fire that I would choose."[19] During the reception after the award presentation, when I was introduced to Tremblay as lanza's biographer, Tremblay commented perceptively, "You are fortunate, for quite apart from the music, [lanza] is such an interesting person." Tremblay proved to be right. lanza is formidably intelligent, fiercely original, courageous in the face of criticism, and resolutely optimistic.

It is sadly true that many composers and performers lose their joy in music as they grow older: whether it is because they are disappointed in their careers, or feel that their style is becoming passé, or simply grow too tired, there is a sense of bitterness. This is definitely not the case with lanza. In terms of sheer joy in music, it is almost as if his biological clock stopped at the age of thirty. He still exhibits the same enthusiasm and youthful curiosity about music as a young man setting out on his career. So, with this character trait in mind, I would like to end this biography by adding to Tremblay's choice of element. Yes, "fire" very much describes lanza's passionate music and energetic personality, but I also think that one could equally choose "water" – the element associated with life, growth, and above all, endurance.

Chronological List
of Compositions by alcides lanza

Angela Adónica (1953) for voice and piano
Text by Pablo Neruda
Publisher: Shelan (Montreal)

[Song for voice and piano] (1955)
Text in Portuguese
Lost; opening phrases quoted in *penetrations VI/VII* (1972–II/III)

Six Preludes and Fugues (1957) for piano
Lost; one of the preludes used for *Preludio y Toccata* (see next two items)

Preludio (1957) for piano
Lost; reconstructed from memory as *preludio (preludio)* (1989–III)

Toccata (1957) for piano
Publisher: Ricordi Americana (Buenos Aires)

La ahogada del cielo (1957) for voice and piano
Text by Pablo Neruda
Publisher: Shelan (Montreal)
Arrangement for mixed choir, 1957, unpublished

Sonata (1958) for two pianos
Lost

Transformaciones (1959) for chamber orchestra
Publisher: Peer/Pan American Union (New York)

Sonata (1959) for violin and piano
[unpublished]

Concierto de Cámara (1960–I) for winds, strings, and percussion
Publisher: EAM (Buenos Aires)

Tríptico (1960–II) for piano
[unpublished]

three pieces (1960–III) for solo clarinet
Publisher: EAM (Buenos Aires), reprinted Shelan (Montreal)

[unknown, lost work] (1961–I)

desplazamientos (1961–II) for flute, clarinet, trumpet, violin, and contrabass
[unpublished]

cuarteto II (1961–III) for flute, clarinet, bassoon, and piano or vibraphone
[unpublished].

[unknown, lost work] (1962–I)

plectros [I] (1962–II) for piano, four hands
Publisher: Barry (Buenos Aires), later Boosey and Hawkes (New York)

trio-concertante (1962–III) for any three instruments
Publisher: Shelan (Montreal)

eidesis sinfónica (1963–I) for orchestra
Publisher: Shelan (Montreal)

invención (1963–II) for piano
[unpublished]

[unknown, lost work] (1963–III)

three songs (1963–IV) for soprano and chamber ensemble
Publisher: Shelan (Montreal)

[unknown, lost work] (1963–V)

let's stop the chorus (1963–VI) for any mixed group of voices
[destroyed]

cuarteto IV (1964–I) for four horns
Commissioned by Guelfo Nalli
Dedicated to the Cuarteto de Trompas Wagner
Publisher: Shelan (Montreal)

piano concerto (1964–II) for piano and orchestra
Publisher: Shelan (Montreal)

[three unknown, lost works] (1965–I, II, and III)

módulos I (1965–IV) for solo guitar
Dedicated to Narcisco Yepes
Publisher: Shelan (Montreal)

exercise I (1965–V)
electronic music (with self developing choreography)
Publisher: Shelan (Montreal)

plectros II (1966–I) for piano and electronic sounds
Commissioned by Carla Hübner
Dedicated to Carla Hübner
Publisher: Boosey and Hawkes (New York)

interferences I (1966–II) for two groups of wind instruments and tape
Publisher: Shelan (Montreal)

acúfenos I (1966–III) for trombone and four instruments
Commissioned by Per Brevig
Dedicated to Per Brevig
Publisher: Boosey and Hawkes (New York)

kromoplásticos (1966–IV), electronic music
Commissioned by Gregorio Dujovni
Publisher: Shelan (Montreal)

interferences II (1967–I) for percussion ensemble and electronic sounds
Commissioned by Paul Price (Manhattan Percussion Ensemble) and Antonio

Yepes (Ritmus Percussion Ensemble, Buenos Aires)
Dedicated to the Manhattan Percussion Ensemble and the Ritmus Percussion Ensemble
Publisher: Boosey and Hawkes (New York)

cuarteto V (1967–II) for string quartet
Dedicated in memoriam Jackson Pollock
Publisher: Shelan (Montreal)

eidesis II (1967–III) for thirteen instruments
Commissioned by Gunther Schuller
Dedicated to Gunther Schuller
Publisher: Boosey and Hawkes (New York)

two times too (1967–IV), electronic music soundtrack
Composed for a documentary film by Jerome Ducrot about the Argentinean painter Luis Felipe Noé
Publisher: Shelan (Montreal)

strobo I (1967–V) for contrabass, percussion, lights and electronic music
Commissioned by Bertram Turetzky
Dedicated to Bertram Turetzky
Publisher: Shelan (Montreal)

strobo II (1968–I) for three contact mikes, any instruments
[unpublished]

ekphonesis I (1968–II) for string and/or keyboard instrument and tape
Dedicated to Manuel Enriquez
Publisher: Shelan (Montreal)

ekphonesis II (1968–III) for voice, piano, and tape
Commissioned by Margarita Gonzalez
Publisher: Shelan (Montreal)

penetrations I (1968–IV)
electronic sounds
Commissioned by the Museum for Contemporary Crafts, New York
Publisher: Shelan (Montreal)

[unknown, lost work] (1969–I)

ekphonesis III (1969–II) for wind, keyboard, and string instruments and tape
Publisher: Shelan (Montreal)

the cement jungle suite (1969–III), electronic music
Recording published by Boosey and Hawkes (London)

four electronic statements (1969–bis), electronic music
Recording of three of the pieces published by Boosey and Hawkes (New York)

penetrations II (1969–IV) for wind, string, percussion, and/or keyboard instruments and tape
Publisher: Shelan (Montreal)

penetrations III (1969–V) for ensemble, two rhythm boxes, tape
Commissioned by the Philadelphia Composers Forum
[unfinished and unpublished]

penetrations IV (1970–I), electronic music
[unavailable]

kron'ikelz 70 (1970–II) for two narrators, chorus, orchestra, and tape
[destroyed]

espontaneidad (1970–III) music for audiovisual
[destroyed]

penetrations V (1970–IV) for a minimum of ten sound sources, voices, lights, electronic extensions, and electronic sounds
Commissioned by Ars Nova, Malmö, Sweden, for their tenth anniversary concert
Dedicated to Hans Åstrand
Publisher: Boosey and Hawkes (New York)

plectros III (1971–I) for piano, synthesizer, and tape
Pub: Shelan (Montreal)

eidesis III (1971–II) for one or two orchestras, tape, and lights
Dedicated to Antonio Tauriello
Publisher: Boosey and Hawkes (New York)

ekphonesis IV (1971–III), electronic sounds (with optional instrumental drone and slide projections of Picasso's *Guernica*)
Publisher: Shelan (Montreal).

acúfenos II (1971–IV) for chamber ensemble, electronic sounds, and electronic extensions
Dedicated to the composers/performers group
Publisher: Boosey and Hawkes (New York)

mantis I (1972–I), electronic sounds, with optional actor, slides
[unpublished]

penetrations VI (1972–II) for actress-singer, tape, and chamber ensemble
Commissioned by Südwestfunk Baden Baden for the Donaueschingen Festival
Dedicated "pour Meg" [Sheppard]
Publisher: Boosey and Hawkes (New York)

penetrations VII (1972–III) for actress-singer and tape
[chamber version of *penetrations VI* (1972–II)]
Dedicated "pour Meg" [Sheppard]
Publisher: Shelan (Montreal)

hip'nos I (1973–I) for one or more instruments
Dedicated to James Fulkerson
Publisher: Boosey and Hawkes (New York)

plectros IV (1974–I) for two pianists of opposite sex, miscellaneous percussion instruments, and tape
Commissioned by the Société de Musique Contemporaine du Québec
Dedicated to Bruce and Pierrette [Mather]
Publisher: Shelan (Montreal)

kron'ikelz 75 (1975–I) for two solo voices, chamber ensemble, and tape
Commissioned by New Music Concerts, Toronto
Dedicated "para los olvidados del mundo"
Publisher: Shelan (Montreal)

sensors I (1976–I) for percussion ensemble
Commissioned by Pierre Béluse and McGill Percussion Ensemble

Dedicated to Pierre Béluse and the McGill Percussion Ensemble
Publisher: Shelan (Montreal)

acúfenos III (1977–I) for flute, piano, and tape
Commissioned by Jorge Caryevschi
Dedicated to Jorge Caryevschi
Publisher: Shelan (Montreal)

eidesis IV (1977–II) for wind ensemble and electronic sounds
Commissioned by Robert Gibson and McGill Wind Ensemble
Dedicated to Robert Gibson
Publisher: Shelan (Montreal)

out of ... (1978–I), electronic music
Publisher: Shelan (Montreal)

acúfenos IV (1978–II) for woodwind quintet
Commissioned by the York Winds
Dedicated to the York Winds
Publisher: Shelan (Montreal)

ekphonesis V (1979–I) for voice, lights, electronic sounds, and electronic extensions
Commissioned by Meg Sheppard
Dedicated "toMeg2, in the year of the child"
Publisher: Shelan (Montreal)

sensors II (1980–I) for multiple trombones
Commissioned by Ted Griffith and the McGill Trombone Studio
Publisher: Shelan (Montreal)

acúfenos V (1980–II) for trumpet, piano, and tape
Commissioned by Robert Gibson
Dedicated to Robert Gibson
Publisher: Shelan (Montreal)

eidesis V (1981–I) for chamber orchestra
Commissioned by Joel Thome and Orchestra of Our Time
Dedicated to Joel Thome and the Orchestra of Our Time
Publisher: Shelan (Montreal)

módulos II (1982–I) for guitar, voice, and tape
Commissioned by Garry Antonio
Publisher: Shelan (Montreal)

sensors III (1982–II) for organ and two percussionists
Commissioned by Leonard Raver
Publisher: Shelan (Montreal)

eidesis VI (1983–I) for string orchestra with piano
Commissioned by Manuel Enriquez for the Foro de Música Nueva, Mexico City
Publisher: Shelan (Montreal)

separata I (1983–II) for piano
Publisher: Shelan (Montreal)

módulos III (1983–III) for guitar, chamber ensemble, and tape
Commissioned by Alvaro Pierri
Dedicated to Alvaro Pierri
Publisher: Shelan (Montreal)

interferences III (1983–IV) for chamber ensemble and tape
Commissioned by Dante Grela and the Agrupación Nueva Música, Rosario
Dedicated to Dante Grela and the Agrupación Nueva Música, Rosario
Publisher: Shelan (Montreal)

sensors IV (1983–V) for choir and computer generated tape
Commissioned by Christopher Reynolds and the McGill Concert Choir
Dedicated to McGill Concert Choir
Publisher: Shelan (Montreal)

interferences IV (1984–I) for clarinets, cello or contrabass, and percussion
Commissioned by Jesús Villarojo and the Grupo LIM (Laboratorio Interpretación Musical, Madrid)
Dedicated to Grupo LIM and Jesús Villarojo
Publisher: Shelan (Montreal)

bour-drones (1985–I) for string orchestra
Commissioned by Wanda Kaluzny and the Montreal Chamber Orchestra

Dedicated to the Montreal Chamber Orchestra, "... Micheline, a tu memoria ..."
Publisher: Shelan (Montreal)

sensors V (1985–II) for solo percussion and percussion ensemble
Commissioned by Pierre Béluse
Dedicated to Pierre Béluse
Publisher: Shelan (Montreal)

ektenes I (1985–III) for columbine and amaranth
Commissioned by Gayle Young
Dedicated to Gayle Young
Publisher: Shelan (Montreal)

módulos IV (1986–I) for amplified or electric guitar and tape
Commissioned by Alvaro Pierri
Dedicated to Alvaro Pierri
Publisher: Shelan (Montreal)

arghanum I (1986–II) for solo accordion, clarinets, synthesizer, and percussion
Commissioned by Joseph Petric
Dedicated to Joseph Petric
Publisher: Shelan (Montreal)

sensors VI (1986–III) for percussion ensemble
Commissioned by Repercussion
Dedicated to Repercussion
Publisher: Shelan (Montreal)

arghanum II (1987–II) for flute and contrabass, with chamber ensemble
Commissioned by Bertram Turetzky
Dedicated "to bert and nancy [Turetzky] and ... robert und clara"
Publisher: Shelan (Montreal)

arghanum III (1987–II) for solo tape
Publisher: Shelan (Montreal)

arghanum IV (1987–III) for solo tape
Publisher: Shelan (Montreal)

ektenes II (1987–IV) for oboe and percussion
Commissioned by Lawrence Cherney
Dedicated to Lawrence Cherney
Publisher: Shelan (Montreal)

guitar concerto (1988–I) for guitar and orchestra
Commissioned by Alvaro Pierri
Dedicated "para Alvaro"
Publisher: Shelan (Montreal)

ekphonesis VI (1988–II) for actress-singer and tape
Commissioned by Meg Sheppard
Dedicated "two Meg, too"
Publisher: Shelan (Montreal)

... there is a way to sing it ... (1988–III) for solo tape
Commissioned by David Olds
Publisher: Shelan (Montreal)

la isla de los arrayanes (1989–I)
for clarinets, digital synthesizer, percussion, and contrabass
Commissioned by ARRAY
Dedicated to ARRAY
Publisher: Shelan (Montreal)

un mundo imaginario (1989–II) for choir and computer-generated tape
Commissioned by Iwan Edwards and the McGill Concert Choir
Dedicated to Iwan Edwards
Publisher: Shelan (Montreal)

preludio (preludio) (1989–III) for piano
[reconstruction of lost "Preludio" of 1957]
Publisher: Shelan (Montreal)

coll'age (1989–IV) "para de uno a cinco ..."
Commissioned by Hans Åstrand, Royal Swedish Academy of Music, for
Luis de Pablo's sixtieth anniversary
Dedicated to luis de pablo
Publisher: Shelan (Montreal)

arghanum Vpet (1990–I) for accordion (or piano) and tape
Commissioned by Joseph Petric
Dedicated to Joseph Petric
Publisher: Shelan (Montreal)
[The version for piano and tape is titled *arghanum Vπ* (1990–I).]

the freedom of silence (1990–II) for voice, piano, and tape
Commissioned by Meg Sheppard
Dedicated "amegtoo"
Publisher: Shelan (Montreal)

son glosas, claro ... (1991–I) for digital synthesizers and tape
Re-composed as *como rocas al sol* (2002–V)
Commissioned by Sergio Barroso
Dedicated "a sergio (... a mano ...?)"
Publisher: Shelan (Montreal)

quodlibet, stylus luxurians (1991–II) for organ and chamber ensemble
Commissioned by Werner Jacob
Dedicated to Werner Jacob
Publisher: Shelan (Montreal)

vôo (1992–I) for acting voice and tape
Text by alcides lanza, adapted from *No olvido do tempo/No ouvido do tempo* by Gil Nuno Vaz
Commissioned by the Centro para la Promoción de la Música Contemporánea, Madrid, for the Festival de Alicante
Dedicated "a los nautas cósmicos, acuáticos e intelectuales ..."
Publisher: Shelan (Montreal)

piano concerto (1993–I) for (MIDI) piano and chamber orchestra
Commissioned by Hugo Goldenzweig
Dedicated to Hugo Goldenzweig
Publisher: Shelan (Montreal)

in ... visible (1994–I) for choir and computer-generated tape
Commissioned by Iwan Edwards and the McGill Chamber Singers
Dedicated to McGill Chamber Singers and Iwan Edwards
Publisher: Shelan (Montreal)

ektenes III (1995–I) for clarinet, tape, and digital signal processing
Commissioned by Jean-Guy Boisvert
Dedicated to Jean-Guy Boisvert
Publisher: Shelan (Montreal)

... the people sang ... (1996–I) for voice and tape
Dedicated "To Meg"
Publisher: Shelan (Montreal)

the big dipper (1996–II) for accordion and tape
Commissioned by Joseph Petric
Dedicated "otra para joseph"
Publisher: Shelan (Montreal)

ontem (1999–I) for voice, tablas, tape, and digital signal processing
Text by alcides lanza, adapted from *No olvido do tempo/No ouvido do tempo* by Gil Nuno Vaz
Commissioned by Meg Sheppard and Shawn Mativetsky
Dedicated "to gil nuno vaz (y para Shawn y Meg)"
Publisher: Shelan (Montreal)

plectros V (2000–I) for amplified prepared piano and percussion en-semble
Commissioned by Pierre Béluse
Dedicated to Pierre Béluse and the McGill Percussion Ensemble
Publisher: Shelan (Montreal)

maderas (2000–II) for marimba and other pieces of wood
Publisher: Smith Publications

metales (2001–I) for vibraphone and other pieces of metal
Commissioned by the Lithium Ensemble
Dedicated to the Lithium Ensemble
Publisher: Shelan (Montreal)

separata II (2001–II) for flute[s] and other pipes
May be performed as a piece for two flutes, or simultaneously with *maderas* (2000–II), *metales* (2001–I), and/or *parches* (2002–IV)
Commissioned by the Lithium Ensemble

Dedicated to Sylvia Niedswiecka and the Lithium Ensemble
Publisher: Shelan (Montreal)

aXenas (2002–I) for clarinet, cello, percussion, and piano
Commissioned by the GEMS Ensemble
Dedicated "a Xenakis, GEMS, chaos"
Publisher: Shelan (Montreal)

aXions (2002–II) for voice, violin, double bass, percussion, and electro-
acoustic sounds
Commissioned by the moTion Ensemble
Dedicated to moTion Ensemble
Publisher: Shelan (Montreal)

eXpançao (2002–III) for voice, electroacoustic sounds, and digital signal
processing
Commissioned by Meg Sheppard
Dedicated "paraMegotravez"
Publisher: Shelan (Montreal)

parches (2002–IV) for drum[s] and other skins
Commissioned by the Lithium Ensemble
Dedicated to the Lithium Ensemble
Publisher: Shelan (Montreal)

como rocas al sol (2002–V) for accordion and electroacoustic sounds
re-composed version of *son glosas, claro ...* (1991–I)
Dedicated to Joseph Petric
Publisher: Shelan (Montreal)

aXents (2003–I) pour ensemble instrumental et sons électroacoustiques
Commissioned by NEM and CCMIX
Dedicated to CCMIX and NEM
Publisher: Shelan (Montreal)

'cantos' ... rodados (2004–I) for accordion and electroacoustic sounds
Commissioned by Joseph Petric
Dedicated to Joseph Petric
Publisher: Shelan (Montreal)

eXerc (2004–II) electroacoustic music
Publisher: Shelan (Montreal)

diastemas (2005–I) for marimba and electroacoustic sounds
Commissioned by Gina Ryan
Dedicated to Gina Ryan
Publisher: Shelan (Montreal)

Notes

The following abbreviations are used in citations throughout the notes and the sources.

ALF alcides lanza fonds, Richard Johnston Canadian Music Archives Collection, University of Calgary Library, Calgary, Alberta.

NG2 *The New Grove Dictionary of Music and Musicians.* 2nd ed. Edited by Stanley Sadie and John Tyrell. London: Macmillan, 2001.

preludio (preludio)

1 Personal information in this section is taken from interviews with alcides lanza (Montreal, 12 Apr. 1996), Enriqueta Ayala Gauna (Rosario, 22 Oct. 1996), and Edgardo Lanza (Rosario, 23 Oct. 1996).

Chapter One

1 This and all further personal information about lanza's early years with his family is taken from interviews with alcides lanza (Montreal, 12 Apr. 1996), Enriqueta Ayala Gauna (Rosario, 22 Oct. 1996), and Edgardo Lanza (Rosario, 23 Oct. 1996).

2 lanza did not know that his father had been a musician; he first learned of it during my interviews with his brother Edgardo Lanza (Rosario, 23 Oct. 1996) and his cousin Enriqueta Ayala Gauna (Rosario, 22 Oct. 1996).

3 In the novels and stories by lanza's uncle, Velmiro Ayala Gauna, many of the characters use Guaraní words, which are translated in notes or glossaries at the back of the books.

4 Until recently lanza was under the impression that his father had won the money betting on horses, but during my interviews with Edgardo Lanza and Enriqueta Ayala Gauna, both agreed that Antonio Lanza

had won a cigarette contest (interviews, Rosario, 22 and 23 Oct. 1996). Antonio later died of a pulmonary oedema caused in part by his heavy smoking; lanza has admitted that, perhaps subconsciously, he did not want to associate his beloved piano with the cigarettes that contributed to his father's death (private conversation, Buenos Aires, 25 Oct. 1996).

5 Personal information about lanza's life in Rosario is taken from my interviews with lanza (Montreal, 27 Apr. and 4 May 1996), Enriqueta Ayala Gauna (Rosario, 22 Oct. 1996), Dante Grela (Rosario, 23 Oct. 1996), and Arminda Canteros and Arminda Farrugia (Rosario, 23 Oct. 1996).

6 For information on Rosario and the composers associated with this city, see Silvia Astuni, Daniel Cozzi, and Claudio Lluan, eds., *100 Años de música Rosarina* (Rosario: Universidad Nacional de Rosario, 1991); Rodolfo Arizaga, *Enciclopedia de la música Argentina* (Buenos Aires: Fondo Nacional de las Artes, 1971); Rodolfo Arizaga and Pompeyo Camps, *Historia de la música en la Argentina* (Buenos Aires: Ricordi Americana, 1990); *Encyclopedia of Latin American History and Culture* (New York: Scribner's, 1996); Miguel Ficher, Martha Furman Schliefer, and John M. Furman, *Latin American Classical Composers: A Biographical Dictionary* (Lanham, MD: Scarecrow Press, 1996).

7 Private conversation with Enrique Belloc, Buenos Aires, 21 Oct. 1996.

8 lanza discusses his relationship with his uncle in interview, Montreal, 27 Apr. and 4 May 1996. For further information on Velmiro Ayala Gauna and his works see Eugenio Castelli, "La narrativa de Ayala Gauna," *El Litoral* (Santa Fe, Argentina), 25 May 1961; Augusto Raúl Cortazar, *Indios y gauchos en la literatura argentina* (Buenos Aires: Instituto Amigos del Libro Argentino, 1956); Fernando Hugo Casullo, *Voces indígenas en el idioma español* (Buenos Aires: Perlado, 1963); *Quién es quién en la Argentina* (Buenos Aires: Kraft, 1958–59).

9 *Don Frutos Gómez, el comesario* (1960) is based on the book of the same title, first published in Rosario by Editorial Hormiga in 1960; second and third editions followed in 1966 and 1975.

10 "A la memoria de mi padre, Ramón Ernesto Ayala Gauna, que aromó los días de mi infancia con el perfume agreste de las leyendas de mi tierra india," Velmiro Ayala Gauna, *La selva y su hombre* (Rosario: Ruiz, 1944).

11 Velmiro Ayala Gauna, *Teatro de lo Esencial* (Santa Fe, Argentina: Castellví, 1953).

12 Interview with Enriqueta Ayala Gauna (Velmiro's widow), Rosario, 22 Oct. 1996.

13 Interview with alcides lanza, Montreal, 27 Apr. 1996.

14 Private conversation with alcides lanza, Montreal, 16 Dec. 1996.

15 Interview with Enriqueta Ayala Gauna, Rosario, 22 Oct. 1996.

16 Interview with Arminda Canteros and Arminda Farrugia, Rosario, 23 Oct. 1996.

17 Ibid.

18 Ibid.

19 *Tangos: Arminda Canteros, Piano* (McGill Records, CD 750035-2); lanza was the producer of this recording.

20 lanza discusses his difficulties at the Profesorado Nacional de Música school in interview, Montreal, 4 May 1996.

21 lanza discusses this incident in interview, Montreal, 27 Apr. 1996.

22 Ibid.

23 Private conversation with alcides lanza, Rosario, 23 Oct. 1996.

24 lanza has been reticent to discuss the illness and death of his first child, but he speaks briefly on the subject in two interviews: Montreal, 18 May 1996 and 25 June 2000. He spoke more openly in an unrecorded conversation in Buenos Aires on 30 Oct. 1996. His first wife, Lydia Tomaíno, discusses the matter in an interview (Buenos Aires, 25 Oct. 1996) but has requested that the recording not be made available to other researchers until after lanza's death. Another source for the information in this section is my unrecorded interview with Guillermo Lanza (Buenos Aires, 20 Oct. 1996).

Chapter Two

1 For information on musical institutions in Buenos Aires and the Latin American composers mentioned in this chapter, see Rodolfo Arizaga, *Enciclopedia de la música argentina* (Buenos Aires: Fondo Nacional de las Artes, 1971); Rodolfo Arizaga and Pompeyo Camps, *Historia de la música en la Argentina* (Buenos Aires: Ricordi Americana, 1990); Gerard Béhague, "Argentina (I. Art Music)," *NG2* 1: 873–5; Gerard Béhague, *Music in Latin America: An Introduction* (Englewood Cliffs, NJ: Prentice-Hall, 1979), 272–8, 328–41; Gilbert Chase, *A Guide to the Music of Latin America* (Washington, D.C.: Pan American Union, 1962), "Argentina," 63–98; *Encyclopedia of Latin American History and Culture* (New York: Scribner's, 1996); Miguel Ficher, Martha Furman Schliefer, and John M. Furman, *Latin American Classical Composers* (Lanham, MD: Scarecrow Press, 1996); Roberto García Morillo, *Estudios sobre música argentina* (Buenos Aires: Secretaría de Cultura, Ministerio de Educación y Justicia, Ediciones Culturales

Argentinas, 1984); Victor Gesualdo, *Breve historia de la música en la* · *Argentina* (Buenos Aires: Claridad, 1998) and *La música en la Argentina* (Buenos Aires: Editorial Stella, 1988); Susana Salgado, "Buenos Aires," *NG2* 2: 555–7.

2 The information on Erlich is taken from Rodolfo Arizaga, *Enciclopedia de la música argentina*, 125, and from recollections of alcides lanza (interview, Montreal, 16 Dec, 1996).

3 Paz later quarrelled with the other composers and left to form his own group, the Conciertos de la Nueva Música, which in 1944 became the Agrupación Nueva Música. This ensemble still exists today under the direction of Francisco Kröpfl.

4 Later that year lanza made an arrangement of "La ahogada del cielo" for solo voice and piano.

5 lanza discusses Bautista in an interview, Montreal, 4 May 1996, and a private conversation, Montreal, 16 Dec. 1996.

6 Interview with alcides lanza, Montreal, 16 Dec. 1996.

7 Juan José Castro had been appointed dean of studies at the newly founded Conservatory of Puerto Rico and he had invited Bautista to teach there.

8 Interview with alcides lanza, Montreal, 4 May 1996.

9 Interview with alcides lanza, Montreal, 4 May 1996. Canteros also remembered this conversation (interview, Rosario, 23 Oct. 1996).

10 Interview with alcides lanza, Montreal, 4 May 1996.

11 Early in 1959 lanza joined a large composers' organization called the Agrupación Argentina de Jóvenes Compositores, but later that year lanza, Krieger, and Gandini broke away to form the Agrupación Euphonia, which they soon renamed Agrupación Música Viva. For discussions on Música Viva, see interviews with alcides lanza, Montreal, 18 May 1996 and with Gerardo Gandini, Buenos Aires, 28 Oct. 1996.

12 Interview with alcides lanza, 4 May 1996.

13 Interview with alcides lanza, 4 May 1996; interview with Gerardo Gandini, Buenos Aires, 28 Oct. 1996.

14 Interview with alcides lanza, Montreal, 4 May 1996.

15 lanza discusses his relationship with Krieger in interview, Montreal, 18 May 1996.

16 In New York, for example, the split was between disciples of Milton Babbitt and those of John Cage.

17 Interview with Francisco Kröpfl, Buenos Aires, 25 Oct. 1996.

18 Juan Carlos Paz, *Introducción a la música de nuestro tiempo* (Buenos Aires: Editorial Nueva Visión, 1955), 380.

19 Interview with Francisco Kröpfl, Buenos Aires, 25 Oct. 1996.

20 Interview with alcides lanza, Montreal, 16 Dec. 1996.

21 Three composers discussed Ginastera's teaching during interviews and other communications: alcides lanza (interviews, Montreal, 4 May and 16 Dec. 1996, and e-mail communication, 18 Jan. 2000); Gerardo Gandini (interview, Buenos Aires, 28 Oct. 1996); and Mariano Etkin (interview, Buenos Aires, 27 Oct. 1996). For more information on Ginastera, see Malena Kuss, *Alberto Ginastera* (London: Boosey & Hawkes, 1999); Pola Suárez Urtubey, *Alberto Ginastera* (Buenos Aires: Ediciones Culturales Argentinas, 1967); Gilbert Chase, "Alberto Ginastera: Argentine Composer," *Musical Quarterly* 43 (1957): 439–60.

22 E-mail communication from alcides lanza to Pamela Jones, 18 Jan. 2000.

23 Ibid.

24 Interview with Fernando von Reichenbach, Buenos Aires, 29 Oct. 1996.

25 Ibid.

26 Interview with alcides lanza, Montreal, 16 Dec. 1996.

27 Interview with alcides lanza, Montreal, 5 Apr. 1997.

28 This meeting also had a strong influence on Gerardo Gandini who, like lanza, has devoted much of his career to promoting the contemporary music of Latin America. In Buenos Aires Gandini later created the Centro de Experimentación de Opera y Ballet, an organization that has commissioned and performed a series of chamber operas by contemporary Argentinean composers, and he also performs recent South American music in his wide-ranging career as a concert pianist.

29 My description of the closing of the Di Tella music department – which differs from that in John King, *El Di Tella y el desarrollo cultural argentino en la década del sesenta* – is based on my interviews with Fernando von Reichenbach (Buenos Aires, 29 Oct. 1996), Francisco Kröpfl (Buenos Aires, 25 Oct. 1996), and alcides lanza (Buenos Aires, 25 Oct. 1996).

30 John King, *El Di Tella y el desarrollo cultural argentino en la decada del sesenta*, trans. Carlos Gardini (Buenos Aires: Ediciones de Arte Gaglianone, 1985), interviews with Francisco Kröpfl, 284–8, and Gerardo Gandini, 289–93. Fernando von Reichenbach was not interviewed for King's book.

31 "Eso a la vez se mezcló con problemas relacionadas con el tipo de gobierno que había en ese momento" (Kröpfl, quoted in King, *El Di Tella*, 285).

32 According to lanza, both von Reichenbach and Kröpfl told him privately, as early as 1971, about the government shutdown of the music school; interview with alcides lanza, Montreal, 16 Dec. 1996.

33 King includes a 1984 interview with an unrepentant Onganía who insists that his closing the visual arts branch of the Di Tella were part of his program to combat the public immorality that was ruining the culture of a great nation (*El Di Tella*, 309).

34 Interview with alcides lanza, Montreal, 16 Dec. 1996.

35 Interview with Mariano Etkin, Buenos Aires, 27 Oct. 1996; interview with Gerardo Gandini, Buenos Aires, 28 Oct. 1996.

36 Interview with alcides lanza, Montreal, 18 May 1996; lanza also discusses this matter briefly in interview, Montreal, 4 May 1996.

37 Interview with Francisco Kröpfl, Buenos Aires, 25 Oct. 1996. The studio was closed in 1973.

38 Interview with alcides lanza, Montreal, 16 Dec. 1996.

39 Interview with alcides lanza, Montreal, 27 Apr. 1996.

40 Interview with alcides lanza, Montreal, 16 Dec. 1996.

41 Interview with alcides lanza, Montreal, 18 May 1996.

Chapter Three

1 Not all the "downtown" composers would have agreed with all these principles, but most would have accepted many of them.

2 Interview with Charles Dodge, Hanover, New Hampshire, 19 May 1997; interview with Jon Appleton, Hanover, New Hampshire, 20 May 1997.

3 Private conversation with George Flynn, Montreal, 10 Nov. 2000. lanza discusses the alienation of composers not interested in serialization in interview, Montreal, 18 May 1996; see also the interviews with Dodge and Appleton (note 2 above).

4 Interview with Jon Appleton, Hanover, New Hampshire, 20 May 1997.

5 Joseph P. Straus, "The Myth of Serial 'Tyranny' in the 1950s and 1960s," *Musical Quarterly* 83 (1999): 301–43.

6 Ibid., 303.

7 Anthony Tommasini, "Midcentury Serialists: The Bullies or the Besieged?" *New York Times*, 9 July 2000, AR23.

8 Milton Babbitt, "Who Cares If You Listen?" (1958), in Leo Treitler, general ed., *Source Readings in Music History*, rev. edition (New York: Norton, 1998), 1308.

9 Interview with Pril Smiley, Mohonk Lake, New York, 20 July 1997.

10 For information on the so-called "New York School" see David Nicholls, "Getting Rid of the Glue: The Music of the New York School," in *The New York Schools of Music and Visual Arts: John*

Cage, Morton Feldman, Edgard Varèse, Willem De Kooning, Jasper Johns, Robert Rauschenberg, ed. Steven Johnson (New York : Routledge, 2002), 17–56; David W. Bernstein, "John Cage and the 'Aesthetic of Indifference,'" in ibid., 113–34; Peter Gena, "Freedom in Experimental Music: The New York Revolution," *TriQuarterly* 52 (1981), 223–43; Michael Nyman, *Experimental Music: Cage and Beyond,* 2nd ed. (Cambridge: Cambridge University Press, 1999), chapter 3, "Inauguration 1950–60: Feldman, Brown, Wolff, Cage," 42–59; Charles Hamm, *Music in the New World* (New York: Norton, 1983), "The American Avant-Garde," 580–617; H. Wiley Hitchcock, *Music in the United States: A Historical Introduction,* 3rd ed., Prentice-Hall History of Music Series (Englewood Cliffs, NJ: Prentice-Hall, 1988), "The Post-War Decades: Into the 1960s," 243–83; Eric Salzman, *Twentieth-Century Music: An Introduction,* 4th ed., Prentice-Hall History of Music Series (Upper Saddle River, NJ: Prentice-Hall, 2002), chapter 15, "Anti-Rationality and Aleaory," 163–9.

11 *La Revista de Letras* is a periodical published by the University of Puerto Rico in Mayagüez.

12 "John Cage in an Exclusive Interview with Alcides Lanza / ... We Need a Good Deal of Silence ..." *Revista de Letras de la Facultad de Artes y Ciencias* 3, 11 (Sept. 1971), 319–32. The tape of the interview is in ALF.

13 Composers/Performers Group, *New Music from South America,* Mainstream Records, MS/5017.

14 Private conversation with alcides lanza, Montreal, 15 Apr. 2001.

15 *Música contemporánea de América,* EDUL Records, Rosario, 030.

16 *New Music from South American,* Mainstream Records, New York, MS/5017.

17 *exercise 1* also incorporates a few fragments that lanza had created in 1964 at the Di Tella's rudimentary electronic music studio.

18 Interview with alcides lanza, Montreal, 15 June 1996.

19 There is a tape recording, unfortunately of very poor quality, of this interview in ALF.

20 The performance was at Hunter College in New York.

21 Interview with alcides lanza, Montreal, 25 June 2005, Montreal.

22 Interview with alcides lanza, Montreal, 15 June 1996.

23 This and the following quotations about *eidesis II* in this section are from my interview with alcides lanza, Montreal, 15 June 1996.

24 Nicolas Slonimsky, *Music since 1900,* 4th ed. (New York: Scribner's, 1971), 1260: Slonimsky's gloss of "icositetraphonic" reads: "As the

etymology of the term indicates, icositetraphony deals with music using 24 equal intervals in an octave (icosi = 20; tetra = 4; phone = sound), i.e., in quarter-tones" (1453).

25 Jacques Thériault, "Une perception plus juste d'Alcides Lanza," *Le Devoir* (Montreal), 18 March 1972: "Ce n'est pas tous les jours qu'on a l'occasion de reviser son opinion sur un compositeur. J'ai dit, à l'occasion d'un concert du Performers Group de New York à McGill, à la fin de janvier, qu'Alcides Lanza s'était escrimé dans le désert ... Or, voici qu'une seule soirée à la Société de Musique Contemporaine du Québec vient d'atténuer totalement ma reticence première à l'égard de Lanza ... L'œuvre qui m'a réconcilié avec ce jeune compositeur argentin s'appelle 'Eidesis II.' Ecrite pour treize instruments, cette musique explore et sonde 'l'analyse spectrale du sons' avec beaucoup d'acuité. Mais, ce qui m'a plus frappé, c'est son caractère électro-acoustique, cette façon avec laquelle Lanza traite les instruments en les dôtant de propriétés nouvelles et en équilibrant toutes ses masses de sons."

26 This and the following quotations in this section about *strobo I* are from my interview with alcides lanza, Montreal, 5 Aug 1996.

27 Frank Hrury, Cleveland *Plain Dealer*, 16 May 1968.

28 Cleveland *Sun Press*, 16 May 1968.

29 This performance was discussed in interviews with Gerardo Gandini, Buenos Aires, 28 Oct. 1996; and with Fernando von Reichenbach, Buenos Aires, 29 Oct. 1996.

30 The meaning of the word *ekphonesis* is "to speak out loud."

31 Kröpfl discusses his career in interview, Buenos Aires, 25 Oct. 1996. See also Rodolfo Arizaga, *Enciclopedia de la música argentina* (Buenos Aires: Fondo Nacional de las Artes, 1972); Rodolfo Arizaga and Pompeyo Camps, *Historia de la música en la Argentina* (Buenos Aires: Ricordi Americana, 1990); Gerard Béhague, *Music in Latin America: An Introduction*, (Englewood Cliffs, NJ: Prentice-Hall, 1979); and Miguel Ficher, Martha Furman Schliefer, and John M. Furman, *Latin American Classical Composers: A Biographical Dictionary* (Lanham, MD: Scarecrow Press, 1996).

32 Interview with alcides lanza, Montreal, 18 May 1996.

33 In 2005 the Faculty of Music of McGill University became the Schulich School of Music of McGill University. Because this change occurred after lanza's retirement, in this book I have retained the name that was in use during lanza's thirty years at the university.

34 Mather discusses his relationship with lanza in interview, Montreal, 16 Oct. 1999.

Chapter Five

1 Interview with Meg Sheppard, Montreal, 17 July 1996. Unless otherwise indicated, all further quotations from Sheppard in this chapter are taken from this interview. lanza describes his meeting with Sheppard in interview, Montreal, 18 July 1996.

2 lanza describes this incident in interview, Montreal, 18 July 1996.

3 lanza speaks about his problems obtaining studio time in Berlin and his conversations with Bertoncini and Shinohara in interview, Montreal, 18 July 1996.

4 lanza gives a detailed description of the project in "Penetrations I (1968–69)," *Source: Music of the Avant Garde*, double issue 7/8, in vol. 4, no. 2 (July 1970), 44.

5 lanza wrote this comment in the margin of an early draft of the present chapter.

6 Interview with alcides lanza, Montreal, 24 Oct. 1998.

7 Ibid.

8 There are some twenty or more reviews of *trilogy* or parts of *trilogy* in ALF.

9 Interview with Sheppard, Montreal, 17 July 1996. lanza discusses Sheppard's commission in interview, Montreal, 24 Oct. 1998.

10 lanza describes the three figures in interview, Montreal, 24 Oct. 1998.

11 Private conversation with alcides lanza, Montreal, 24 Oct. 1998.

12 The square brackets around the "L" are lanza's; in the prefatory notes to the score he states that the brackets indicate a consonant that is to be "only hinted at, with unclear emission."

13 Private conversation with alcides lanza, Montreal, 25 Oct. 1998.

14 Interview with alcides lanza, Montreal, 24 Oct. 1998.

15 *The Children like Marbles Tumble into Life*, broadsheet (Vancouver, BC: Pulp Press, 1979).

16 Interview with alcides lanza and Meg Sheppard, Montreal, 1 Nov. 1998.

17 alcides lanza, *trilogy* (Shelan eSp-9201-CD, 1992).

18 *Glass Houses* (Columbia Records, 1980).

19 Interview with Meg Sheppard, Montreal, 17 July 1996; Sheppard also discusses this in interview with lanza and Sheppard, Montreal, 1 Nov. 1998.

20 Robert Frost, "Fire and Ice," *Harper's Magazine*, December 1920.

21 "Let us go forth, the tellers of tales, and seize whatever prey the heart long for, and have no fear." W. B. Yeats, "A Teller of Tales," *The Celtic Twilight*, 2nd, expanded ed. (London: Bullen, 1902), p. 7.

22 "Es inevitable asociarla con Cathy Berberian; no solo por su tremenda sensualidad sino por una relación con la obra: Luciano Berio escribió para Berberian, como Lanza lo hace *para* Sheppard. La obra de Lanza diseña una gran curva dramática ... que culmina con unas preguntas sobre la suerte del planeta ... Pero no es ... la importancia de esas preguntas lo que confiere fuerza y profundidad a la obra de Lanza, sino una extraña materialidad, ... de la cual no es posible separar la voz y el cuerpo de Sheppard." Federico Monjeau, "Lanza en acción," *Página 12* (Buenos Aires), 13 Aug. 1989.

Chapter Six

1 Private conversation with alcides lanza, Montreal, 12 Aug. 1996.
2 For a good summary of the diversity of aesthetic and technical approaches to electroacoustic composition among the pioneers in the field, see the early chapters of Peter Manning, *Electronic and Computer Music*, rev. ed. (Oxford: Oxford University Press, 2002).
3 "Semaine que ne peut qualifier autrement qu'une semaine délirante, littéralement délirante"; Serge Garant, quoted in Marie-Thérèse Lefebvre, *Serge Garant et la révolution musicale au Québec* (Montreal: Louise Courteau, 1986), 75.
4 Saint-Marcoux died of a brain tumour at age forty-six. Her friendship with lanza is discussed in chapter 7. The lives of a number of significant Quebec composers have been regrettably short; in addition to Mercure and Saint-Marcoux, André Mathieu (1929–68) died at age thirty-nine from complications due to alcoholism, Claude Vivier (1948–83) was murdered at age thirty-three, and Michel-Georges Brégent (1948–1993) died at age forty-five.
5 Private conversation with alcides lanza, Montreal, 6 Oct. 2004.
6 Le Caine often continued to tinker with his machines for decades after their invention. In this list I give the dates that these machines were first produced.
7 lanza discusses *plectros III* in interview, Montreal, 5 Aug. 1996.
8 lanza made this comment during a rehearsal of *penetrations II* in Montreal, 3 Apr. 1997.
9 lanza discusses *ekphonesis IV* in interview, Montreal, 5 Aug. 1996.
10 *Two Times Too* (1967), a documentary on Argentinean painter Luis Felipe Noé, directed by Jerome Ducrôt with an electronic music soundtrack by lanza. There is a copy of this film in ALF.
11 Interview with alcides lanza, Montreal, 5 Aug. 1996.

12 Bruce Mather discusses *plectros IV* in interview, Montreal, 16 Oct. 1999; lanza, Mather, and Lepage discussed it with me during rehearsals for the work in Montreal, 6–8 Feb. 2000.

13 Jacob Sisskind, Montreal *Gazette*, 21 Jan. 1974.

14 Private conversation with alcides lanza, Montreal, 10 Apr. 1999.

15 The following information concerning the troublesome rehearsals for the first performances of *kron'ikelz 75* comes from a series of telephone conversations with Robert Aitken and Erica Goodman in Toronto and with lanza in Montreal (10 Sept. to 18 Oct. 2000).

16 Kathleen McMorrow, librarian of New Music Concerts, has informed me that the petition is now lost; telephone conversation, 17 Oct. 2000.

17 The amount might have been as high as $2,000.

18 Eric Salzman, *Twentieth-Century Music: An Introduction*, 4th ed. (Upper Saddle River, NJ: Prentice-Hall, 2002), 195.

19 Taruskin introduces the term "atonal triad" (for the 016 trichord) in *The Oxford History of Western Music* (Oxford: Oxford University Press, 2005), IV: 331.

20 The other favourite trichord of the early atonalists, the 013 "major-minor third" cell (for example, D–F–F-sharp) also occurs frequently in *sensors III*; one instance is the first three notes (both hands): E-flat–D–F-sharp, which is also part of the "doodle" motive. Because this cell seems to me to have less structural significance than the atonal triad I have avoided calling attention to its frequent appearances in my examples.

21 The six-note chord also includes the 013 "major-minor third" trichord G–E-flat–F-sharp.

Chapter Seven

1 lanza's recollections of Saint-Marcoux are in three interviews: Montreal, 28 Apr. 1998; 22 Oct. 1999; and 25 June 2000. The interview of 25 June 2000 also includes a detailed discussion of *bour-drones*. For more information on Saint-Marcoux, see "Micheline Coulombe Saint-Marcoux," *Compositeurs au Québec*, no. 7 (Montreal: Canadian Music Centre, 1986); Gilles Potvin, "Micheline Coulombe Saint-Marcoux," in *Compositeurs canadiens contemporains*, ed. Louise Laplante, trans. Véronique Robert (Montreal: Les presses de l'université du Québec, 1977) , 305–8; Jacques Thériault, "Saint-Marcoux, Micheline Coulombe," *Encyclopedia of Music in Canada*, 2nd ed., 1173–4; Micheline Coulombe Saint-Marcoux, "Réflexions d'une jeune compositrice," *Vie Musicale* 8 (1968), 13–16.

2 lanza describes this conversation in interview, Montreal, 25 June 2000.

3 *transmutations*, Shelan eSp-9601-CD.
4 Micheline Coulombe Saint-Marcoux, [introductory note to program brochure], Journées de musiques nouvelles d'Amérique Latine, Montreal, 1982.
5 lanza discusses *un mundo imaginario* in interview, Montreal, 25 June 2000.

Chapter Eight

1 lanza discusses the McGill Contemporary Music Festivals in interview, Montreal, 22 Oct. 1999; all quotations from lanza in this section are from that interview.
2 Jesús Villa Rojo, *El clarinete y sus posibilidades: Estudio de nuevos procedimientos*, 2nd ed. (Madrid: Alpuerto, 1984).
3 Appleton was the musical advisor for the project, Sydney Alonso was in charge of hardware design, and Cameron Jones the software.
4 *Percussion Music from the Americas*, McGill Records CD 7500-52-2.
5 Claude Gingrass, "L'impression finale: Hambraeus fait de la musique, lanza fait du bruit"; *La Presse*, 14 Mar. 1986.
6 In the late 1990s Denys Bouliane, a composition professor at McGill, organized two small-scale but impressive festivals that depended in large part on performers from outside the university. In more recent years these festivals have grown to become co-productions between McGill and the SMCQ.
7 lanza discusses the founding of GEMS and its organization in interview, Montreal, 18 May 1996.
8 ALF holds thirty-four pages of documents (letters, memos, petitions, etc.) pertaining to incidents discussed in this section. I also discussed the issue in interviews with lanza (Montreal, 16 Oct. 1999) and Bruce Mather (Montreal, 16 Oct. 1999), and in conversations with Robert F. Jones (16 Oct. 1999), Bruce Minorgan (10 May 2000), Tom Plaunt (10 Aug. 2000), and Christine Vanderkooy (10 July 2000).
9 Memo, [fall] 1977; copy in ALF.
10 See, for example, Richard Bunger, *The Well-Prepared Piano*, 2nd ed. (San Pedro, CA: Litoral Arts Press, 1981).
11 "The Non-Conventional Pianist" [interview with Margaret Leng Tan], *The Dominion Post* (Wellington, NZ), 22 July 2005 <www5.stuff.co.nz/stuff/0,1478,3354172a14195,00.html>.
12 Edwin M. Ripin and Hugh Davies, "Prepared piano," *NG2* 20: 298.
13 Memo, 14 Nov. 1986; copy in ALF.
14 Memo, Maria Jerabek to John Rea, 14 Nov. 1986; copy in ALF.

15 The petition reads: "We, the undersigned, express our concern about the abuse of pianos in PCH [Pollack Concert Hall], as outlined in Prof. Plawutsky's memo to you and request you convene a meeting prior to the forthcoming gems concert to establish regulations governing the use of the Faculty of Music pianos." Memo to John Rea, 20 Jan. 1987, signed by Elizabeth Dawson, Tom Plaunt, Luba Zuk, Norair Artinian, Helmut Blume, Dale Bartlett, Kenneth Woodman, Charles Reiner, Louis-Philippe Pelletier, and Esther Masters; copy in ALF.

16 Letter, lanza to John Rea, 24 January 1987; copy in ALF. The full text of lanza's letter reads as follows:

> dear John: i was very surprised to hear from you that once again the "abuse" of the pianos in Pollack Hall is being laid at the door of those who play contemporary music. when this issue came up previously a compromise was reached during dean Blume's tenure as dean whereby if any preparation of a piano is required for a concert, we would use the old "red" piano for preparation. this has been done despite the added cost of moving this piano each time it is needed. this compromise seems to have worked to everyone's satisfaction to date. now it seems that this whole issue is once again a subject for complaint.
>
> first, i must express my disappointment that instead of a meeting to discuss concerns, this protest took the form of a petition. McGill has always been noted for the mutual tolerance of different musical aesthetics that are evident among staff members. instead of circulating petitions against one another, i feel that differences of opinion should be the subject of frank discussion among colleagues. to have my competency and professionalism questioned in such a manner after some thirty-five years as a professional musician has – to be frank – offended me.
>
> i understand that the concert ... is objected to on the grounds that the pianos were damaged due to preparation ... unfortunately most of those who signed a petition protesting the "abuse" of the pianos were not present to hear those pianos being played. in any event, the piano tuner put in a brief appearance at the dress rehearsal and the preparation as done was approved by him. i was more than a little surprised to read his comments after the fact. if he had such concerns, why not tell me at the time? the specific "charges" i take to be: (1) that a string was broken (this string broke on one of the pianos that were not prepared, while playing on the keyboard – a not uncommon occurrence even if one is playing Liszt!) (2) the dampers were twisted (again, as everyone knows, this can also happen during the usual wear and tear

on a piano. this was the same complaint made against a student two years ago – not one of my concerts – and i didn't buy it *then*) (3) certain metal fittings were removed (this i categorically deny – who had the tools? the time? the need?) ...

as an afterthought, i believe that it is well known that the greatest cause of deterioration in pianos is overuse. the pianos at Pollack Hall are played from morning to night three hundred plus days every year – piano recitals, chamber ensembles, opera workshops – you name it. (fortunately – or unfortunately depending on one's point of view – new music concerts average only some ten of those concerts per year. at least we are not contributing overmuch to the normal wear of the pianos!) ...

if there are any further concerns about the preparation of pianos for new music and the potential for damage to the instrument, i would be happy to give a master class demonstration to all interested staff. let's give the lie once and for all to this source of seemingly perpetual discord.

now, John, we have worked together for too many years for you to consider me some sort of musical vandal. my reputation must speak for me. i am a little long in the tooth to submit to any supervision of my professional conduct by those who are uninformed in the contemporary keyboard techniques and whose motives are questionable.

17 Memo, François Robitaille to lanza, Denys Bouliane, Eugene Plawutsky, Louis-Philippe Pelletier, and Isolde Lagacé, 24 Nov. 1997; copy in ALF. It is interesting to note the plucking of piano strings is now permitted on all of the pianos in McGill's concert halls; the greasy residue theory has been put to rest.

18 Statement read by lanza in Clara Lichtenstein Hall, 24 Nov. 1997; copy in ALF.

19 Mike Somerville, "Trying to Break the Sound Barrier in the Music Department," McGill Daily, 28 Jan. 1998.

The man who holds the golden key to McGill's electronic music studio ... is the internationally renowned electronic music composer and performer alcides lanza ... Recently, one of his compositions sparked a controversy which provided an apt example of the struggle between the establishment and the vanguard in musical academia ... The controversy revolves around lanza's 1996 [sic] composition entitled "Plectros II" ... The piece contains sections in which the performer must reach in to the piano and pluck specified harmonics on the piano strings, which offers a distinctive complementary texture to the electronic sounds whirling about the room. lanza planned on performing this piece at one of McGill's Studio Exchange Concerts in the Clara Lichtenstein Recital Hall ... Two weeks before the show, however, lanza received word from "higher administration" that his piece could not be performed.

Why? ... They said that lanza's piece was too aggressive for the expensive Yamaha grand pianos in Lichtenstein Hall and they were afraid that he might damage a string, or detune it ...

On the night of the performance, after hearing that his 25-year-old position as artistic director of the ems would be at stake should he break the rules, lanza gave in. He stood before an almost full house and read rather solemnly from a piece of paper, that he would not be playing the original version of the piece ... He ended his speech by conveying his sincere hope that we will be able to hear twentieth century music before the twenty-first century and was greeted with enthusiastic applause from all members of the audience

20 "Guidelines for effective institutional piano maintenance," College and University Technician's Committee of the Piano Technicians Guild, 1990. Reproduced (1998) at <www.overspianos.com.au/ inst_mnt.html>.

21 lanza discusses his piano marathons briefly in interview, Montreal, 18 May 1996, and in depth in interview, Montreal, 12 Sept. 1999. This section is also based on my recollections of the events as a member of the audience.

22 lanza gives a detailed account of how he went about compiling a sound collage for the film faithful to Ray's quite explicit instructions in interview, Montreal, 12 Sept. 1999.

23 Interview with alcides lanza, Monteal, 12 Sept. 1999.

24 Ibid.

25 Ibid.

26 All quotations in this section are from an interview with alcides lanza, Montreal, 22 April 1998.

27 Interview with Osvaldo Budón, Montreal, 9 Dec. 1996.

Chapter Nine

1 Interview with alcides lanza, 14 June 1999.

2 Examples include the operatic quotations in *ekphonesis II* and the Schumann quotations in *plectros IV.*

3 Interview with alcides lanza, Montreal, 15 May 2005.

4 Interview with Joseph Petric, Montreal, 9 June 2001.
5 lanza discusses *arghanum I* in interview, Montreal, 14 June 1999; all quotations from lanza in this section are from that interview. lanza found the word "arghanum" in Sibyl Marcuse's dictionary *Musical Instruments*, where she defines it as an "Arabic name for the Byzantine organ ... It had bellows of skin and iron, and the word arghanum was interpreted as meaning 1000 voices ... The Byzantines reputedly used the arghanum to disconcert their enemies, and it is reported to have been audible sixty miles away." Sibyl Marcuse, *Musical Instruments: A Comprehensive Dictionary*, corrected edition (NY: Norton, 1975), p. 21.
6 Constant Lambert, *Music ho!* (London: Faber, 1934), p. 213.
7 lanza discusses *arghanum V* in interview, Montreal, 14 June 1999; all quotations from lanza in this section are from that interview.
8 Petric recorded the second version of *arghanum V* on his CD, *Orbiting Garden* (Centrediscs CMCCD 7802, 2002).
9 To lanza, the Islas Malvinas are Argentinean.
10 In my interview with Petric (Montreal, 9 June 2001) he describes the work as "amazingly organic."
11 In a 1997 lecture on his MIDI piano concerto (a work that incorporates much of *arghanum V*) lanza pointed out many of the connections with *El monito*. Much "inside information" in the following discussion comes from his notes for this lecture (copy of notes in ALF).
12 In order to distinguish between the different versions of *arghanum V* lanza added suffixes to the roman numeral: the second version for Petric is called *arghanum Vpet* (*pet* for Petric), and the piano version is called *arghanum Vπ* (*π* for *piano*). lanza recorded *arghanum Vπ* for his CD, *Music of the Americas, 1* (Shelan eSp-9301-CD, 1993).
13 lanza discusses his *concerto for midi piano and orchestra* in interview, Montreal, 22 Oct. 1999; all quotations from lanza in this section are from that interview.
14 lanza discusses his feelings about Columbus in interview, Montreal, 15 Dec. 1997.
15 Gil Nuno Vaz, *No olvido do tempo / No ouvido do tempo* (Santos, Brazil: private publication, 1984).
16 *vôo* is discussed in three interviews: lanza and Sheppard, Montreal, 15 Dec. 1997; lanza, Montreal, 15 Dec. 1997; and lanza, Montreal, 22 Apr. 1998.
17 lanza used the excerpt found in Gerard Béhague, *Music in Latin America: An Introduction* (Englewood Cliffs, NJ: Prentice-Hall, 1979), 49.

The original is in E minor, but lanza reworked the music in C-sharp minor. The text of the original aria begins with the words, "*Con las alas*" [with wings]. lanza was attracted to both the music and the flight imagery of the text.

18 Interview with Meg Sheppard, Montreal, 15 Dec. 1997.

19 "Ses œuvres aux titres évocateurs – penetrations, eidesis, acúfenos, plectros – témoignent à la fois de recherches poussées et d'un mode de pensée très intuitif, voire frénétique: une sorte de frénésie organisée. Si j'avais à l'associer à l'un des quatre éléments que sont la terre, l'air, l'eau et le feu, c'est sûrement le feu que je choisirais." Address given at McGill University, Montreal, 9 Dec. 1996; a copy of Tremblay's manuscript is in ALF.

Sources

Interviews

Recorded Interviews with alcides lanza
Montreal: 27 Apr. 1996, 4 May 1996, 18 May 1996, 15 June 1996, 18 July 1996, 5 Aug. 1996, 27 Apr. 1997, 15 Dec. 1997 (with Meg Sheppard), 22 Apr. 1998, 24 Oct. 1998 (side 2 with Meg Sheppard), 14 June 1999, 12 Aug. 1999, 22 Oct. 1999, 25 June 2000

Unrecorded Interviews with alcides lanza
Montreal: 12 Aug. 1996, 16 Dec. 1996, 5 Apr. 1997, 10 Apr. 1999, 5 June 2005
Buenos Aires: 25 Oct. 1996

Other Recorded Interviews
Appleton, Jon: Hanover, New Hampshire, 20 May 1997
Ayala Gauna, Enriqueta: Rosario, Argentina, 22 Oct. 1996
Budón, Osvaldo: Montreal, 9 Dec. 1996
Canteros, Arminda, and Arminda Farrugia: Rosario, Argentina, 23 Oct. 1996
dianda, hilda: Buenos Aires, 29 Oct. 1996
Dodge, Charles: Hanover, New Hampshire, 19 May 1997
Etkin, Mariano: Buenos Aires, 27 Oct. 1996
Gandini, Gerardo: Buenos Aires, 28 Oct. 1996
Ginastera, Aurora: Buenos Aires, 30 Oct. 1996
Grela, Dante: Rosario, Argentina, 23 Oct. 1996
Kröpfl, Francisco: Buenos Aires, 25 Oct. 1996
Lanza, Edgardo: Rosario, Argentina, 23 Oct. 1996

Mather, Bruce: Montreal, 16 Oct. 1999
von Reichenbach, Fernando: Buenos Aires, 29 Oct. 1996
Sheppard, Meg: Montreal, 17 July 1996; interviews with lanza 15 Dec. 1997 and 24 Oct. 1998.
Smiley, Pril: Mohonk Lake, New York, 20 July 1997
Tomaino, Lydia: Buenos Aires, 25 Oct. 1996

Other Unrecorded Interviews

Aitken, Robert: series of telephone conversations Sept. and Oct. 2000.
Goodman, Erica: telephone conversation, 19 Sept. 2000.
Lanza, Guillermo: Buenos Aires, 20 Oct. 1996
Petric, Joseph: Montreal, 9 June 2001
Vanderkooy, Christine: Montreal, 10 July 2000

Writings by alcides lanza

(in chronological order)
"A New Notational System." *Parámetros* (Caracas, April 1969).
"Consideraciónes sobre la música en su relación con el tiempo presente." *Revista de Letras* (Univ. of Puerto Rico) 3 (1969): 384–91.
"Primer festival de música de las Americas." *Revista de Letras* (Univ. of Puerto Rico) 3 (1969): 466–72.
"Penetrations I (1968–69)." *Source: Music of the Avant Garde*, 4, no. 2 (July 1970): 44.
"John Cage in an Exclusive Interview with Alcides Lanza / ... We Need a Good Deal of Silence ..." *Revista de Letras* (Univ. of Puerto Rico). 3, no. 11 (Sept. 1971): 319–32.
"Music Theatre: A Mixed Media Realization of Kagel's 'ludwig von.'" *Interface* 8 (1979): 237–48.
"auditory perceptions: fringe benefits: a number of sonic events at the edge of (Montréal's) reality." *Musicworks* 60 (Fall 1994): 57–9.
"auditory perceptions: fringe benefits 2: a number of sonic events at the edge of reality." *Musicworks* 61 (Spring 1995): 68–9.
"auditory perceptions: fringe benefits 3: a number of sonic events at the edge of reality." *Musicworks* 64 (Spring 1996): 54–5.
"auditory perceptions: fringe benefits 4, a number of sonic events at the edge of reality: a visitor, ... Three hommages, ... and g.e.m.s. ... " *Musicworks* 65 (Summer 1996): 40–2.
"auditory perceptions: fringe benefits, 5. a number of sonic events at the edge of reality." *Musicworks* 68 (Summer 1997): 53–5.

"auditory perceptions: fringe benefits 6: a number of sonic events at the edge of reality." *Musicworks* 69 (Dec. 1997): 58–9.

"auditory perceptions: fringe benefits 7: a number of sonic events at the edge of reality." *Musicworks* 70 (Spring 1998): 47.

"auditory perceptions: fringe benefits, 8: a number of sonic events at the edge of reality." *Musicworks* 71 (Summer 1998): 52–3.

"eclectic electric montreal: auditory perceptions: fringe benefits, 9: a number of sonic events at the edge of reality." *Musicworks* 73 (Spring 1999): 51–2.

"electroacoustics galore: auditory perceptions: fringe benefits 10: a number of sonic events at the edge of reality." *Musicworks* 74 (Summer 1999): 52–3.

"Etkin, Mariano." *Latin American Music* (New York, 1999).

"eclectic electric montreal: auditory perceptions: fringe benefits, 11: a number of sonic events at the edge of reality." *Musicworks* 76 (Spring 2000): 56–8.

"Etkin, Mariano." NG2 8: 407–8.

Writings by Other Authors

Appleton, J. "Reevaluating the Principle of Expectation in Electronic Music." *Perspectives of New Music* 8 (1969): 106–11.

Arizaga, Rodolfo. *Enciclopedia de la música Argentina.* Buenos Aires: Fondo Nacional de las Artes, 1971.

Arizaga, Rodolfo, and Pompeyo Camps. *Historia de la música en la Argentina.* Buenos Aires: Ricordi Americana, 1990.

Astuni, Silvia, Daniel Cozzi, and Claudio Lluán, eds. *100 Años de música Rosarina.* Rosario: Universidad Nacional de Rosario, 1991.

Austin, Kevin. "Capturing, Crystalizing and Fragmenting Time: An Introduction to Sonic Arts." [introductory notes for Concordia University course FFAR250]. 1999. http://music.concordia.ca/FFAR_Reading_Ea.html.

Ayala Gauna, Velmiro. *Don Frutos Gómez, el comesario.* 1st ed., Rosario: Editorial Hormiga, 1960; 2nd ed., 1966, 3rd ed., 1975.

– *La selva y su hombre.* Rosario: Ruiz, 1944.

– *Teatro de lo esencial.* Santa Fe, Argentina: Castellví, 1953.

Babbitt, Milton. "The Revolution in Sound: Electronic Music." *Music Journal* 18 (1960): 7.

– "Who Cares If You Listen?" (1958). In *Source Readings in Music History,* general ed. Leo Treitler, 1305–11. Rev. ed. New York: Norton, 1998.

Baruch, Gerth-Wolfgang. "Was ist Musique concrète?" *Melos* 20 (1953): 9–12.

Beckwith, John. "Udo Kasemets: A Portrait." *Musicanada* 22 (1969): 8–9.

Beckwith, John, and Udo Kasemets. *The Modern Composer and His World*. Toronto: University of Toronto Press, 1961.

Béhague, Gerard. "Argentina (I. Art Music)." *NG2* 1: 873–75.

– "Music." In *Latin America and the Caribbean: A Critical Guide to Research Sources*. ed. Paula Hattox Covington, 567. Westport, CT: Greenwood, 1992.

– *Music in Latin America: An Introduction*. Prentice-Hall History of Music Series. Englewood Cliffs, NJ: Prentice-Hall, 1979.

Berio, Luciano. "The Studio di Fonologia Musicale of Milan." *The Score* 15 (1956): 83.

Bernstein, David W. "John Cage and the 'Aesthetic of Indifference.'" In *The New York Schools of Music and Visual Arts: John Cage, Morton Feldman, Edgard Varèse, Willem De Kooning, Jasper Johns, Robert Rauschenberg*, ed. Steven Johnson, 113–34. New York: Routledge, 2002.

Bethell, Leslie, ed. *A Cultural History of Latin America: Literature, Music and the Visual Arts in the 19th and 20th Centuries*. Cambridge: Cambridge University Press, 1998.

Bunger, Richard. *The Well-Prepared Piano*. 2nd ed. San Pedro, CA: Litoral Arts Press, 1981.

Burns, Kristine H., comp. and annotator. "History of Electronic and Computer Music Including Automatic Instruments and Composition Machines." http://music.dartmouth.edu/~wowem/electronmedia/music/eamhistory.html.

Cage, John. *Selected Texts*. ed. Richard Kostelanetz. New York: Cooper Square Press, 1983.

Castelli, Eugenio. "La narrativa de Ayala Gauna." *El Litoral* (Santa Fe, Argentina), 25 May 1961.

Casullo, Fernando Hugo. *Voces indígenas en el idioma español*. Buenos Aires: Perlado, 1963.

Chase, Gilbert. "Alberto Ginastera: Argentine Composer." *Musical Quarterly* 43 (1957): 439–60.

– *A Guide to the Music of Latin America*. Washington, DC: Pan American Union, 1962.

College and University Technician's Committee of the Piano Technicians Guild. "Guidelines for Effective Institutional Piano Maintenance" (1990). Reproduced 1998 at <www.overspianos.com.au/inst_mnt.html>.

Compositores de América / Composers of the Americas. Washington, DC: Pan American Union, 1971.

Cortázar, Augusto Raúl. *Indios y gauchos en la literatura argentina*. Buenos Aires: Instituto Amigos del Libro Argentino, 1956.

de la Vega, A. "Latin American Composers in the United States." *Latin American Music Review / Revista de música latinoamericana* 1 (1980): 162–75.

Dobinson, Michael R. "A Trilogy from Shelan" [review of *trilogy* CD]. *Musicworks* 62 (Summer 1995): 55.

Drucker, Joanna. "Collaboration without Object(s) in the Early Happenings." *Art Journal* 52, no. 4 (Dec. 1993): 51–58.

Eimert, Herbert. "Was ist elektronische Musik?" *Melos* 20 (1953): 1–5.

Emmerson, Simon, ed. *Music, Electronic Media, and Culture*. Aldershot (England): Ashgate, 2000.

Encyclopedia of Latin American History and Culture. Barbara A. Tenenbaum, editor in chief; associate editors, Georgette Magassy Dorn et al. New York: Scribner's, 1996.

Encyclopedia of Music in Canada. 2nd ed., ed. Helmut Kallmann, Gilles Potvin, Kenneth Winters et al. Toronto: University of Toronto Press, 1992; updated version available at http://www.thecanadianencyclopedia.com/index.cfm?PgNm=EMCSubjects&Params=U1.

Ernst, David. *The Evolution of Electronic Music*. New York: Schirmer Books, 1977.

Ferguson, Sean. "Extra Sensory Percussion: The Percussion Music of alcides lanza." *Musicworks* 61 (Spring 1995): 20–8.

Ficher, Miguel, Martha Furman Schliefer, and John M. Furman. *Latin American Classical Composers: A Biographical Dictionary*. Lanham, MD: Scarecrow Press, 1996.

García Morillo, Roberto. *Estudios sobre música argentina*. Buenos Aires: Secretaría de Cultura, Ministerio de Educación y Justicia, Ediciones Culturales Argentinas, 1984.

Gena, Peter. "Freedom in Experimental Music: The New York Revolution." *TriQuarterly* no. 52 (1981): 223–43.

Gesualdo, Victor. *Breve historia de la música en la Argentina*. Buenos Aires: Claridad, 1998.

– *La música en la Argentina*. Buenos Aires: Editorial Stella, 1988.

"Gilles Tremblay," *Compositeurs au Québec*, no. 1. Montreal: Canadian Music Centre, 1974, rev. ed. 1985.

Griffiths, Paul. *A Guide to Electronic Music*. London: Thames & Hudson, 1979.

Hamm, Charles. *Music in the New World*. New York: Norton, 1983.

Haskell, Barbara. *Blam! The Explosion of Pop, Minimalism and Performance, 1958–1964*. Exhibition Catalogue. New York: Whitney Museum of American Art and W.W. Norton, 1984.

Hitchcock, H. Wiley. *Music in the United States: A Historical Introduction.* 3rd ed. Prentice-Hall History of Music Series. Englewood Cliffs, NJ: Prentice-Hall, 1988.

Johnson, Roger, ed. *Scores: An Anthology of New Music.* New York: Schirmer, 1981.

Johnson, Steven, ed. *The New York Schools of Music and Visual Arts: John Cage, Morton Feldman, Edgard Varèse, Willem De Kooning, Jasper Johns, Robert Rauschenberg.* New York: Routledge, 2002.

Jones, Pamela. "lanza/Sheppard's Canadian Tour a Voyage of Discovery." *Words & Music* 5, no. 2 (February 1998): 10.

– "À la recherche des racines: La vie et la carrière d'alcides lanza en Argentine." *Circuit: Revue Nord-Américaine de Musique du XXe Siècle* 10, no. 2 (1999): 9–15.

Kaprow, Allan. *Assemblages, Environments, and Happenings.* New York: Abrams, 1966.

Kasemets, Udo. "Tuning of Systems to Systems of Tuning." *Musicworks* 57 (Winter 1994): 24–29.

King, John. *El Di Tella y el desarrollo cultural argentino en la década del sesenta.* Trans. Carlos Gardini. Buenos Aires: Ediciones de Arte Gaglianone, 1985.

Kuss, Malena. *Alberto Ginastera.* London: Boosey & Hawkes, 1999.

"lanza, alcides." *Dizionario enciclopedico universale della musica e dei musicisti,* ed. Alberto Basso. 4: 200. Torino: UTET, 1986.

Laurier, Andrée. "The Composer and the Computer." *The Canadian Composer* 189 (March 1984): 14–19.

Le Caine, Hugh. "Synthetic Means." In *The Modern Composer and his World,* ed. John Beckwith and Udo Kasemets, 109–133. Toronto: University of Toronto Press, 1961.

Lefebvre, Marie-Thérèse. *Serge Garant et la révolution musicale au Québec.* Montreal: Louise Courteau, 1986.

Lillington, Tom. "Sheppard Shines" [review of *Transmutations* CD]. *Musicworks* 71 (Summer 1998): 59.

Lippard, Lucy R., ed. *Six Years: The Dematerialization of the Art Object from 1966 to 1972: A Cross-Reference Book of Information on Esthetic Boundaries.* New York, Praeger, 1973.

Manning, Peter. *Electronic and Computer Music.* Rev. ed. Oxford: Oxford University Press, 2002.

Marcuse, Sibyl. *Musical Instruments: A Comprehensive Dictionary.* Corrected ed. New York: Norton, 1975.

McGee, Timothy J. *The Music of Canada.* New York: Norton, 1985.

Meyer-Eppler, Werner. "Elektronische Kompositionstechnik." *Melos* 20 (1953): 5–9.

"Micheline Coulombe Saint-Marcoux." *Musicworks* 18 (Winter 1982): 24.

"Micheline Coulombe Saint-Marcoux." *Compositeurs au Québec*, no. 7. Montreal: Canadian Music Centre, 1986.

Monjeau, Federico. "Lanza en acción." *Página 12* (Buenos Aires), 13 Aug. 1989.

Morillo, R. García. *Estudio sobre música argentina.* Buenos Aires, 1984.

"Musicircus." John Cage Database. http://www.johncage.info/workscage/musicircus.html

Nattiez, J.J. "Montréal: Musiques actuelles – Editorial." *Circuit* 1/2 (1990): 5–6.

Nicholls, David. "Getting Rid of the Glue: The Music of the New York School." In *The New York Schools of Music and Visual Arts: John Cage, Morton Feldman, Edgard Varèse, Willem De Kooning, Jasper Johns, Robert Rauschenberg,* ed. Steven Johnson, 17–56. New York: Routledge, 2002.

Nyman, Michael. *Experimental Music: Cage and Beyond.* 2nd ed. Cambridge: Cambridge University Press, 1999.

Paz, Juan Carlos. *Alturas, tensiones, ataques, intensidades (Memorias, I).* Buenos Aires: Ediciones de la Flor, 1972.

– *Introducción a la música de nuestro tiempo.* Buenos Aires: Editorial Nueva Visión, 1955.

"Pierre Mercure." *Compositeurs au Québec*, no. 9. Montreal: Canadian Music Centre, 1976.

Pousseur, Henri. "Musique électronique musique sérielle." *Cahiers musicaux* 12 (1957): 50–53.

Potvin, Gilles. "Lanza, Alcides." *Encyclopedia of Music in Canada*, 2nd ed., ed. Helmut Kallmann, Gilles Potvin, Kenneth Winters et al., 717. Toronto: University of Toronto Press, 1992.

– "Micheline Coulombe Saint-Marcoux." In *Compositeurs canadiens contemporains.* Rev. enl. ed. Ed. Louise Laplante, trans. Véronique Robert, 305–8. Montreal: Les presses de l'université du Québec, 1977.

Quién es quién en la Argentina. Buenos Aires: Kraft, 1958–59.

Ripin, Edwin M., and Hugh Davies. "Prepared piano." *NG2* 20: 298–99.

Saint-Marcoux, Micheline Coulombe. Introductory note to program brochure. *Journées de Musiques Nouvelles d'Amérique Latine.* Montreal, 1982.

– "L'influence de la machine sur la musique du XXe siècle." *Le Devoir* (Montreal), 27 June 1970: 21–2.

- "Réflexions d'une jeune compositrice." *Vie Musicale* 8 (1968): 13–16.
Salgado, Susana. "Buenos Aires." *NG*2 2: 555–57.
- "Lanza, Alcides." *NG*2 14: 257–58.
Salzman, Eric. *Twentieth-Century Music: An Introduction*, 4th ed. Prentice-Hall History of Music Series. Upper Saddle River, NJ: Prentice-Hall, 2002.
Schwartz, Elliott. *Electronic Music: A Listener's Guide*. Rev. ed. New York: Da Capo, 1989.
"Serge Garant," *Compositeurs au Québec*, no. 6. Montreal: Canadian Music Centre, 1975.
Shreffler, Anne C. "The Myth of Empirical Historiography: A Response to Joseph N. Straus," *Musical Quarterly* 84 (2000): 30–9.
Slonimsky, Nicolas. *Music Since 1900*. 4th ed. New York: Scribner's, 1971.
Somerville, Mike. "Trying to Break the Sound Barrier in the Music Department." *McGill Daily* (Montreal), 28 Jan. 1998.
Strange, Allen. *Electronic Music: Systems, Techniques, and Controls*. 3rd ed. New York: McGraw-Hill, 2000.
Straus, Joseph N. "The Myth of Serial 'Tyranny" in the 1950s and 1960s." *Musical Quarterly* 83 (1999): 301–43.
Suárez Urtubey, Pola. *Alberto Ginastera*. Buenos Aires: Ediciones Culturales Argentinas, 1967.
Taruskin, Richard. *The Oxford History of Western Music*. Oxford: Oxford University Press, 2005.
Thériault, Jacques. "Saint-Marcoux, Micheline Coulombe." *Encyclopedia of Music in Canada*, 2nd ed., ed. Helmut Kallmann, Gilles Potvin, Kenneth Winters et al., 1173–4. Toronto: University of Toronto Press, 1992.
- "Une perception plus juste d'Alcides Lanza." *Le Devoir* (Montréal), 18 March 1972.
Tommasini, Anthony. "Midcentury Serialists: The Bullies or the Besieged?" *New York Times*, 9 Jul. 2000, AR23.
Ussachevsky, Vladimir. "Columbia-Princeton Electronic Music Center." *Revue Belge de Musique* 13 (1959): 129–31.
Villa Rojo, Jesús. *El clarinete y sus posibilidades: Estudio de nuevos procedimientos*. 2nd ed. Madrid: Alpuerto, 1984.
Vinton, John. *Dictionary of Contemporary Music*. New York: Dutton, 1971.
Whittall, Arnold. *Music since the First World War*. London: Dent, 1977.
Wick, Robert L. *Electronic and Computer Music: An Annotated Bibliography*. Westport, CT: Greenwood, 1997.
Young, Gayle. *The Sackbut Blues: Hugh Le Caine: Pioneer in Electronic Music*. Ottawa: National Museum of Science and Technology, 1989.

Index

A page reference in italics indicates the presence of an illustration.